Kant and the Reach

Studies in Kant's Theory of Ratio

The essays collected in this volume have interpretative unity. Their underlying conc nature of Kant's philosophical system, and ...is deepest intentions and basic commitments.

The book falls into three parts. The first three essays deal with Kant's approach to things-in-themselves and with the realm of noumenal causality. The second part considers Kant's approach to the methodology of rational inquiry, and, in particular, his views on cognitive systematization and the limits of philosophizing itself. The third section focuses on the role played by the Categorical Imperative in both the theoretical and practical philosophy.

The aim throughout, one that many Kant scholars and students will find provocative, is to show that in an important sense Kant is prepared to assert the primacy of practical over theoretical philosophy.

Nicholas Rescher is University Professor of Philosophy at the University of Pittsburgh.

Kant and the Reach of Reason

Studies in Kant's Theory of Rational Systematization

NICHOLAS RESCHER

University of Pittsburgh

CAMBRIDGE UNIVERSITY PRESS

PUBLISHED BY THE PRESS SYNDICATE OF THE UNIVERSITY OF CAMBRIDGE
The Pitt Building, Trumpington Street, Cambridge, United Kingdom

CAMBRIDGE UNIVERSITY PRESS
The Edinburgh Building, Cambridge CB2 2RU, UK   http://www.cup.cam.ac.uk
40 West 20th Street, New York, NY 10011–4211, USA   http://www.cup.org
10 Stamford Road, Oakleigh, Melbourne 3166, Australia
Ruiz de Alarcón 13, 28014 Madrid, Spain

First published 2000

Printed in the United States of America

Typeface Palatino 10.5/13 pt.   *System* QuarkXPress™ 4.04 [AG]

A catalog record for this book is available from the British Library.

Library of Congress Cataloging in Publication Data
Rescher, Nicholas.
Kant and the reach of reason : studies in Kant's theory of
rational systematization / Nicholas Rescher.
p.   cm.
Includes bibliographical references and index.
ISBN 0-521-66100-5. – ISBN 0-521-66791-7 (pbk.)
1. Kant, Immanuel, 1724–1804.   I. Title.
B2798.R426   1999
193–dc21   99-25919
                                              CIP

ISBN 0 521 66100 5   hardback
ISBN 0 521 66791 7   paperback

Contents

Acknowledgments

This book gathers together various essays on the philosophy of Kant that I have written over a period of some thirty years. Almost all of them have appeared in print, and I am grateful to the publishers concerned for permission to reprint this material in the slightly revised form appropriate to a collection of this sort. I am indebted to Estelle Burris for her help in preparing this material for publication and grateful to an anonymous referee from Cambridge University Press for offering constructive suggestions for improvement.

NOTES ON TEXT QUOTATIONS AND TRANSLATIONS

A word of explanation may be in order regarding my practice of giving extensive quotations from Kant's texts instead of mere references to them. These discussions present some rather unorthodox interpretations of Kant's philosophical position, and I believe that it is conducive to the prospects of persuasion to make the textual support for these interpretations manifest, presenting then and there the evidence for thinking that Kant actually holds the views I attribute to him.

The Kant of the present book uses English, courtesy of the following translations:

1. *Critique of Pure Reason,* tr. Norman Kemp Smith (London: Macmillan, 1929). Cited as *CPuR.*
2. *Critique of Practical Reason,* tr. Lewis White Beck (New York: Bobbs-Merrill, 1956). Cited as *CPrR.*

3. *Critique of Judgment,* tr. J. H. Bernard (London: Macmillan, 1892). Cited as *CJ.*
4. *Prolegomena to any Future Metaphysic,* tr. Lewis White Beck (New York: Bobbs-Merrill, 1950). Cited as *Prolegomena.*
5. *Foundations of the Metaphysics of Morals,* tr. Lewis White Beck (New York: Bobbs-Merrill, 1959). Cited as *Grundlegung.*
6. *Metaphysical Foundations of Natural Science,* tr. James Ellington (New York, 1970). Cited as *Metaphysical Foundations.*
7. *The Metaphysics of Morals,* pt. II, tr. James Ellington (New York, 1964).

Use of these translations has not, however, been slavish. On frequent occasions they have been modified in the interests of accuracy.

In the case of *CPuR,* references are given in the pagination of the first (A) and second (B) editions. In all other cases, references are given in the pagination of the edition of the erstwhile Royal Prussian Academy of Science (Königliche Preussische Akademie der Wissenschaften) in Berlin.

September 1998
Pittsburgh, PA

Introduction

An oft-repeated truism has it that every important thinker of the past needs to be reinterpreted in the light of the changed intellectual circumstances of a later present. But there is not only a diachronic variation of circumstances; there is also a perspectival variation of philosophical outlooks in the present. Sooner or later, a student who becomes closely engaged with the work of one of the great thinkers of the past tends to develop a characteristic vision of its impact and bearing. And so it is in this case. For the Kant depicted here is a protopragmatist who differs in significant respects from the Kant envisioned by various other contemporary interpreters.

First and foremost, these essays see Kant as a problem solver whose favored instrument of work is the distinction. Whenever we look to Kant we find him preoccupied with what he sees as essential distinctions: analytic–synthetic, a priori–a posteriori, formal–material, efficient–final, knowledge–belief, theoretical–practical, means–ends, moral–prudential, categorical– factual – the list goes on and on. And all of these distinctions afford tools for addressing philosophical problems that must – as Kant sees it – be resolved through the development of suitable conceptual and doctrinal instrumentalities. The Kant I envision is one who is pervasively concerned with solving philosophical problems by undoing knots of thought by means of distinctions.

A second key point is that the Kant envisioned here is a dedicated systematizer. A follower of Leibniz and Wolff, he not merely seeks answers to questions and solutions to problems, but answers and solutions that fit into a coherent and systematic whole. And this systematic approach indicates that the proper way to illuminate a Kantian position is not just from the local context of its treatment in a particular Kantian work, but by adducing cognate discussions in Kantian texts in areas that may seem remote from the particular discussion at hand.

Though produced on various occasions over many years, the essays collected together here exhibit a thematic and interpretative unity. While most of them are topically focused on specific issues (on things-in-themselves, moral causality, the Categorical Imperative), all of these essays are somehow concerned – and most of them centrally concerned – with the overall nature of Kant's system, his deepest philosophical intentions and most basic commitments. More than most past and recent commentators have done, these essays stress the specifically practical aspect of Kant's idealism, interpreting this as an explicative idealism that brings his thought into touch with the sort of pragmatism espoused by Peirce.

The book falls into three parts. Chapters 1–3 deal with Kant's approach to things-in-themselves and the realm of noumenal causality. Chapters 4–6 consider his approach to the methodology of rational inquiry and, in particular, his view of the methods of cognitive systematization, with special attention to his position regarding the limits and prospects of philosophizing itself. Finally, the third division, Chapters 7–9, deals with the role played by the Categorical Imperative alike in Kant's theoretical as in his practical philosophy. The aim, throughout, is to show that in an important sense Kant is prepared to assert the primacy of practical over theoretical philosophy.

Taken together, these studies accordingly unfold a continuous story line with a characteristic overall plot of its own, which runs roughly as follows: the conception of things-in-themselves or noumena, is not a doorway through which we can project our knowledge from the phenomenal realm into the problematic sphere of mind-independent reality (Chapter 1). Kant's use of causal expressions in relation to noumena represents a use of the "Principle of Sufficient Reason" grounded in the cognitive approaches of reason itself, rather than rooted "dogmatically" in an ontologically independent reality that reason endeavors to know (Chapter 2). The ideas projected by pure reason do not represent

objects proper (real things in space time) but serve merely to furnish reason with thought instrumentalities. For objectification one
must look not to pure reason as such, but to the contingently given
resources of the human intellect (Chapter 3). Pure reason's concern is not with the obtaining of knowledge, but with its systematization (Chapter 4). And it is a peculiar feature of the human
mind that it requires that such systematization proceed in the purposive terms of a design that provides for a causality of purpose
behind the causality of nature (Chapter 5). Since philosophizing
itself is an exercise in pure reason that prescinds from theoretical
reason's focus on issues of real-world applicability, it follows that
the proper work of philosophy lies on the side of practical reason
(Chapter 6). And it is thus crucial for Kant that the reach of pure
reason is greater in practical than in strictly theoretical/cognitive
matters, so that the range of warranted acceptability (of what we
can and must think to be so) is greater than that of actual knowledge (Chapter 7). This is vividly illustrated in the way in which
the necessity and universality of moral principles is rooted in the
Categorical Imperative fundamental to Kantian morality (Chapter 8). For the universality of the Categorical Imperative is absolute; what is fundamentally at issue here is a principle of reason
that holds not just for moral/practical matters, but across the
whole board of reason's concerns; theoretical as well as practical
(Chapter 9).

The general theme of the approach to Kant taken in these pages
is that of demystification. Kant's project, as portrayed here, is
not one projecting a realm of mysterious items detached from the
reality of this world: things-in-themselves, noumenal causes or
transcendent purposes, or unrealizable duties. He is not the pro-
jector of a theoretical zoo populated by strange philosophical entities that are not of this world. His procedure is the effective opposite of this: to project on the screen of mind certain ideas that
are serviceable in clarifying what the things of this world are
through a contrast with what they are not. His use of idealizations
is always negative: to provide an explanatory contrast with the
actualities of the realm of our knowledge and existence. His ide-
alities accordingly have a status that is not ontological, but functional and, if you will, pragmatic – to provide thought tools that

are serviceable in clarifying the world's realities. Thus, for, example, even his highly idealized ethics is portrayed here as part of the stage setting of a wider moral theory, which, as such, contrasts with an applicative casuistry indispensable to rational decision about the acceptability of actions amidst the difficult circumstances of an uncooperative world.

In this way, the essays gathered here provide for a unified account that views the ideal of comprehensive systematization which Kant deems a characteristic of reason in general as also providing the key to the articulation of his own philosophy. Systematization is pivotal both *in* Kant's thought about the nature of knowledge and also *for* Kant's philosophy itself, whose central formative concept mechanism it provides.

The book is the product of the labors of a working philosopher who has for many years found the periodic preoccupation with Kantian texts to be a source of stimulus and inspiration. Its main concern is not with current controversies in Kant interpretation and the critique of rival Kant exegetes. Rather it endeavors to set out a systemically cohesive line of Kant interpretation as suggested by the author's own efforts to get clear on the issues. To a large extent the book keeps its distance from current scholarly debates and controversies and concentrates on setting out its own characteristic effort at a comprehensive reading of Kant.

Chapter 1

On the Status of "Things-in-Themselves" in Kant's Critical Philosophy

1. ARE THINGS-IN-THEMSELVES MERELY VESTIGIAL DOGMATISM?

Kant's distinction between "appearances" and "things-in-themselves" is construed by various commentators along the lines of the traditional philosophical contrast between appearance and reality. There are, on the one hand, the phenomena of the "realm of appearance" (whose status is mind correlative and whose being lies in their being present to a mind) and, on the other hand, the realm of extramental reality, the domain of "what really exists as it really exists," wholly and entirely apart from the sphere of human thought and knowledge.[1] Now if this be so, then the conception of things-in-themselves encounters grave difficulties because of the obvious problem of "getting there from here," where "here" represents the fundamental commitment of Kant's critical philosophy. Thus A. C. Ewing flatly asserts: "Kant gives no grounds for believing in things-in-themselves, but merely asserts their existence dogmatically."[2] And if things-in-themselves indeed constitute a domain of altogether mind-external reality, it is hard to see how the matter could be otherwise on Kantian principles. Accordingly, it is often held that Kant's thing-in-itself is the (highly questionable) concession to a dogmatically rooted extra-mental reality of a philosophy whose "Copernican Revolution" everywhere else rejects metaphysical dogmatism and puts the creative activity of the human mind at center stage.

This chapter is a slightly revised version of an essay published under the same title in Gerhard Funke (ed.), *Akten des 5. Internationalen Kant Kongresses: Mainz 1981* (Bonn: Bouvier, 1981), pp. 437–47. Reprinted by permission of Bouvier Verlag.

This discussion will endeavor to show that the preceding perspective is very much mistaken. It will argue that it is quite incorrect to think of Kant's conception of a thing-in-itself as an inappropriate concession to a metaphysical stance that is totally at odds with the fundamental thrust of Kant's philosophy.

2. NOUMENAL REALITY AS AN INSTRUMENTALITY OF THOUGHT

For Kant, human thought proceeds at three (closely interrelated and interconnected) levels, corresponding to the three major faculties of the human mind:

1. *Sensibility,* which conforms our sense perception of objects to the (characteristically human) "forms of sensibility," namely space and time.
2. *Understanding* (*Verstand*), which conforms our various individual judgments regarding objects to the (characteristically human) categories of thought.
3. *Reason* (*Vernunft*), which conforms the collective totality of our judgments regarding objects to certain structural requirements of systemic unity.

Their interrelation is crucial in Kant's theory of the thing-in-itself.

As Kant sees it, the conception of a thing-in-itself arises through abstraction, through removing in thought and by hypothesis certain conditions which are there in fact – namely, the particular limiting conditions of operation of our human sensibility (*CPuR*, B307). Specifically, what we can "think away" are, in the first instance, our particular forms of sensibility (sight, touch, and the rest) and then, by extension, any and all forms of sensibility. We thus arrive at the hypothesis of a being (God?) who does not perceive objects sensuously at all, but "intuits" them "directly," in a sensuously unmediated act of the mind (*CPuR*, B310). Now, when the conditions of sensibility are thus thought away, what remains is the conception of an object that is accessible to a mind that can apprehend things nonsensuously, and this in turn engenders the conception of objects that are purely intelligible or noumenal in nature:

6

> [I]f we entitle certain objects, as appearances, sensible entities [*Sinneswesen:* phenomena], then since we thereby distinguish the mode in which we intuit them from the nature that belongs to them in themselves it is implied in this distinction that we place the latter, considered in their own nature, although we do not so intuit them . . . , which are not objects of our senses but are thought as objects merely through the understanding, in opposition to the former, and that in so doing we entitle them intelligible entities [*Verstandeswesen:* noumena]. (*CPuR,* B306)

We might (mistakenly) reify such items into genuine yet unexperientable things – things as a pure, sensuously unmediated, wholly intuitive understanding perceives them:

> If by "noumenon" we mean a thing so far it is *not an object of our sensible intuition,* and so abstract from our mode of intuiting it, this is a noumenon in the negative sense of the term. But if we understand by it an *object* of a *non-sensible intuition,* we thereby presuppose a special mode of intuition, namely, the intellectual, which is not that which we possess, and of which we cannot comprehend even the possibility. This would be a "noumenon" in the *positive* sense of the term. (*CPuR,* B307)

This positive approach is wholly improper, since we cannot even begin to conceive of such an intuition. A negative variant, however, is quite legitimate:

> The concept of a *noumenon* is thus a merely *limiting concept,* the function of which is to curb the pretensions of sensibility; and it is therefore only of negative employment. At the same time it is no arbitrary invention; it is bound up with the limitation of sensibility, though it cannot affirm anything positive beyond the field of sensibility. (*CPuR,* A255 = B310–11)

When we "think away" the particular conditions of our own sensibility, this still leaves us with something (*CPuR,* B312 = A254). And what we arrive at is the conception of a thing-in-itself, a noumenon in its negative guise:

> [A]ppearance can be nothing by itself, outside our mode of representation. Unless, therefore, we are to move constantly in a circle, the word appearance must be recognized as already indicating a relation to something, the immediate . . . which . . .

7

must be something in itself, that is, an object independent of sensibility. There thus results the concept of a *noumenon*. It is not indeed in any way positive, and is not a determinate knowledge of anything, but signifies only the thought of something in general, in which I abstract from everything that belongs to the form of sensible intuition. (*CPuR*, A251–52)

And again:

[W]e must bear in mind that the concept of appearances, as limited by the Transcendental Aesthetic, already of itself establishes the objective reality of *noumena* and justifies the division of objects into *phaenomena* and *noumena,* and so of the world into a world of the senses and a world of the understanding [*mundus sensibilis et intelligibilis*], . . . For if the senses represent to us something merely *as it appears,* this something must also in itself be a thing and an object of a non-sensible intuition, that is, of the understanding. In other words, a "knowledge" must be possible, in which there is no sensibility, and which alone has reality that is absolutely objective. Through it objects will be represented *as they are,* whereas in the empirical employment of our understanding things will be known only *as they appear.* (*CPuR*, A249–50)

The thing-in-itself is accordingly a creature of understanding (*Verstandeswesen: ens rationis*) – a product of abstraction – arrived at by prescinding from the conditions of sensibility.

To be sure, such "creatures of the understanding" do not carry us beyond the domain of phenomena and their grounding:

The understanding . . . does indeed think for itself an object in itself but only as transcendental object, which is the ground of appearance . . . The critique of the pure understanding accordingly does not permit us to create a new field of objects beyond those which may be presented to it as appearances, and so to stray into intelligible worlds: of these it does not even allow us to entertain a concept. (*CPuR*, A288–89 = B344–45)

The only objects with which we can even deal are therefore those connected – however tenuously – to the domain of appearances.

Of course, we could not possibly *know* about noumenal objects.

For, as Kant sees it, knowledge, strictly speaking, is confined to the objects of (sensory) experience. And given that they are, *ex hypothesi,* sense inaccessible, noumena lie beyond the reach of that sensibility through which alone objects can be given to us. But we can certainly *think* them – that is, we can meaningfully assume or suppose (and indeed posit or postulate) such things. We thus have a cognitive (or, at any rate, intellectual) route to things-in-themselves independent of outright knowledge of them, and fortunately so, since knowledge of them is altogether unrealizable.[3] This think versus know distinction is thus crucial. Were Kant to hold that we can know things in themselves, or even that we can know something of them (e.g., that they exist), then this would contradict his characteristic critical doctrine that any and all positive knowledge of objectively real things must, for us, be mediated by the sensibility.

However, this denial of positive knowledge of noumena does not produce a complete vacuum of information. There is (as Kant's own practice makes clear) a good deal that can be said about them, seeing that we have no alternative but to suppose that there indeed are noumena (that appearances are appearances of something) and that they are somehow grounded in a nonphenomenal reality. To be sure, this does not go very far. And the rest of what we have is negative and generic – that noumena are not spatiotemporal, subject to the categories, etc. Moreover, note that all this is not a matter of things in themselves as individual things, but is always something generic, something pertaining to the concept of noumena as such. At the level of particularity (of concrete objectivity) we can know nothing of noumena, for such knowledge would have to be synthetic, and this sort of knowledge simply cannot be obtained in regard to noumena.

The information we have regarding noumena is always packaged in analytic, objectively vacuous, negative stipulations to the effect that nothing of such and such a sort (phenomenal, spatiotemporal, subjectively conditioned, etc.) could validly be counted by us as a noumenon. The idea of a noumenal reality is thus something of which we can make no positive applications of any sort. Nevertheless it is a highly useful device:

What our understanding acquires through this concept of a noumenon, is a negative extension; that is to say, understanding is not limited by sensibility; on the contrary, it itself limits sensibility in calling things in themselves (things not regarded as appearances) *noumena.* But it at the same time sets limits to itself, recognizing that it cannot know them through any of the categories, and that it must therefore think them only under the title of an unknown something. (*CPuR,* A256 = B312)

The thing-in-itself, as such, is literally vacuous, "since that X (the [mind-external] object) which corresponds to them [viz. to our representation] is nothing to us, being, as it is, something that has to be distinct from all our [sense-based] representation" (*CPuR,* A105). Things-in-themselves are, accordingly, literally nothing for us in their status of identifiable "things." But the conception of things in themselves (at the generic level) is quite another matter – something we can certainly get a grip on. It is a contrivance of the mind, a creature of our understanding to which we stand fully and irrevocably committed:

The understanding, when it entitles an object in a [certain] relation mere phenomenon, at the same time forms, apart from that relation, a representation of an *object in itself,* and so comes to represent itself as also being able to form *concepts* of such objects. And . . . the understanding . . . also supposes that the object in itself must at least be *thought* . . . and so is misled into treating the entirely *indeterminate* concept of an intelligible entity, namely, of a something in general outside our sensibility, as being a *determinate* concept of an entity that allows of being known in a certain [purely intelligible] manner by means of the understanding. (*CPuR,* B306–7)

And again:

We cannot call the noumenon such an *object;* signifying as it does, the problematic concept of an object for a quite different intuition [namely, *nonsensuous* intuition] and a quite different understanding from ours, it is itself a problem. (*CPuR,* B334 = A287)

To assume a change with regard to our forms of sensibility means that the understanding too will not be unaffected, because our forms of judgment (categories) can no longer be supposed to apply (nor, for that matter, our principles for the systemic unity of reason). But of course to abrogate our particular categories of understanding is not necessarily to abrogate all categories of understanding. So when contemplating a change with respect to the operation of sensibility, we must contemplate a change with respect to the operation of the understanding as well: the prospect of different categories must now also be brought into (hypothetical) play. However, alteration is not total abrogation. Something yet remains.

After all, to be fully objective and authentic, an appearance must be an appearance *of* something; there must be an underlying something that does the appearing – that grounds it in an extraphenomenal order. The phenomena are representations (appearances), and where there is representation, there must be something that is represented (something that appears): "When we say that the senses represent objects *as they appear*, and the understanding objects *as they are*, the latter statement is to be taken . . . as meaning that the objects must be represented as [mere] objects of experience, that is, as [mere] appearances" (*CPuR*, A258 = B314), or again: "[T]hough we cannot *know* these objects [of experience] as things in themselves, we must yet be in a position at least to *think* them as things in themselves; otherwise we should be landed in the absurd conclusion that there can be appearances without anything that appears" (*CPuR*, Bxxvi).

But of course noumena are not particular (individuated) things about which we have positive information. We can, and so must, have the concept of a noumenal realm or order, but not a concept of noumenal things. As individuated particulars, noumena are not even possible: "For to substitute the logical possibility of the *concept* (namely that the concept does not contradict itself) for the transcendental possibility of *things* (namely that an object corresponds to that concept) can deceive and leave satisfied only the simpleminded" (*CPuR*, A244 = B302). We can appropriately entertain and deploy the generic conception of "things-in-themselves," but we can never concretely apply it (e.g., to "this chair in itself"). For Kant this would involve a contradiction in terms. Accordingly, things-in-themselves are not a part of knowable reality (nature):

"Since we can apply to it [the noumenon] none of the concepts of understanding, the representation remains for us empty." The "thing" at issue with the thing-in-itself is "a concept without an object," a mere *ens rationis* that is the mere shell of an object without content, without reality, indeed without as such being genuinely possible, "although they must not for that reason be declared also to be impossible" (*CPuR*, A290 = B347; cf. A291 = B347).

But of course knowledge is not the only cognitive modality at our disposal. For one thing, there is assumption and hypothesis. And, for another, there is positing and postulation. On this basis, the availability of things-in-themselves emerges as a postulate of the human understanding and the conception thereof as its indispensable tool. Kant summarizes the position as follows:

> The cause of our not being satisfied with the substrate of sensibility, and of our adding to the phenomena noumena which only the pure understanding can think, is simply as follows. The sensibility . . . is itself limited by the understanding in such a fashion that it does not have to do with things in themselves but only with the mode in which, owing to our subjective constitution, they appear. The *Transcendental Aesthetic,* in all its teaching, has led to this conclusion; and the same conclusion also, of course, follows for the concept of an appearance in general; namely that something which is not in itself appearance must correspond to it. (*CPuR,* A251)

Our understanding is committed to the postulate or supposition that things-in-themselves have a place in an experience-external nonsensuous noumenal realm, however little we may know about them (*CPuR*, A253 = B309). Noumena are "things the understanding must think" (*CPuR*, B307) – given the modus operandi of the human mind. Our understanding cannot operate without supposing things-in-themselves, any more than our sensibility can operate outside the space-time framework at the perceptual level. But to postulate something as an instrumentality for use is very different from claiming to know of its actuality.

To be sure, we do not and indeed cannot possibly – as a matter of principle – *know* anything concretely about an experience-external order of things. But that is neither here nor there. What counts is that the operations of our mind are so structured that we do and must take our representations as actually representative. We do and must *think* of our experience as the product of a mind-external reality that somehow impinges upon our mind *ab extra*. And it is just this fundamental tendency of the human mind to objectification and externalization that is the sole and sufficient basis of things-in-themselves. Postulation and presupposition can appropriately enter in where knowledge of actual existence leaves off. In sum, the conception of a thing-in-itself is a thought tool: what we have here are validatable thought objects, theoretical entities that we can and must make use of in order to make sense of a knowable reality of which they themselves are emphatically not a determinable part.

3. THE FUNCTIONAL ROLE OF THE CONCEPTION OF THINGS-IN-THEMSELVES

As Kant saw it, the central and crucial task of the mind's realistic commitment to things-in-themselves is "to keep phenomena in their place" as phenomena, to enforce a recognition that appearances are just that – appearances – by providing for the contrast between the appearance as such and a something that appears, thus blocking the way to an idealism (in its phenomenalist configuration) that rests content with a fabric of appearance. The prime role and function of his recourse to things-in-themselves is thus viewed by Kant in a negative mode, as a means for marking the limits of the human understanding:

> [T]he concept of a noumenon is necessary, to prevent sensible intuition from being extended to things in themselves, and thus to limit the objective validity of sensible knowledge. The remaining things, to which it does not apply, are entitled noumena, in order to show that this knowledge cannot extend its domain over everything which the understanding thinks . . . The concept of a noumenon is thus a merely *limiting concept,* the function of which is to curb the pretensions of sensibility; and it is therefore only of negative employment. At the same time there is no arbitrary invention; it is bound up with the limitation of sensibility though it cannot affirm anything positive beyond the field of sensibility. (*CPuR*, A255 = B310)

Noumena serve to curb the pretensions of sensibility. And they do this by providing for two crucial factors: objectivity and externality.

Objectivity is needed to implement the real–fictitious distinction. This turns on the coherence and orderliness internal to our experience. As A. C. Ewing puts it, Kant holds that "for us the reference to an object . . . must . . . be understood as an expression of the unity of experience."[4] This objectivity is provided by the "transcendental object," of which Kant says:

> All our representations are . . . referred by the understanding to some object . . . as the object of sensible intuition. But this goes no further than the transcendental object; and by that is meant a something = X, of which we know, and with the present constitution of our understanding we can know nothing whatsoever, but which, as a correlate of the unity of apperception, can serve only for the unity of the manifold in sensible intuition. (*CPuR*, A250)

But this objectivity of experiential unity is only half the story.

Externality enters in because objectivity must be supplemented by the mind's insistence that our representations do actually represent – that they are somehow grounded in an extraphenomenal reality. (The "externality" at issue is clearly not a matter of spatiality, but one of grounding.)[5] And this externality has its roots in the fact that the human understanding necessarily and inexorably postulates things-in-themselves (i.e., commits itself in thought to an endorsement of their reality). Exactly this – the provision of externality – is the reason for being of Kantian things-in-themselves.

Our thought is inherently "intensional" (to borrow Husserl's term) – that is, aimed at matters that are (as we see it) themselves positioned outside the domain of the mental. In unifying the materials of sensibility into actual units or items (not mere phenomenal constellations or ordered collages of sense qualities, but integrated and interrelated wholes), the understanding does something useful. But such a unity, indicated by an integrated sense manifold – a "transcendental object," as Kant calls it – is not enough. What is still lacking is externalizing intentionality, that pointing at something external through which an appearance (however unified) is referred to something extraphenomenal as being an appearance of *something* (*CPuR*, A252). It is this second demand that the conception of a thing-in-itself is designed to meet.

The conception of things-in-themselves is a creature of mind – a self-imposed demand of the human understanding needed to implement its commitment to the objectivity and externality of those things with which it has to deal on the basis of the deliverances of sensibility and understanding. The task of this postulate is to ensure the fact that "we have *experience*, and not merely *imagination* of other things," as Kant puts it at the start of the "Refutation of Idealism" (*CPuR*, B275). The fundamental role of the conception of things-in-themselves is thus to preclude ontological idealism, to provide for that essential idea of an independently self-sufficient object through which alone the "objects" of our thinking become genuine objects, conceived of as being more than mere mental constructions.

We accordingly not only can have credence in things-in-themselves – can think them as actual – but we must do so. As rational inquirers we cannot but *postulate* their availability – though, to be sure, we can never *know* it, for that would be to bring them within the phenomenal orbit. We not only can endorse the conception of things-in-themselves, but we must do so to operate within our "conceptual scheme." They represent an ineluctable imperative of our cognitive reason. Our mind being so constituted that it must impute objectivity to the objects of our experience, it cannot but regard them as the cognition-internal representations of cognition-external realities. Our reason is committed to that espousal, that *postulation* of things-in-themselves without which the conception of a thought-external reality could not be implemented. We cannot – must not – claim knowledge about a manifold of mind-independent reals that exist altogether "in themselves." What is at issue here is a matter of a (practically) rational commitment to an indispensable useful conceptual resource.

To keep a precritical dogmatism in check we must stipulate the unknowability of noumena: to keep feckless idealism in check we must postulate their existence. The conception of things-in-themselves must be applicable at the generic level (even without our being in a position ever to apply it at the level of particulars). It is a concept we can only employ *sub ratione generalitatis*. There is no particularization – no prospect of identification – at this level: quite literally "we can have no knowledge of any object as a thing in itself" (*CPuR*, Bxxvi). And even in the case of our own selves, where we come into closest proximity to noumena, we can secure no knowledge whatever:

> [W]e must admit and assume behind the appearances some-
> thing else which is not appearance, namely things in themselves;
> we do so although we must admit that we cannot approach them
> more closely and can never know what they are in themselves,
> since they can never be known by us except as they affect us.
> This must furnish a distinction, though a crude one, between a
> world of sense and a world of understanding. The former, by
> differences in the sensuous faculties, can be very different among
> various observers, while the latter, which is its foundation, re-
> mains always the same. A man may not presume to know even
> himself as he really is by knowing himself through inner sen-
> sation . . . Thus in respect to mere perception and receptivity to
> sensations he must count himself as belonging to the world of
> sense; but in respect to that which may be pure activity in him-
> self (i.e., in respect to that which reaches consciousness directly
> and not by affecting the senses) he must reckon himself as be-
> longing to the intellectual world. But he has no further knowl-
> edge of that world. (*Grundlegung,* p. 451, Akad.)

Kant would have viewed the labors of his successors toward clarifying the thing-in-itself and providing information about its nature as utterly misguided. A thing-in-itself whose nature is brought within the reach of the categories of understanding is ipso facto unable to do the job of endowing the appearances with the intentionality of indicating something that stands altogether outside the phenomenal order, and thus to ensure that appearances are appearances *of* something. A cognitively domesticated thing-in-itself would (*ex hypothesi*) not be able to accomplish the important mission assigned to such things in the Kantian framework – namely, that of providing a basis of *mind externality* for the objects at issue in our knowledge.

4. THE STATUS OF THE CONCEPTION
OF THINGS-IN-THEMSELVES

Let us now return to the purported difficulty mooted at the out-set – the charge that Kant's recourse to things-in-themselves is not only gratuitous and dogmatically undefended, but even involves a certain inconsistency or incongruity with his basic commitments. For, all that he is entitled to on his theory, so the objection goes, is a variety of "creatures of the human mind," and yet what he wants and needs to have is an assured extramental reality for certain identifiable individual things that are entirely mind independent "in themselves."

It deserves emphatic stress that this line of objection is very much mistaken. Kant is not hankering after what he cannot have. He is content with what he can get. As he sees it, the understanding delivers into our hands (or, rather, our minds) the concept of things-in-themselves as a conceptual resource of its own devising that is the fruit of its insistence on objectivity and externality. But to claim knowledge of their existence is inappropriate: we certainly cannot claim to know that such things exist. For "In the *mere concept* of a thing no mark [token, "character"] of its existence is to be found. For ... existence ... has ... to do only with the question of whether such a thing be so given us that the perception of it can, if need be, precede the concept" (*CPuR*, A225 = B272). But while the understanding cannot *know* things in themselves, it indeed must think or, more precisely, *postulate* such things by way of imputation. What we can get from the understanding is the *conception* of things in themselves and the *conception* of them as real (*CPuR*, A249). Still, our commitment to this conception does not involve knowledge: it does not settle or prejudice any ontological issues, since "to substitute the logical possibility of the *concept* (namely that the concept does not contradict itself) for the transcendental possibility of *things* (namely that an object corresponds to the concept) can deceive and leave satisfied only the simple-minded" (*CPuR*, A244 = B302).

And this brings us to the crux of the matter. The realm of things-in-themselves is not a realm of which we are in a position to say that we *know* it to exist in the demanding Kantian sense of

"know" – at best it can be said that we do and must *think* it to be
there (in Kant's essentially postulational sense of "think"). With
things-in-themselves *as such* we are beyond our depths. The *conception* of a thing in itself, however, is a creature of the understanding to which we stand irrevocably committed in viewing our
experience as an experience of *something* that is itself experience
external. Things-in-themselves are the creatures of mind, or rather
(and perhaps more exactly), the *conception* of things-in-themselves
is a mental contrivance to which our reason finds itself unavoidably committed.

Put in a nutshell, the matter stands thus: just as space and time
are forms of sensibility (creatures of man's perceptual faculty),
and causality, unity, spontaneity, and the rest are forms of man's
understanding or faculty of judgment, so also is the very conception of a thing-in-itself a creature of the human mind, a *Verstandeswesen*, an *ens rationis* – a (negative) *noumenon*, in the ety-
mological sense of the term, that is, something created by the
understanding in its in-built insistence upon operating with a
conceptual scheme of objective, mind-external foci of knowledge.

On Kantian principles, positive noumena are out. There is just
no prospect of establishing any cognitive contact with mind-
independent *realia* that exist altogether "in themselves"; and even
if there were, *we* could have nothing to do with them – they would,
literally, be nothing to us. Even the mere possibility of noumena
in any positive construction of this conception stands outside the
realm of what we can get – and of what we need.

But what there is, and for us (given the modus operandi of our
intellect) must be, is the commitment to a conception of things-in-
themselves for use as a limiting concept. For it is of the very nature
of human reason to construe the things of experience, the phenomena, as representations – that is, to take them to be correlative
with underlying reality, to be not just appearances but appearances
of things as they are in themselves (an sich selbst genommen). The
mind-generated conception of things-in-themselves is the basis
on which the human understanding erects that postulate that
can alone underwrite the genuine (authentic) externality of things
which their merely phenomenal (seeming) externality can suggest
but never guarantee, seeing that the stability and permanence

of objective experience demands that "the existence of actual things which I perceive outside me" is something that can never be obtained from the mere representation of such things (*CPuR*, B275–76).

Accordingly, the thing-in-itself enters into the system of Kant not as a certain type of existing thing, correlative with an onto-logical category of some sort. Rather it provides an intellectual tool in that the conception reflects the inherent stance of a reason committed to viewing the things of the world (its world) in a certain sort of way – to wit, in terms of their representational aspect as appearances *of* something. The thing-in-itself is the product of our mind's commitment to thinking about the phenomena (the items of our experience) as *mere* phenomena, as appearances – which, of course, can only be done on the basis of a commitment to the idea that there is something that appears, seeing that an appearance must, by the very meaning of the term, be an appearance *of* something. It is the conception of things-in-themselves that counts, and that does indeed have an ontological *locus standi* in the operational processes of the human mind. And it is via this conception that we must postulate things in themselves and think of them as beings wholly independent of us.

All that Kant is entitled to on his principles, but also all that he needs for the purposes of his position, is a thought-indispensable conception of things-in-themselves. The Kantian thing-in-itself is to be understood not as part of the furniture of the real world as such, of nature, but rather as an instrumentality of our thought about this real world. And such a thing-in-itself, something intro-duced in this way to play this sort of role, is the product of an in-tellectual insistence upon – that is, a postulation of – a certain way of thinking about things, the product of a certain "conceptual scheme" to which our reason stands committed. Things-in-them-selves as such are not natural objects but themselves entities, mere *Verstandeswesen* – putative correlates of certain mechanisms of our understanding. Paradoxical though it may sound, things-in-themselves are – as Kant saw it – not in the final analysis real things at all, but thought things, whose legitimacy lies in their being not fictions, but inherent and inevitable commitments of the human understanding.

To interpret "things-in-themselves" differently – as representing an ontological category of actual things – would indeed do violence to Kant's whole outlook. It would in truth lead to something dogmatic and unassimilable to the critical philosophy. But Kant certainly does not commit the mistake that beckons here. His discussion of the thing-in-itself is not a response to the injunction "Tell me about things as they actually are – really and mind independently – quite apart from our conceptual framework and its involvement and presuppositions." From Kant's point of view this injunction is absurd – it formulates an altogether nonsensical demand. His theory is designed not to fulfill but to abolish this sort of question.

5. CONCLUSION

For Kant, then, the concept of things-in-themselves or noumena is not a doorway through which we can project our knowledge from the phenomenal realm into the problematic sphere of mind-independent reality. Rather, it is a postulational, mind-imposed contrivance through which alone we are able to operate our conceptual scheme – a scheme in which objectivity and externality play a crucial role. To reemphasize: Kant's things-in-themselves form part not of the furniture of a realm of mind-independent reality, but rather of the machinery of thought. The Kantian thing-in-itself is, in effect, an *ens rationis,* a postulate of reason based on the fact that our human mind does and must think of the things of everyday experience in a certain sort of way.

Chapter 2

Kant on Noumenal Causality

1. THE PROBLEM OF NOUMENAL CAUSALITY

As apart from the manifold of things as we encounter them in ordinary experience, Kant envisioned a realm of things-in-themselves that are grounded in the operations of human reason – noumenal mind things (*entia rationis*), as it were. And at this level he also envisioned result-productive activity. As he saw it, noumenal causality can take three forms:

1. The quasi-causal agency of things-in-themselves in producing the phenomena
2. The agency of a rational will in making free choices (the "causality of freedom")
3. The agency of a creative intelligence in the pursuit of purposes within nature (the "causality of purpose")[1]

The conception of noumenal causality accordingly operates in the Kantian system at three levels: that of things-in-themselves, that of persons, and that of a creator God. Each of these poses characteristic difficulties of understanding. However, the present chapter is concerned with the first two alone. (The second is addressed in Chapter 8 and the third in Chapter 5.)

In the *Critique of Pure Reason*, Kant repeatedly characterizes the thing-in-itself (*Ding an sich* or noumenon) in such terms as "the non-sensible cause" of representations or as "the purely intelligible

This chapter is a slightly revised version of an essay on "Noumenal Causality in the Philosophy of Kant," in the *Proceedings of the Third International Kant Congress* (Dordrecht: Reidel, 1972), pp. 462–70; reprinted in L. W. Beck (ed.), *Kant's Theory of Knowledge* (Dordrecht: Reidel, 1972), pp. 462–70. (With kind permission from Kluwer Academic Publishers.)

21

cause" of appearances (*CPuR*, A494 = B522). Again and again he employs the language of causal efficacy with regard to things-in-themselves. Thus he speaks of "the representations through which they [things-in-themselves] *affect* us" (*CPuR*, A190 = B235; italics added) and elsewhere says that while things-in-themselves "can never be known by us except as they *affect* us" (*Grundlegung*, p. 452, Akad.; italics added) they nevertheless represent "a transcendental object, which is the *cause* of appearance and therefore not itself appearance" (*CPuR*, A288 = B344; italics added). Accordingly Kant writes in the *Prolegomena*:

> And we indeed, rightly considering objects of sense as mere appearances, confess thereby that they are based upon a thing in itself, though we know not this thing in itself but only know its appearances, namely the way in which our senses are affected by this unknown something. The understanding, therefore, by assuming appearances, grants the existence of things-in-themselves also. (*Prolegomena*, sect. 32; p. 314, Akad.)

But, on the other hand, Kant is repeatedly and emphatically insistent that the cause–effect relationship is coordinate with the categories of understanding, and that, in consequence, any and all applicability of the principle of causality is to be strictly confined to the phenomenal sphere. Causality, properly understood is, so Kant teaches, always temporally conditioned and thus cannot apply to noumena, which are not spatiotemporal at all. For, as he tells us in the *Prolegomena*:

> [I]f we should occupy ourselves about the object in itself, there is not a single possible attribute by which I could know that it is determined under any of these aspects [i.e., the categories], that is, under the concept either of substance, or of cause. (*Prolegomena*, sect. 28)

The categories and all that depends upon them accordingly just cannot be applied to things-in-themselves. And so noumena cannot be the literal cause of anything whatever.

From the very outset, perceptive students of the Kantian philosophy, such as J. S. Beck, have been troubled by the question of how these two seemingly conflicting positions are to be reconciled. And critics down to the present day continue to charge Kant with outright inconsistency on this head. P. F. Strawson, for example, objects as follows in *The Bounds of Sense:*

> For the resultant transportation of the terminology of objects "affecting" the constitution of subjects takes that terminology altogether out of the range of its intelligible employment, viz., the spatio-temporal range . . . the original model, the governing analogy is perverted or transposed into a form which violates any acceptable requirement of intelligibility, including Kant's own principle of significance.[2]

The issue of noumenal causality obviously poses a basic and important problem for any cohesive interpretation of Kant's philosophy and accordingly deserves closer examination.

2. SUFFICIENT REASON

The present discussion argues that the sensible construction of Kant's position is that in fact two quite different sorts of "causality" are at issue here, viz. (1) *authentic causality,* which is genuinely experientiable and is governed by the experientially *constitutive* Principle of Causality, and (2) a not properly causal *generic grounding,* which is merely intelligible (i.e., can be thought but not known) and is governed by a *regulative* Principle of Sufficient Reason. The kinship between the two sorts of "causality," authentic causality and generic grounding, is sufficiently remote that the employment of the same terms – such as "affecting" – in both cases must be regarded as merely analogical (in the manner in which Kant speaks at *CPuR*, A206 = B252). Thus, the grounding at issue is, strictly speaking, not causal at all, but merely quasi-causal.

The key to a proper understanding of the role that Kant maintains for the things-in-themselves lies in his insistence that reason itself compels us to accept their acceptance: "For what necessarily forces us to transcend the limits of experience and of all appearances is the *unconditioned,* which reason, by necessity and by right, demands in things-in-themselves, as required to complete the series of conditions" (*CPuR*, Bxx). This passage not only says that reason demands that there be things-in-themselves, but also hints *why* this is so. For Kant, the conception of a perceived object freed from the operative conditions of perception is every bit as sense-less as would be that of a view of an object that is freed from any and every point of view, and so regarded in separation from one of the essential conditions of viewability. But correlative with the conception of the conditioned object of perception goes that of an unconditioned noumenon. Employment of this conception is warranted and justified because it answers to the inexorable de-mands of a Principle of Sufficient Reason ("the unconditioned, which reason, by necessity and by right, demands . . . to complete the series of conditions").[3] As Kant puts the matter in one key passage,

> The principle of (sufficient) reason is thus properly . . . a rule, prescribing a regress in the series of conditions of given ap-pearances, and forbidding it (viz., reason) from bringing the regress to a close by treating anything at which it may arrive as absolutely unconditioned. (*CPuR*, A508–9 = B536–37)[4]

And in the *Prolegomena*, Kant articulates the line of thought at is-sue in the following terms:

> Reason through all its concepts and laws of the understanding which are sufficient to it for empirical use, that is, within the sen-sible world, finds in it no satisfaction, because ever-recurring questions deprive us of all hope of any completion . . . The sen-suous world is nothing but a chain of appearances . . . It is not the thing in itself, and consequently must point to that which contains the basis of this appearance, to beings which cannot be known merely as appearances, but as things-in-themselves. In the knowledge of them alone can reason hope to satisfy its de-sire for completeness in proceeding from the conditioned to its conditions. (*Prolegomena*, sect. 57; pp. 353–54, Akad.)

There is a significant parallel between these passages and cog-nate discussions in Leibniz. Thus in explaining the workings of the Principle of Sufficient Reason in his important essay "On the Ultimate Origin of Things" Leibniz maintains:

> the sufficient reason of existence can not be found either in any particular things or in the whole aggregate or series . . . And even if you imagine the world eternal, and containing an infi-nite series of states, you will nevertheless find a sufficient rea-

son for them in none of them whatsoever, and as any number of them whatsoever does not aid you in giving a reason for them, it is evident that the reason must be sought elsewhere . . . From which it follows that . . . an ultimate extramundane reason of things . . . cannot be escaped.

The reason of the world, therefore, lies hidden in something extramundane different from the chain of states or series of things, the aggregate of which constitutes the world.[5]

It is noteworthy – and characteristic of the writers involved – that whereas Leibniz here applies the Principle of Sufficient Reason ontologically, to establish an extramundane source of existence (i.e., God), Kant applies it epistemologically, to establish an extramundane ground of perceptual experience (i.e., the noumenon).

Of course, for Kant any such application of the Principle of Sufficient Reason would not succeed in bringing the *Ding an sich* within the orbit of experience. It remains a pure creature of theory (*ens rationtis*), located quite outside the rationale of experienced existence – and so unknowable – which, by the very workings of reason we not only can but must think, that is to say, must *postulate* (esp. *CPuR*, Bxxvi–xxvii).

It is essential to recognize that Kant's step from appearances to the thing-in-itself is accomplished through the Principle of Sufficient Reason and not through the Principle of Causality. For causality, according to Kant, is operative only between phenomena, so that causal relations only obtain within the phenomenal realm. Any recourse to causality could never point outside the area of the phenomenal. With the Principle of Causality, then, we must remain squarely inside the domain of experience.

Because the Principle of Sufficient Reason underpins it as a support, the Principle of Causality admits of a demonstration of sorts – specifically of the sort given to it in the Second Analogy. However, the Principle of Sufficient Reason itself admits of no demonstration.

[The rationale of the principle of Causality lies in] rules of synthetic unity *a priori,* by means of which we can anticipate experience. For lack of this approach [*Methode*], in the delusive urge to seek to demonstrate dogmatically the synthetic proposition which empirical employment of reason recommends as its principle, the attempt has frequently been made – always in vain! – to provide a proof for the Principle of Sufficient Reason. (*CPuR*, A217 = B264–65)

But the operation of a Principle of Sufficient Reason can endow the phenomena with an intentional character that points toward an external something outside the phenomenal domain. It does so by coming into play in a limited but very important way: by establishing the pivotal point that the phenomenal order must itself be grounded, and so producing the result *that* an underlying noumenal order must be accepted, without thereby going very far toward throwing light on the issue of *what* the nature of this noumenal order could be and *how* it is constituted. Of course, such a principle cannot, on Kantian lines, be *known*, but it can, and indeed *must*, be *thought*. Kant here once more deploys his crucial distinction between "items of knowledge" that we can expect to encounter in actual experiential confrontation and "creatures of theory" that we cannot expect to encounter experientially, but rather project theoretically in the contexts of explanatory understanding.

A careful heed of this perspective – and so of the distinction between a generic (and temporally unschematized) Principle of Sufficient Reason and a specific (and temporally schematized) Principle of Causality – enables us to see how Kant can be freed from the charge of inconsistency in regard to noumenal causality. The answer is simply that the relationship of things-in-themselves to the phenomena is actually not to be construed in causal terms at all – at any rate insofar as the causality at issue is specifically that associated with the Kantian category. Kant's own occasional looseness of formulation notwithstanding, it is clear that although things-in-themselves somehow "affect" the sensibility so as to bring representations of objects into being, the relationship here at issue is definitely not to be construed in properly causal terms. No real "agency" is involved: the matter is one of grounding rather than of causing. The linkage between phenomenon and thing-in-itself, rather than being in fact specifically causal in character, is mediated by a generic Principle of Sufficient Reason. This principle provides an (essentially) noncausal principle of grounding to which Kant time and again makes appeal. And – use of activity-oriented language notwithstanding – an appeal to actual causality is just not at issue here, any more than it is when one says that 5 is "produced" by the addition of 3 and 2. The relationships involved are essentially static linkages in a purely conceptual order.

The generic grounding at issue here is pre- or subcategorical; it itself is not (as yet) temporally schematized. For this reason, this sort of grounding is not something that lies within the province of our actual knowledge, but something pre- or subcategorical that is merely thinkable. As Kant puts it, it rests on no more than " a lame appeal to a logical condition, which, though necessary to the concept, is very far from being sufficient for real possibility" (*CPuR*, A244 = B302). We do not *know* things-in-themselves and *discover* their causal agency; instead we *think* things-in-themselves and *impute* explanatory efficacy to them.[6] Only when this generic grounding becomes temporally specified in the context of the materials of our actual experience do we indeed arrive at genuine causality.

Useful light is shed upon the issue in the *Critique of Practical Reason*. Here Kant writes:

> Now the concept of a being which has a free will is that of a *causa noumenon;* and we are assured that this concept does not contradict itself, because the concept of a cause originates exclusively in pure understanding, and its objective reality with reference to objects in general is guaranteed by the Deduction [in the *Critique of Pure Reason*]. As independent in origin from all sensuous conditions, it is in itself not to be restricted to phenomena, so that, unless a definite theoretical use of it is to be made, it could certainly be applied to things as pure beings of the understanding. But because no intuition, which could only be sensuous, can support this application, *causa noumenon* is, for the theoretical use of reason, an empty concept although a possible and thinkable one. Through it I do not strive to know theoretically the characteristic of a being in so far as it has a pure will; it is enough for me to denote it as such by means of this concept and thus to couple the concept of causality with that of freedom (and with what is inseparable from it, i.e., the moral law as its determining ground). I have this right by virtue of the pure nonempirical origin of the concept of cause. (*CPrR*, 55–56)

Just like the "causality" of the thing-in-itself in the *Critique of Pure Reason,* so the "causality" of the free agent in the *Critique of Practical Reason* represents a conception that is empirically empty but methodologically (i.e., procedurally or practically) indispensable – indispensable if we are to make sense of our experience as an agent or observer, respectively.

Even with Kant we still sail in the backwash of the linkage – inherent in the scholastic use of the Latin *causa* – between a generic *grounding* of reasons and a specifically efficient *causality* of natural process. With Kant, the Principle of Sufficient Reason is an unschematized version of the Principle of Causality, even as an abstractly intelligible conception of grounding constitutes an unschematized counterpart to the categorical conception of cause. The Principle of Sufficient Reason is a generic-framework principle guaranteeing only some sort of grounding in general: the Principle of Causality is a specific implementation of this principle indicating that in one specific area (nature's domain of sense-based experience) a certain specific mode of grounding (viz. causal explanation) is always forthcoming.[7]

Kant's position as a (transcendental) idealist also comes into the picture here. As he sees it, we do have before us one familiar conceptual model or paradigm of noumenal causality – namely, our own putative causality as rational choosers in relation to our actions within the sphere of free agency. It is precisely because our reason is able to initiate actions *sua sponte* that it can also prove to be sufficient in the order of rationalization in a way that no appeal to causal explanation within the phenomenal order can possibly manage to achieve:

> Reason therefore acts freely; it is not dynamically determined in the chain of natural causes through either outer or inner grounds antecedent in time. This freedom ought not, therefore, to be conceived only negatively as independence of empirical conditions. The faculty of reason, so regarded, would cease to be a cause of appearances. It must also be described in positive terms, as the power of originating a series of events. In reason itself nothing begins; as unconditioned condition of every voluntary act, it admits of no conditions antecedent to itself in time . . . [W]e regard reason as a cause that, irrespective of all the above-

mentioned empirical conditions, could have determined, and ought to have determined, the agent to act . . . This causality of reason we do not regard as only a co-operating agency, but as complete in itself, even when the sensuous impulses do not favor but are directly opposed to it; the action is ascribed to the agent's intelligible character. (*CPuR*, A553–54 = B581–83)

Kant's thinking in this connection rests on the fundamental proportion of analogy that things-in-themselves are to phenomena as the rational will is to its free acts, and that the "causality of freedom" actually provides us with a model for noumenal causality in general. Thus consider the following passage:

If . . . appearances are not taken for more than they actually are; if they are viewed not as things-in-themselves, but merely as representations, connected according to empirical laws, they must themselves have grounds which are not appearances. The effects of such an intelligible cause appear, and accordingly can be determined through other appearances, but its causality is not so determined. While the effects are to be found in the series of empirical conditions, the intelligible cause, together with its causality, is outside the series. Thus the effect may be regarded as free in respect of its intelligible cause, and at the same time in respect of appearances as resulting from them according to the necessity of nature. (*CPuR*, A537 = B565)

Although Kant is here writing of the causality of freedom, his observations apply every bit as much to the noumenal operation of things-in-themselves producing phenomena as to the noumenal causality of free wills in producing phenomenal actions.

3. THE IMPETUS TO ONTOLOGICAL AUTONOMY AND INSUPERABLE PROPENSITIES TO THINK

The Kantian doctrine of noumenal causality roots in the final analysis in the structure of a conceptual scheme that is woven around the very concept of knowledge. For *knowledge* of objects would not be knowledge *of objects* if the "objects" at issue did not have an ontological foothold outside the knowledge situation. But what is at issue here is not a matter of actually learned existence, but of conceptually warranted postulation. Kant in effect makes a subtle but critical shift from the ontological to the epistemological order; from "did not in fact have" to "were not warrantedly thought to have." And what provides the warrant for such a shift is a deployment of the Principle of Sufficient Reason.

Now if this leap toward the unconditioned behind conditioned objects as given in experience were not justified, then knowledge, objective knowledge, would collapse with it. For we could then not legitimately regard the experience of objects as a transaction – the upshot of a genuine encounter between mind and object – since it would be a mere production of the mind alone. (If there were no mind-independent basis, experience would lose all its claim to objectivity.) It is the fact that a justification can be given that shifts the Kantian position from a subjective to a transcendental idealism.

An object of experience – as it presents itself within the orbit of our sensory contact with things – is inevitably subject to the conditions of experientiability. In the framework of Kant's philosophy, it makes no sense even to consider this object, the experienced object, as somehow self-subsistent in the full bloom of its mind-dependent qualifications – any more than it would make sense to contemplate a word as existing in a language-disconnected setting. For Kant, an experienced object is ineradicably heteronomous, it is inevitably subject to an unshakable belief in a reality somehow hidden away under the superficial appearances we humans take hold of. The mind engaged in the quest for knowledge approaches its experience with an insuperable impetus for ontological heteronomy, in virtue of which it insists upon (i.e., "necessarily postulates") the presence of an object that meets the demand for a realm of reality behind that of appearance.

It is crucially important for Kant that the ontological leap from appearance to underlying reality is in fact justified. Yet for him this justification proceeds not in terms of the ontology of nature, but rather in terms of the ontology of mind. (The Copernican Revolution comes to the fore again.) The mind not only can, but it must postulate an experientially untouched reality underlying the experienced appearance by way of providing its grounding. Both the key terms here – "must" and "postulate" – require comment.

The "must" is critical here – because what goes on here is no matter of choice but represents an essential feature of the human mind. In one key passage, Kant puts the matter as follows:

> [The] unconditioned is not, indeed, given as being in itself real . . . ; it is, however, what alone can complete the series of conditions when we proceed to trace these conditions to their grounds. This is the course which our human reason, by its very nature, leads all of us, even the least reflective, to adopt. (*CPuR*, A584 = B612)

And again in the *Prolegomena* Kant puts the matter as follows:

> And we indeed, rightly consider objects of sense as mere appearances and confess thereby that they are based upon a thing in itself . . . The understanding, therefore, by assuming appearances, grants the existence of things-in-themselves also; and to this extent we may say that the representation of such things as are the basis of appearances, consequently of mere beings of the understanding, is not only admissible but unavoidable. (*Prolegomena*, Sect. 32, p. 314, Akad.)

This unavoidability is centrally important: we would have a very sorry defense of objectivity if we could not even secure intersubjective universality.

At first thought, this unavoidability seems not to be a matter of logical compulsion. For logical compulsion is hypothetical, whereas this the presently operative compulsion seems not hypothetical but categorical. But this appearance in misleading. We have here the sort of compulsion through rational presuppositions that is operative at many places in Kant. The necessitation at issue is thus not absolute but relative: If you are going to claim genuinely objective knowledge, then you must also be prepared to claim a genuine object whose existence, at any rate, is something independent of the conditions of thought. That is, you "must" do this if experience is to be thought of in a certain way – that is, is to count as knowledge producing. In a key passage, Kant wrote:

> In the first place, it is evident beyond all possibility of doubt, that if the conditioned is given, a regress in the series of all its conditions is *set* up *as a task*. For it is involved in the very concept of the conditioned that something is referred to a condition,

and if this condition is again itself conditioned, to a more remote condition, and so through all the members of the series. The above proposition is thus analytic, and has nothing to fear from a transcendental criticism. It is a logical postulate of reason, that through the understanding we follow up and extend as far as possible that connection of a concept with its conditions which directly result from the concept itself. (*CPuR*, A497–98 = B525–26)

In sum, the "must" of "must postulate" resides in the mind, which by the very nature of its constitution cannot but work accordingly in its quest for objective knowledge.

So much for the "must." Next we must consider "postulate" – for it is just this that Kant means by "think" in the present context. Kant described the postulation at issue in the following terms:

Appearances, so far as they are thought as objects according to the unity of the categories, are called *phaenomena*. But *if I postulate* things which are mere objects of understanding, and which, nevertheless, can be given as such to an intuition, although not to one that is sensible ... such things would be entitled *noumena* [*intelligibilia*]. Now we must bear in mind that the concept of appearances, as limited by the Transcendental Aesthetic, already of itself establishes the objective reality of *noumena* and justifies the division of objects into *phaenomena* and *noumena*, and so of the world into a world of the senses and a world of the understanding [mundus sensibilis et intelligibilis] ... For if the senses represent to us something merely *as it appears*, this something must also in itself be a thing, and an object of a non-sensible intuition, that is, of the understanding ... All our representations are, it is true, referred by the understanding to some object; and since appearances are nothing but representations, the understanding refers them to a *something*, as the object of sensible intuition. But this something, thus conceived, is only the transcendental object; and by that is meant a something = X, of which we know, and with the present constitution of our understanding can know, nothing whatsoever. (*CPuR*, A248–50)

Clearly, when we postulate a thing, the very use of the word "postulate" concedes that (1) we certainly do not encounter this thing in experience, and in fact (2) we do not actually know that it exists. The "things" which our understanding projects are clearly not items of which we have any independent knowledge. But, of course, projective postulation is a step not to be taken at random; it must have some rational foundation, some validation. The operation of the Principle of Sufficient Reason in its regulative guise can provide such warrant for a necessary postulation because it carries essentially conceptual (i.e., logical) force, via its rooting in the very nature of the workings of our mind.

The idea of an existential postulation may seem strange – so much so that the whole process may be thought illegitimate. But an example can help to show that this is not the case. Consider the question of "the sum" of an infinite series such as

$$\frac{1}{2} = \frac{1}{4} + \frac{1}{8} + \cdots + \frac{1}{2} + \cdots$$

Clearly we can never actually sum the series up to show that the sum total in question exists: we not only cannot actually carry out the infinite summation process so as to produce the infinite sum; we cannot even demonstrate (and so know) its existence by the standard machinery of arithmetic. (All we can demonstrate is that *if* the sum exists, then it can neither be > 1 nor < 1; we cannot demonstrate that it does indeed exist and equals 1.) But if we *postulate* the existence of infinite sums – whose existence we admittedly cannot *prove* in the usual way – then we are in a position to make coherent claims regarding the sum total of our series. This example, then, may serve to motivate by way of analogy the conception of an existential postulation.

And the example has a close kinship to Kant's line of thought. We can show that the infinite sum at issue is subject to a limit (i.e., cannot exceed 1). But the actuality of a limit to a series does not establish the existence of something *at* the limit, something that *does* the limiting – as Kant himself clearly says (*Prolegomena*, sect. 45; p. 332, Akad.). Similarly, the limitedness of a regress of grounds does not establish the existence of an ultimate ground, knowable in the same manner as the grounds themselves. To say that such a limit can – and in certain cases must – be thought to exist is not to say that its existence can be known. A limit of known grounds does not constitute a known limit of grounds.

4. CONCLUSION

The crux of the present interpretation, then, is that Kantian noumenal causality is not actual causality at all, in the strict sense on which causality is governed by the specific, experientially constitutive Principle of Causality of the Second Analogy. Rather, it is only analogical causality, governed by a generic and regulative principle of grounding, a Principle of Sufficient Reason, a principle that controls what we must think to be the case, rather than what we can claim to know regarding nature. Hence this use of the Principle of Sufficient Reason does not demonstrate the existence of noumenal grounding. Rather the Principle of Sufficient Reason provides the basis for a commitment that is – as Kant sees it – both inevitable and rationally warranted, the necessary postulation of noumenal causality in terms of Kant's know versus think distinction. It does not establish the real existence of things-in-themselves and their causal operation, but rather commits our mind to the concept of a thing-in-itself – and thus a noumenal causality – as a conceptual resource that is both available and applicable. Kant is concerned to argue that the realm of our *information* – of what we can and must appropriately think – is wider than the realm of our experiential *knowledge.*

The Principle of Sufficient Reason accordingly does a job that needs doing for Kant and that other elements of his system are not prepared to do. But it is for him merely regulative and not knowledge productively constitutive. It represents a divine discontent, the unwillingness – nay inability – of the mind seeking for objective knowledge to rest satisfied with conditions – with less than the unconditioned. But it also marks a critical limit – that which sets knowing off from thinking (sc., postulating). The fact that a principle with a systematically solid standing is involved is pivotal here, for only through a principle of this nature could one obtain a rational warrant for the postulation that calls noumenal causality into operation.

If this view that a Principle of Sufficient Reason is importantly at work in Kant's teaching is correct, it points toward a much closer kinship of his philosophy with that of Leibniz and Wolff than is generally acknowledged. For it indicates that Kant's system of critical philosophy needs a Principle of Sufficient Reason every bit as much as that of his "dogmatic" predecessors. To be sure, however, he can and does place this ongoing commitment within the aegis of his Copernican Revolution, by grounding sufficient reason "critically," in the modus operandi of the cognitive apparatus of reason itself, rather than "dogmatically," in that of an ontologically independent reality that it endeavors to know.

Chapter 3

Kant's Cognitive Anthropocentrism

1. SENSIBILITY ANTHROPOCENTRISM

In the initial part of the *Critique of Pure Reason*, Kant insists that we must accept, if only by way of presumption, that there is such a thing as a characteristic modus operandi of the human mind – that the human mind, by its very nature as such, functions in a certain specific sort of way in its cognitive operations. And he goes on to hold that, in consequence, any question about how matters may stand "in themselves" – apart from the conditions of knowability set by the human mind – is something about which we can hope to achieve no information whatsoever. We therefore face the situation of an agnosticism regarding the nature and machinations of things as they are in themselves, apart from the conditions imposed by our human cognitive faculties. Moreover, Kant goes on to insist that we can secure no basis for understanding why the modus operandi of our human cognitive faculties has the features it does through appeal to some more fundamental level of known fact. While we can discern what the conditions of human cognition are, we cannot possibly secure any information about how and why they obtain, seeing that any explanation of these issues would require some deeper involvement in inaccessible information about how matters stand "in themselves."

The implications of this agnostic position – and in particular those regarding its specifically anthropocentric nature – often go

This chapter is an expanded version of an essay entitled "Kant and the 'Special Constitution' of Man's Mind," published in the author's *Studies in Modality* (Oxford: Blackwell, 1974), *American Philosophical Quarterly* monograph no. 8, pp. 71–83. Reprinted by permission of Blackwell Publishers.

unappreciated. The present discussion explores somewhat more fully the nature of Kant's agnosticism regarding the roots of human knowledge and examines its implications for the coherence of Kant's overall argument.

There is no need to go to great lengths to establish Kant's acknowledgment that the forms of sensibility at issue in the Transcendental Aesthetic are forms of human sensibility specifically relating to the perceptual experience enjoyed by us. He could scarcely be more explicit on this point:

> But intuition takes place only in so far as the object is given *to us*. This again is possible, *for us humans at any rate* [uns Menschen wenigstens] in so far as the mind is affected in a certain way. The capacity (receptivity) for receiving representations through the mode in which *we* are affected by objects, is called "sensibility." Objects are given *to us* by means of sensibility, and it alone yields *us* intuitions . . . But all thought must, directly or indirectly . . . , relate ultimately to intuitions, and therefore, *with us*, to [our human] sensibility, because in no other way can an object be given *to us*. (*CPuR*, A19 = B33; italics added.)

It is accordingly perfectly clear that, on Kant's view, the way in which objects are "given" in perceptual experience is relativized to the particular features characterizing our specifically human faculty of perception. He is quite explicit on this point: "*Our nature is so constituted* that *our* mode of perception [or "intuition"] can never be other than sensible; that is, it contains only the mode in which *we* are affected by objects" (*CPuR*, A51 = B75, italics added). Whatever things may be, in and by themselves, outside the range of this particular us-coordinated setting, is terra incognita for us humans. For Kant the materials with which our sensibility deals are known to us only – and just exactly – insofar as our human sensibility presents them:

> What matter may be as a thing in itself (transcendental object) is completely unknown to us, though, owing to its being represented [by us] as something external, its permanence *as appearance* can indeed be observed. (*CPuR*, A366, italics added)

We can (indeed, must) think of knowledge as transactionally grounded – as rooted in some sort of interaction between our minds ("in themselves") and things ("in themselves"). But we can only come to know the products of these interactions; about those interagents themselves we can learn nothing whatsoever. Thus Kant writes:

> What we maintain is that all our perception is nothing but the representation of appearance; that the things which we perceive are not in themselves what we perceive them as being, nor their relations so constituted in themselves as they appear to us, and that if the subject, or even only the subjective constitution of the senses in general, be removed, the whole constitution and all the relations of objects in space and time, nay space and time themselves, would vanish. As appearances, they cannot exist in themselves, but only in us. What objects may be in themselves, and apart from all this receptivity of our sensibility, remains completely unknown to us. We know nothing but our mode of perceiving them. (*CPuR*, A42 = B59)

That other sorts of intelligent creatures (e.g., such higher intelligences as angels or gods) would inevitably have to intuit objects in the forms of spatiality and temporality characteristic of us humans is something that Kant would expressly deny. He emphasizes of space and time that "they belong only to the form of intuition, *and therefore to the subjective constitution of our mind,* apart from which they could not be ascribed to anything whatsoever" (A23 = B38; italics added). Thus space is "the subjective condition of [our] sensibility, under which alone outer intuition is possible *for us*" (A26 = B43; italics added), so that "it is, therefore, *solely from the human standpoint* that we can speak of space" (A26 = B42; italics added). And the same holds of time, which "is nothing but the subjective condition under which alone intuition can take place *in us*" (A33 = B49; italics added). Accordingly, "if we abstract from *our* mode of inwardly intuiting ourselves. . . and so take objects as they may be in themselves, then time is nothing" (A34 = B51; Kant's italics), so that "time is *a purely subjective condition of our human intuition*" (A35 = B51; italics added). Space and time accordingly relate specifically to human sensibility:

> What objects may be . . . apart from all this receptivity of *our* sensibility, remains completely unknown to us. We know nothing

> but our mode of perceiving them [i.e., objects] – *a mode which is
> peculiar to us, and not necessarily shared in by every being, though,
> certainly, by every human being.* (*CPuR*, A42 = B59; italics added)

The specific relativization to the first person plural "we/us" pervades Kant's discussion of these themes.

It is, to be sure, imaginable that cognizing beings other than
people also possess a sensibility that is subject to these same conditions, but this is something about which we cannot, in principle,
obtain any information:

> This mode of intuiting in space and time need not be limited to
> human sensibility. It may be that all finite, thinking beings nec-
> essarily agree with man in this respect, although we are not in
> a position to judge whether this is actually so. (*CPuR*, B72)

This of course means that the extra-experiential features of
perceived objects – preeminently their location in space and time –
can never validly be related to things as they may be in themselves, outside the realm of human experience. Our knowledge of
reality reaches only as far as our experience. The things of the
world as we know it – and the spatiotemporal framework that
embraces them – are alike wholly empirical and experience-
bound. Where experience cannot reach, the objective knowledge
too is unrealizable:

> I do not . . . at all profess to disprove void space, for it may exist
> where perceptions cannot reach, and where there is, therefore,
> no empirical knowledge of coexistence. But such a space is not
> for us an object of any possible experience. (*CPuR*, A 214 = B 261)

For Kant, the idea of mentally provided substantive knowledge of
extramental reality is a contradiction in terms.

In particular, as regards the human sensibility, "[There is no
way for us to achieve any] further explanation for . . . why space
and time are the *only* forms of our possible perception" (*CPuR*,
B146; italics added). There is nothing about sensibility as such that
requires it to be spatiotemporal, this is simply – as best we can
tell – a feature of the specifically *human* sensibility. And again:

It is not given to us to observe our own mind with any other apprehension than that of inner sense; and . . . it is yet precisely in the mind that the secret of the source of our sensibility is located. The relation of sensibility to an object and what the transcendental ground of this [objective] unit may be, are matters undoubtedly so deeply concealed that we, who after all know even ourselves only through inner sense and therefore as appearance, can never be justified in treating sensibility as being a suitable instrument of investigation for discovering anything save always still other appearances – eager as we yet are to explore their non-sensible cause. (*CPuR*, A278 = B 334)

The long and short of it is that

[n]o one . . . can have the right to claim that he knows anything in regard to the transcendental cause of our representations of the outer senses; and their assertion is therefore entirely groundless. (*CPuR*, A391)

And so, the particular forms of our sensibility, namely space and time, are – as best we can tell – of specifically anthropoid bearing. And accordingly, the cognitive disciplines that fall within their orbit (viz. geometry, arithmetic) embrace propositions whose necessity and universality is specifically *humanly* relative.

So much for the ramification of the anthropocentrism of sensibility. Let us now turn to the understanding.

2. CATEGORIAL ANTHROPOMORPHISM

Human understanding is inherently conceptual: "The knowledge yielded by understanding, or at least by the human understanding, must therefore be by means of concepts, and so is not intuitive, but discursive" (*CPuR*, A68 = B93). Our understanding-provided knowledge is thus inherently categorial in nature – that is, subject to the fundatmental categories of human thought. Kant is perfectly explicit as to the anthropocentric nature of the categories:

The categories . . . are nothing but forms of thought . . . [A]part therefore from the only intuition that is possible *to us*, they have even less meaning than the pure sensible forms. Through these [sensuous] forms an object is at least given, whereas a [cate-gorical] mode of combining the manifold – *a mode peculiar to our understanding* – by itself, in the absence of that intuition whereby the manifold can alone be given, signifies nothing at all. (*CPuR*, B305–6; italics added)

The situation as regards the formal concepts of "the under-standing" thus substantially parallels that of the forms of "the sen-sibility" – it is specifically our human understanding that is at issue here. The *Critique of Pure Reason* is very explicit on this point. Whether other sorts of creatures have our mode of understanding is an issue about which we have no information whatsoever. But we do know that they need not necessarily have it:

> The manifold to be intuited must be given prior to the synthesis of understanding, and independently of it. How this takes place, remains here undetermined. For were I to think an understand-ing which is itself intuitive (as, for example, a divine under-standing which should not represent to itself given objects, but through whose representation the objects should themselves be given or produced), the categories would have no meaning whatsoever in respect of such a mode of knowledge. They are merely rules for an understanding whose whole power consists in thought, consists, that is, in the act whereby it brings the syn-thesis of a manifold, given to it from elsewhere in intuition, to the unity of apperception – a faculty, therefore, which by itself knows nothing whatsoever, but merely combines and arranges the material of knowledge, that is, the intuition, which must be given to it by the object. This peculiarity of our understanding, that it can produce *a priori* unity of apperception solely by means of the categories, and only by such and so many, is as little ca-pable of further explanation as why we have just these and no other functions of judgment, or why space and time are the only forms of our possible intuition. (*CPuR*, B145–46)

The tabulated categories as such are contingently conditional factors outside the jurisdiction of reason. For there is not – and cannot be – a rational explanation of why just those twelve cate-gories must be exactly and specifically as they are:

> Other forms of intuition than space and time, other forms of understanding (different from the discursive), other forms of

thought or of cognition through concepts, although they are possible, we nevertheless can in no way render conceivable and comprehensible to ourselves; and even if we could do so, they still would not belong to experience – the only mode of cognition in which objects are given to us. Whether other perceptions than those belonging to *our* whole possible experience, and therefore a quite different subject-matter field, could exist, the [human] understanding is not in a position to decide. (*CPuR*, A230–32 = B283)

And so, in contemplating the categories from the vantage point of the question "Why these and not others?" we are condemned to total and irremediable ignorance. We face here a barrier that the explanatory resources of reason have no hope of penetrating.

In some passages, indeed, Kant apparently states that the categories are valid for any and every sensuously conditioned understanding, and not the human alone:

The pure concepts of understanding appertain, through the mere understanding, to objects of intuition in general, irrespective of whether this is our own or any other, as long as it is sensuous. But for this very reason they are mere *forms* of thought, through which alone no determinate object can be known. (*CPuR*, B150)

And again:

Space and time, as conditions under which alone objects can possibly be given to us, are valid no further than for objects of the senses, and therefore only for [human] experience. Beyond these limits they represent nothing; for they are only in the senses, and beyond them have no reality. The pure concepts of understanding, however, are free from this limitation, and extend to objects of intuition in general, be the intuition like or unlike ours, if only it be sensible and not intellectual. (*CPuR*, B148)

In such passages, however, we must construe Kant to be talking about categoricity in general, and not about the particular definite entries of his tabulation of particular categories. For how other sorts of categories might function apart from their role in regard to *our* conceptualization of things is something we cannot even meaningfully speculate about. This would carry us into the

noumenal realm, and of noumena we can know nothing whatsoever, seeing that genuine knowledge of particular things always
involves experiential contact. The overall situation parallels that
of space and time:

> Other forms of intuition than space and time, other forms of un-
> derstanding than the discursive forms of thought, or of knowl-
> edge through concepts, even if they should be possible, we
> cannot render in any way conceivable and comprehensive to
> ourselves; and even assuming that we could do so, they still
> would not belong to experience – the only kind of knowledge
> in which objects are given to us. Whether other perceptions than
> those belonging to our whole possible experience, and therefore
> a quite different field of matter, may exist, the [human] under-
> standing is not in a position to decide. It can deal only with the
> synthesis of that which is given [to us]. (*CPuR*, A230–31 = B283)

Like space and time – the crucial forms of human sensibility – so
also the specifically tabulated categories, the crucial forms of
human understanding, are utterly inexplicable on rational principles. To be sure, categories of some sort are indeed essential to any
prospect for the sensuous apprehension of objects. (Demonstrat-
ing this is the task of the Deduction of the Categories.) But with
the particular categories of understanding as specifically tabulated by Kant we face a very different situation. For here we once
again reenter the secure domain of what is specifically correlative
with the specifically human mode of cognition.[1] The salient point
is that although we do (and, given the nature of our cognitive
faculties, must) think the categories to apply to sensuous objects
unrestrictedly, they – as they stand – can in fact be applied validly
only to objects given in our particular mode of intuition:

> The categories . . . are nothing but forms of thought . . . [A]part
> therefore from the only intuition that is possible *to us*, they have
> even less meaning than the pure sensible forms. Through these
> [sensuous] forms an object is at least given, whereas a [categor-
> ical] mode of combining the manifold – *a mode peculiar to our un-
> derstanding* – by itself, in the absence of that intuition whereby
> the manifold can alone be given, signifies nothing at all. (*CPuR*,
> B305–6; italics added)

43

Against such a portrayal of the Kantian position, someone may be tempted to object as follows: "How can you say that the categories of understanding are inexplicable? What of the celebrated Deduction of the Categories? Does this not establish the operation of those various categories on the basis of fundamental general principles?" By no means. For as Kant himself puts it,

> [Categories] are merely rules for an understanding whose whole power consists in thought, consists, that is, in the action whereby it brings to the unity of apperception the synthesis of a manifold that is given to it from elsewhere in intuition. This faculty accordingly by itself knows nothing whatsoever, but merely combines and orders the material for cognition, that is, the intuition, which must be given to it through the object. For the peculiarity of our understanding, that it can produce *a priori* unity of apperception solely by means of the categories, [tabulated] and only by just those of this nature and number, is as little capable of further explanation as why we have just these and no other functions of judgment, or why space and time are the only forms of our possible intuition. (*CPuR*, B145–46)

Kant's so-called Deduction of the Categories is thus not at all a deduction of those particular categories that Kant's table of categories invents, but a deduction of categoricity at large. As Kant sees it, the forms of sensibility and the categories of understanding must be taken as they come; there is no prospect of securing any deeper rationale for them.

The salient point is that although we think the categories to apply to sensuous objects unrestrictedly, they can in fact be applied validly only to objects given in our particular mode of intuition. All that a "deduction of the categories" manages to achieve is to show that some categories are necessary to objective knowledge, but it does nothing to address the issue of why it is those particular items of Kant's table of categories rather than possible others. The specific constitutive features of the human mind manifested on the side of intuition by the two forms of sensibility and on that of the understanding by the twelve categories must accordingly be accepted as contingent – as given ultimates incapable of explanation or rationalization of any sort. The categories are thought instruments by which alone we humans achieve knowledge of objects. But we cannot get behind them to comprehend why it is that a certain particular mode of categorization is a feature of our mind. The crucial fact bears repetition:

> This peculiarity of our understanding, that it can produce *a priori* unity of apperception solely by means of the categories, and only by such and so many, is as little capable of further explanation as why we have just these and no other functions of judgment, or why space and time are the only forms of our possible intuition. (*CPuR*, B146)

Critics who object that Kant does not deduce his particular twelve categories depict this as a shortcoming and failing. In so doing they fail to heed his explicit strictures about the in-principle infeasibility of such a project. It is categoricity alone – the need for some categories or other – that Kant's Deduction of the Categories establishes. The specificity of those particular categories is for Kant a contingent matter with which on account of this very fact reason has nothing to do, seeing that such matters lie outside the range of its jurisdiction. The project of such successors as Fichte and Hegel to rationalize particular categories would be seen by Kant as fundamentally misguided. For while with Hegel nothing lies beyond the range of reason – "the real is rational" – it is pivotal for Kant that there are important pockets of such irrationalizable contingency in nature, forms of sensibility and categories of understanding among them. For Kant as for the Founding Fathers of the American republic there is a separation of powers, and as a consequence of it there is no way in which reason could rationalize the resources, mechanisms, or operations of the human understanding – let alone for our sensibility.

3. THE REACH OF AGNOSTICISM

Although we can grasp that the human mind works in a certain way, on the issue of why it works that way we are plunged into deepest agnosticism:

> We can say of the thinking "I" (the soul) – which regards itself as substance, as simple, as numerically identical at all times, and as the correlate of all existence, from which all other existence

must be inferred – that it does *not* know *itself through the categories,* but knows the categories, and through them all objects, in the absolute unity of apperception, and so *through itself.* Now it is, indeed, very evident that *I cannot know as an object that which I must presuppose in order to know any object,* and that the determining self (the thought) is distinguished from the self that is to be determined (the thinking subject) in the same way as knowledge is distinguished from its object. Nevertheless there is nothing more natural and more misleading than the illusion which leads us to regard the unity in the synthesis of thoughts as a perceived unity in the subject of these thoughts. (*CPuR,* A 402; some italics added)

We cannot come to know the mind as an object and therefore cannot achieve any sort of explanation of why it functions as it does.

Reason can indeed grasp that forms and categories of some sort are needed for it to be able to accomplish its own work in the context of finite intelligences. But it cannot rationalize the details and explain why those particular forms and categories of ours are as they are. Reason can speak only for itself. The details of sensibility and understanding lie beyond its range – outside its jurisdiction (to employ a legal metaphor much favored by Kant). Ours not to reason why with regard to the modus operandi of human cognition. We can note that the human sensibility and understanding has certain features, but we have no means for – and thus no prospect of – explaining why those features obtain as they do. The human understanding has no means for penetrating in back of the proscenium curtain of the stage upon which our experiential affairs transpire.

And so, with Kant, not only knowledge but even reason has its limits. To be sure, for aught we know there may be some deeper potency at work here, but we humans have no viable prospect of penetrating to it:

It is not given to us to observe our own mind with any other intuition than that of inner sense; and . . . it is yet precisely in the mind that the secret of the source of our sensibility is located. The relationship of sensibility to an object and what the transcendental ground of this [objective] unity may be, are matters undoubtedly so deeply concealed that we, who after all know even ourselves only through inner sense and therefore as appearance, can never be justified in treating sensibility as being a suitable instrument of investigation for discovering anything save always still other appearances – eager as we yet are to explore their non-sensible cause. (*CPuR*, A277–78 = B333–34)

Kant insists "that it is not given to us to observe our own mind with any other intuition than that of the inner sense [whose data are empirical and a posteriori]; and that it is yet precisely in the mind that the secret source of our sensibility is located" (*CPuR*, A278 = B334). We have no way of penetrating beyond or behind the realities of our mind. For aught we can ever tell, "*sensibility* and *understanding* . . . perhaps spring from a common, but to us unknown, root" (*CPuR*, A15 = B29). Here we come to depths that our intellect simply cannot plumb. We have no alternative but to accept the modus operandi of the human mind as it stands. And in particular:

> We cannot form the least conception of any other possible understanding, either of such as is itself intuitive or of any that may possess an underlying mode of sensible intuition which is different in kind from that in space and time. (*CPuR*, B139)

The fact that we cannot grasp things-in-themselves means also – and most importantly – that we cannot explain (rationalize, understand) why the modus operandi of the human mind is as it is. We can obtain no deeper information about the makeup of our minds apart from their modus operandi in cognition. This is something that we must simply recognize and accept; we can hope for no explanation in deeper principles that are somehow more fundamental than and explanatorily basic to the workings of our mind. We can discover how the mind relates to its objects, but why it does so in that particular way is a total mystery for us – all that we have, and all that we can have, is an awareness of the product that emerges:

> The much-discussed question of the communion between the thinking and the extended, if we leave aside all that is merely fictitious, comes then simply to this: *how in a thinking subject outer intuition, namely, that of space, with its filling-in of shape and motion, is possible.* And this is a question which no man can

47

possibly answer. This gap in our knowledge can never be filled; all that can be done is to indicate it through the ascription of outer appearances to that transcendental object which is the cause of this species of representations, but of which we can have no knowledge whatsoever and of which we shall never acquire any concept. In all problems which may arise in the field of experience we treat these appearances as objects in themselves, without troubling ourselves about the primary ground of their possibility (as appearances). But to advance beyond these limits the concept of a transcendental object would be indispensably required. (*CPuR*, A393)

The upshot of Kant's critical analysis is thus in these regards deeply skeptical. It insists that some of our most fundamental questions regarding human knowledge lie beyond the possibility of resolution. Specifically, there are three fundamental questions we cannot possibly answer:

- What is the nature of things in themselves?
- Why are our forms of sensibility what they are (viz. space and time)?
- Why are the categories of understanding what they are?

And in this context it warrants reemphasis that it is one of the cardinal aims and objects of Kant's critical enterprise to establish limits to cognitive comprehension. Any and all hope of achieving knowledge of experience-underpinning reality must be abandoned:

[While sensibility] must not presume to reach things-in-themselves but only appearances, the understanding does indeed think for itself an object in itself, but only as transcendental object, which is [somehow] the appearance-distinct ground of appearance and therefore not itself appearance . . . But we are completely ignorant whether this is to be met with in us or outside us and whether it would be removed with the cessation of sensibility, or whether it would still remain. If we are pleased to name this [putative] object noumenon for the reason that its representation is not sensible, we are free to do so. But since we can apply to it none of the concepts of our understanding, the representation remains for us empty, and is of no service except to mark the limits of our sensible knowledge and to leave open a space which we can fill neither through possible experience nor through pure understanding. (*CPuR*, A288–89 = B344–45)

And Kant regards all of this agnosticism as simply a fact of life that must be understood as such. It requires explanation but needs no apology:

> If by the complaint – *that we have no insight whatsoever into the inner [nature] of things* – it be meant that we cannot conceive by pure understanding what the things which appear to us may be in themselves, they are entirely illegitimate and unreasonable. For what is demanded is that we should be able to know things, and therefore to intuit them, without senses, and therefore that we should have a faculty of knowledge altogether different from the human, and this not only in degree but as regards intuition likewise in kind – in other words, that we should be not men but beings [*Wesen*] of whom we are unable to say whether they are even possible, much less how they are constituted. (*CPuR*, A277–78 = B333–34)

4. THE ULTIMATE SOURCE

Every philosophical system is bound to come up against the realities of surd fact sooner or later, somewhere along the line. And with Kant we reach it at the level of the modus operandi of the human mind. In fact, this relativization of the a priori facets of our knowledge to the basic resources of the human intellect is exactly what Kant's Copernican Revolution is all about. For at just this point, a reference to "the special constitution" of our human faculties of intuition and of understanding becomes crucial (cf. *CPuR*, Bxvii–xviii). In the *Critique of Judgment*, Kant formulates this key point with quite explicit bluntness:

> If we look merely to the way in which anything can be *for us* (accordingly to the subjective constitution of our representative powers) an object of knowledge [*res cognoscibilis*], then our concepts will not be confronted with objects, *but merely with our cognitive faculties* and the use which they can make of a given representation (in a theoretical or practical point of view). Thus the question whether anything is or is not a cognizable object is not a question concerning the possibility of things, but of *our*

knowledge of them. (*CJ*, sect. 91, at start; p. 467, Akad.; italics added)

At the same time, it must be stressed that our human intellect is loath to acknowledge its own finitude and to admit its limitations. "It is humiliating to human reason that it achieves nothing [objective] in its pure employment, and indeed stands in need of a discipline to check its extravagances" (*CPuR*, A794 = B872). Reason would fain think that its projections are universal – that the concepts peculiar to its own peculiar modus operandi hold of finite intelligences in general. But this universality is spurious, since it does not and cannot relate to finite intelligences as such, but only to finite intelligences as we conceive of them:

> Reason is a faculty of principles and proceeds in its furthest demand to the unconditioned; on the other hand, the understanding stands at its service always only under a certain condition which must be given. . . We soon see that where the understanding cannot follow, the reason is transcendent and shows itself in ideas formerly established (as regulative principles), but not in objectively valid concepts. But the understanding which cannot keep pace with reason but yet is requisite for the validity of objects, limits the validity of these ideas to the subject. . . . According to the concept which *we ourselves* can *make* of the faculty of a finite intelligent being, nothing else can or must be thought, though this is not to assert that the ground of such a judgment lies in the object. (*CJ*, sect. 76, at start; p. 401, Akad.)

Throughout the realm of factual cognition (in all its dimensions of sensibility, understanding, and cognitive reason), the universality and necessity of our *knowledge* is, as Kant sees it, inevitably restricted to the realm of *our* knowledge.

The explanatory basis of human sensibility – the root of its being and the underlying rationale of its modus operandi – is something entirely beyond our range of achievable information. All that Kant has to offer here is said in the contention "that there are two items of human knowledge, *sensibility* and *understanding*, which perhaps spring from a common, but to us unknown root" (*CPuR*, A15 = B29). And the crucial point is not just that this common root is "to us unknown," but that it is to us unknowable. What we have

here is ultimately a matter of brute fact, namely the "special constitution" of the human mind. But this raises big problems for his
overall position.

5. KANT'S DILEMMA

The key premise of Kant's critical reasoning is a contention of the
form "Our mind operates K-wise [has a certain particular mode
of sensibility, understanding, etc.]." Clearly, we ought not – on
Kantian principles – to allow this crucial anthropocentrism to rest
on the basis of an empirical, survey-based determination of the
factual situation. Somehow we have to establish its necessity and
show that it must obtain for all of us, with "us" understood as "the
members of the species *Homo sapiens.*" But unfortunately the quest
for necessitation here proves profoundly problematic.

To be sure, one potentially promising way to secure the requisite basis of universality and necessity would be to contemplate
the possibility of a deeper explanation of why people (members
of *Homo sapiens*) – in virtue of certain features that define them as
such – must universally and necessarily possess K-type minds.
But this tactic is unavailable to Kant because of his explicit and
repeated insistence that a total agnosticism must prevail with respect to the question of why we humans possess K-type minds.
He explicitly insists that we can give no deeper explanation of our
specific anthropocentrism – that there is no way for us to get behind it to discover the reason why this circumstance obtains. Time
and again Kant indicates that here we face a mystery that defies
human comprehension. To its seeming undoing, then, Kant's
reasoning is defeated by the fact that his position is agnostic at exactly its pivotal point.

Of course, if we were to take the somewhat desperate expedi-
ent of construing anthropocentrism as analytic – through letting
its "us" be (by definitional fiat, as it were) just exactly those whose
members operate K-wise – then we would indeed secure the requirements of universality and necessity here. However, the difficulty would now simply be deflected to another point. For the
problem would now be whether this conveniently specified "us"
encompasses the category to which we ourselves – the members

of *Homo sapiens* – actually belong. And this issue of whether our human species is the one to which that functionally characterized "us" pertains now arises once again in a way that inescapably introduces the necessity-undermining aspect of empirical factuality.

Kant is caught up in a dilemma here. If we define humans as being the possessors of a K-type mind, then we confront the empirical question whether people (members of *Homo sapiens)* are humans (possessors of K-type minds). On the other hand if we define humans as people (members of *Homo sapiens*), then we confront the empirical question whether people have K-type minds. Either way, Kant's claim that we (humans) have certain a priori synthetic knowledge purely and simply because all possessors of K-type minds do so comes apart at the seams.

But could Kant not use a "transcendental argument" to do the job? That is to say, an argument of the presuppositional if–then form: "If synthetic a priori knowledge of objective fact is to be available at all to (any of us) humans, then all of us must exhibit a uniform commonality of fundamental cognitive operations." So far so good. But there is clearly a residual difficulty here. For we clearly cannot put this conditional to work in any actual implementation without somehow making that initial condition (viz. that specieswide commonality) actually available. And just here is where the difficulty lies. For it is one thing to identify a "condition under which alone" something transpires and quite another thing to establish that this condition is satisfied in a particular case. It is one thing to stand committed to a presupposition and another to validate such a commitment.

Yet what of a turning in the regulative direction? What of the prospect of addressing to rational beings a categorical imperative of theoretical reason: "See all of *Homo sapiens* in your own image! Impute to all eligible-seeming fellows the same cognitive powers and capacities that you claim for yourself." This strategy has much (perhaps everything!) to be said for it. But taking this tack calls for a dissolution of the barrier between theoretical and practical reason, subordinating (in the final analysis) the necessities of knowledge to the requirements of praxis. If Kant's system is to be rendered coherent, this, in the end, is the only way to proceed. Perhaps it is something that Kant is not quite prepared to assert in these stark terms. Nevertheless, it is a conclusion to which the whole tenor and tendency of his deliberations inexorably leads: in the end, the through and through practicalization of the theoretical appears to be Kant's best available option.

6. THE CATEGORIES OF EVALUATIVE JUDGMENT AND PRUDENTIAL PRACTICAL REASONING

The preceding discussion indicates that, in Kant's system, both the forms of our intuition and the categories of our understanding alike rest on the ultimately factual basis of the makeup of the human intellect. However, this circumstance, obtaining with respect to the realm of theoretical (inquiring) reason, also extends to embrace prudential reasoning and evaluative judgment.

Specifically, any application of the conceptions of means to ends and of aims and purposes (*Ziele* and *Zwecke*) calls for a specification to the characteristically human frame of reference. Kant is emphatically explicit in insisting that purposiveness is a necessary feature of our human understanding and has a validity that stands strictly relativized to it:

> the concept of the purposiveness of nature in its products is necessary for human judgment in respect of nature, but has not to do with the determination of objects. It is, therefore, a subjective principle of reason for the judgment, which as regulative (not constitutive) is just as necessarily valid for our human judgment as if it were an objective principle. (*CJ*, sect. 76, at end; p. 404, Akad.)

Accordingly, purposiveness is not a feature of the world *an sich*, but represents a projection that reflects a certain characteristic bias peculiar to the human mind in its conceptualization of "nature":

> Hence it is merely *a consequence of the particular constitution of our [human] understanding* that it represents products of nature as possible, according to a different kind of causality from that of the natural laws of matter namely, that of purposes and final causes. (*CJ*, sect. 77, middle; p. 408 Akad.; italics added)

And again:

> It is then one thing to say, "the production of certain things of nature or that of collective nature is only possible through a cause which determines itself to action according to design," and quite another to say, "I can, *according to the peculiar constitution of my cognitive faculties,* judge concerning the possibility of these things and their production in no other fashion than by conceiving for this a cause working according to design, i.e., a Being which is productive in a way analogous to the causality of an intelligence." In the former case I wish to establish something concerning the object and am thereby bound to confirm the objective reality of an assumed concept; in the latter, reason only determines the use of my cognitive faculties, conformably to their peculiarities and to the essential conditions of their range and their limits. (*CJ*, sect. 75, at start; pp. 397–98, Akad.)

Purposiveness is thus not something we learn from the study of nature, but something we bring to it in virtue of the intrinsic special "constitution" of the human mind:

> We confront, therefore, [with regard to purposiveness] a peculiarity of *our* (human) understanding in respect of the judgment in its reflection upon things of nature. But if this be so, the idea of a possible understanding different from the human must be fundamental here. (Just so in the critique of pure reason we must have in our thoughts another possible [kind of] intuition if ours is to be regarded as a particular species for which objects are only valid as phenomena.) And so we are able to say: Certain natural products, from the special constitution of our understanding, *must be considered by us,* in regard to their possibility, as if produced designedly and as purposes. But we do not, therefore, demand that there should be actually given a particular cause which has the representation of a purpose as its determining ground, and we do not deny that an understanding, different from (i.e., higher than) the human, might find the ground of the possibility of such products of nature in the mechanism of nature, i.e., in a causal combination for which an understanding is not explicitly assumed as cause. We have now to do with the relation of *our* understanding to the judgment, viz. we seek for a certain contingency in the constitution of our understanding, to which we may point as a peculiarity distin-

54

guishing it from other possible understandings. (*CJ* sect. 77, nr. start; p. 405, Akad.)

The standing of purposiveness – and of God as a designer-creator who underwrites its applicability to nature – is consequently altogether "subjective" in being specifically correlative with the makeup of human cognitive faculties:

> Hence the concept of an absolute necessary Being is no doubt an indispensable idea of reason, yet it is a problematical concept unattainable by the human understanding. It is indeed valid for the employment of our cognitive faculties in accordance with their peculiar constitution, but not valid of the object. Nor is it valid for every knowing being, because I cannot presuppose in every such being thought and intuition as two distinct conditions of the exercise of its cognitive faculties, and consequently as conditions of the possibility and actuality of things. An understanding into which this distinction did not enter might say: All objects that I know *are,* i.e., exist; and the possibility of some which yet do not exist . . . might never come into the representation of such a being at all. But what makes it difficult for our understanding to treat its concepts here as reason does is merely that, for it, as human understanding, that is transcendent (i.e., impossible for the subjective conditions of its cognition) which reason makes into a principle appertaining to the object. Here the maxim always holds that all objects whose cognition surpasses the faculty of the understanding are thought by us according to the subjective conditions of the exercise of that faculty which necessarily attach to our (human) nature. If judgments laid down in this way (and there is no other alternative in regard to transcendent concepts) cannot be constitutive principles determining the object as it is, they will remain regulative principles adapted to the human point of view. (*CJ,* sect. 76, middle; p. 403, Akad; cf. sects. 88 and 91)

This purpose-oriented aspect of our understanding is accordingly contingent upon the specific constitution of our peculiarly human understanding. Other sorts of intelligences whose concepts of the "natural world" in which they operate is devoid of the aspect of purposiveness are certainly in principle conceivable, though how

55

this possibility could be realized is something that is altogether inconceivable for us:

> But for us men there is only permissible the limited formula: We cannot otherwise think and make comprehensible the purposiveness which must lie at the bottom of our cognition of the internal possibility of many natural things than by representing it and the world in general as a product of an intelligent cause [a God]. Now, if this proposition, based on an inevitable necessary maxim of our judgment, is completely satisfactory from every *human* point of view for both the speculative and practical use of our reason, I should like to know what we lose by not being able to prove it as also valid for higher beings, from objective grounds (which unfortunately are beyond our faculties). It is indeed quite certain that we cannot adequately cognize, much less explain, organized beings and their internal possibility according to mere mechanical principles of nature . . . We must absolutely deny this insight to men . . . So much only is sure, that if we are to judge according to what is permitted us to see by our own proper nature (the conditions and limitations of our reason), we can place at the basis of the possibility of these natural purposes nothing else than an intelligent Being. This alone is in conformity with the maxim of our reflective judgment and therefore with a ground which, though subjective, is inseparably attached to the human race. (*CJ*, sect. 75, middle; pp. 399–400, Akad.)

The final terminus of this finalistic purposiveness inherent in our understanding is God, conceived of as the ultimate designer of nature and causal source of purpose within it. But this does not prove the existence of God, but only the inexorability of the idea of God as an instrument of human thought:

> Hence it is merely a consequence of the particular constitution of our understanding that it represents products of nature as possible, according to a different kind of causality from that of the natural laws of matter, namely, that of purposes and final causes. Hence, also, this principle has not to do with the possibility of such things themselves (even when considered as phenomena), according to the manner of their production, but merely with the judgment upon them which is possible to our understanding . . . It is here not at all requisite to prove that such

an *intellectuas archetypus* is possible, but only that we are inexorably led to the idea of it. (*CJ*, sect. 77, middle; p. 408, Akad.)

Seen from this angle, the necessity of a postulation of the deity is
of a status altogether coordinate with the general man relativization of our a priori knowledge of matters of fact. In this concept of
a deity as creator-planner, the practical category of purposiveness
reaches toward that ideal of reason that represents its ultimate
vanishing point (*focus imaginarius*):

> [I]t is absolutely impossible for us to produce from nature itself
> grounds of explanation for purposive combinations, and it is
> necessary by the constitution of the human cognitive faculties
> to seek the supreme ground of these purposive combinations in
> an originating understanding as the cause of the world. (*CJ*,
> sect. 77, at end; p. 410, Akad.)

So much, then, for the ultimately contingent, factual, and anthropocentric basis of our judgments of purposiveness in nature.
It deserves remark that the prudential (i.e., nonmoral) sector of our
practical reasoning – which ultimately revolves about the recognition of happiness as the goal of human life and activity[2] – also rests
on a foundation of exactly the same man-relativized sort:

> Pure reason, as a practical faculty . . . supplies us at the same
> time with a subjective constitutive principle in the concept of
> an object which [our] reason alone can think and which is to be
> actualized by our actions in the world according to that law. The
> idea of a final purpose in the employment of freedom accord-
> ing to moral laws has therefore subjective *practical* reality. We
> are a *a priori* determined by reason to promote with all our
> powers the *summum bonum* [*das Weltbest*], which consists in the
> combination of the greatest welfare of rational beings with the
> highest condition of the good in itself, i.e., in universal happi-
> ness conjoined with morality most accordant to law. (*CJ*, sect. 88,
> at start; p. 453, Akad.)

Accordingly, Kant's theory of the necessity and universality of
our synthetic a priori judgments is such that on the purposively
practical side also, such judgments inhere in something that is ultimately a matter of brute fact, namely the "special constitution"
of the human mind. Purposiveness is a matter of objectivity all

right, but of the objective validity and emphatically not the objective reality of purpose.

As these deliberations show, Kant's program of Copernican Revolution works itself out in such a way that, outside the analytic domain, a priori truth can and does root in the characteristic makeup and "special constitution" of the human mind. And this general circumstance specifically prevails throughout each of the following spheres:

1. Cognition (i.e., our speculative or theoretical knowledge of nature) in the realm of sensibility and understanding
2. Prudential practical reason (i.e., practical reasoning in its teleologically conditioned, goal-directed bearing)
3. Judgment (i.e., evaluation in both its aesthetic and purposive dimensions)

There is only one omission here, albeit a major one – namely, pure practical reason in its moral (i.e., categorical and purposively unconditioned) bearing. Let us consider more closely the situation that obtains here.

7. REASON IS IN A DIFFERENT BOAT: TRANSCENDENTAL IDEAS AND THEIR ROLE AS TOOLS OF SYSTEMATIZATION

For Kant, reason and its range of transcendental ideas reach beyond the sensory sphere. Access to real things (objects) demands sensibility, but thought things (*Gedankenwesen*) are products of reason alone – and Kant is perfectly content to characterize the thing-in-itself as a thought thing (*Gedankending; ens rationis*) along with the ideas of reason.[3]

For Kant, the inherent commitments of reason must of course be rational, and thereby rationalizable and explainable. Moreover, reason is inherently universal; one cannot meaningfully distinguish between our human reason and other modes. Reason as such is of a piece – always and everywhere.

As Kant sees it, ideas of reason are operative preeminently in three realms: psychology, cosmology, and theology. And in each case they point toward an all-encompassing totality: a ground totalization in one comprehensive unity. But their unifying role proceeds not in the manner of a substantial *is*, but in that of a procedural *as if*. They are not really actual things-in-the-world. They are matters of virtual reality, mere thought things. Three items are preeminently at issue: the ego (I) as unifier, on the side of experiencing, the world (nature) as unifier, on the side of what is experienced; and the supernatural (God) as unifier, on the side of grounding and explanation (see *CPuR*, A672–73 = B700–1). To be sure, ideas of this sort, while indeed objective, are neither actual (i.e., experientially accessible) objects nor matters of objective knowledge:

> Human knowledge begins with intuitions, proceeds from thence to concepts, and ends with ideas. Although in respect of all three elements it possesses *a priori* sources of knowledge, which on first view seem to scorn the limits of all experience, a thoroughgoing critique convinces us that reason, in its speculative employment, can never transcend the field of possible experience with these resources, and that the proper vocation of this supreme faculty of knowledge is to use all methods and their ground rules solely to investigate nature *au fond* in accordance with all possible principles of unity – that of purposiveness preeminently. But we must never transgress the boundary of nature beyond which there is, *for us*, nothing [there to be *known*] save emptiness. (*CPuR*, A702 = B730)

Ideas accordingly do not indicate furnishings of our experiential world. And cognitive (i.e., theoretical/speculative) reason cannot touch them, owing to its dependence on materials provided by sensibility via the processing of understanding. But of course practical reason is something else again – something quite distinctive, in Kant's view. For these ideas are not mere fictions or idle fabrications but indispensably serviceable artifacts of intellect. Kant is deeply committed to a dual-jurisdiction view of cognition: we are dual subjects, so to speak, living in the spheres of theoretical and practical reason. Each has its own legislation and makes its own demands upon us: we are answerable to both, though neither abrogates the jurisdiction of the other.[4] This aspect of the matter requires closer examination.

Reason, as Kant sees it, aims at totality and completeness:

> Reason concerns itself exclusively with absolute totality in the employment of the concepts of the understanding, and endeavors to carry the synthetic unity, which is thought in the category, up to the completely unconditioned . . . Reason accordingly occupies itself solely with the employment of understanding . . . solely to prescribe to the understanding its direction towards a certain unity of which it has itself no concept, and in such manner as to unite all the acts of the understanding, in respect of every object, into an absolute whole. (*CPuR*, A326 = B383)

Reason's tools in the pursuit of its mission are the "ideas of reason." The pivotal and characteristic work of ideas is to put principles of completeness and unity at the disposal of a mind committed to the systematization of experience:

> If we place these principles of systematic unity in the order appropriate to their empirical employment, they will stand thus; *manifoldness, affinity, unity,* each being taken, as an idea, in the highest degree of its completeness. Reason presupposes the knowledge which is obtained by the understanding and which stands in immediate relation to experience, and seeks for the unity of this knowledge in accordance with ideas which go far beyond all possible experience . . . The remarkable features of these principles, and what in them alone concerns us, is that they seem to be transcendental, and that although they contain mere ideas for the guidance of the empirical employment of reason – ideas which reason follows only as it were asymptotically, *i.e.,* ever more closely without ever reaching them – they yet possess, as synthetic *a priori* propositions, objective but indeterminate validity, and serve as rules for possible experience. They can also be employed with great advantage in the elaboration of experience. (*CPuR*, A662–63 = B690–91)

It is in this regard that the ideas obtain a theological coloration. For Kant, the cardinal instance of an idea is that of God, yet not the God of Christianity but that of deism – the author of nature and of nature's laws:

> The regulative law of systematic unity would have us study nature *as if* systematic and purposive unity, combined with the

greatest possible manifoldness, were to be met with every-where *in infinitum,* to the very greatest possible extent. For al-though we may succeed in discerning and realizing but little of this perfection of the world, yet it is nevertheless required by the legislation of our reason that we must always search for and surmise it . . . and it must always be beneficial, and can never be harmful, to form our view of nature in accordance with this principle . . . But it is clear that in this way of conceiving the un-derlying idea of a supreme Author, I do not base the principle upon the existence and upon the knowledge of such a being, but upon its idea only, and that I do not actually derive anything from this being, but only from the idea of it – that is, from the nature of the world's arrangements according to such an idea. (*CPuR,* A700–1 = B728–29)

The work of ideas – as Leibniz already emphasized – is to pave the way for the use of principles of systematization such as ho-mogeneity, taxonomy, continuity, and similar instrumentalities of cognitive systematization:

If we consider in its whole range the knowledge obtained for us by the understanding, we find that what is peculiarly distinc-tive of reason in its attitude to this body of knowledge, is that it prescribes and seeks to achieve its *systematization,* that is, to exhibit the connection of its parts in conformity with a single principle. This unity of reason always presupposes an idea, namely, that of the form of a whole of knowledge – a whole which is prior to the determinate knowledge of the parts and which contains the conditions that determine *a priori* for every part its position and relation to the other parts . . . These con-cepts of reason are not derived from nature; on the contrary, we interrogate nature in accordance with these ideas, and consider our knowledge as defective so long as it is not adequate to them. (*CPuR,* A645–46 = B673–74)

Kant has it that, appearances to the contrary notwithstanding, ideas do not appertain to actual and authentic substances; what they indicate are not substances but thought functions.

The ideas represent beings of reason, not objects of knowledge, which, Kant emphatically insists, can arise only from the conjoint operation of sensibility and understanding:

> The concept of pure and merely intelligible objects is completely lacking in all that might make possible its application [to physical objects]. For we cannot conceive how such intelligible objects might be given [in experience]. The problematic thought which leaves open a place for them serves only, like an empty space, for the limitation of empirical ground-rules [*Grundsätze*], without itself containing or revealing any other object of knowledge beyond their sphere. (*CPuR*, B315)

Objectivity accordingly comes upon reason's stage – though only for a short distance:

> Reason cannot think the systematic unity (of nature's laws) otherwise than by giving to the idea of this unity an object; and since experience can never give an example of complete systematic unity, the object which we have to assign to the idea is not such as experience can ever supply. This object, as thus entertained by reason [ens rationis ratiocinatae], is a mere idea; it is not assumed as a something that is real absolutely and *in itself*, but is postulated only problematically (since we cannot reach it through any of the concepts of the understanding) in order that we may view all connection of the things of the world of sense *as if* they had their ground in such a being. In thus proceeding, our sole purpose is to secure that systematic unity which is indispensable to reason, and which while furthering in every way the empirical knowledge obtainable by the understanding can never interfere to hinder or obstruct it. (*CPuR*, A681 = B709)

The Kantian ideas are objective not in the sense of signifying objects – concrete physical things in space and time – but in providing reason with thought instrumentalities essential to and effectively indispensable for the systematization of our knowledge of such objects. Not objective reality but objective utility is the crux of their validity. For ideas fall into the domain not of cognitive but of practical reason. As far as theoretical/speculative reason is concerned, ideas are no more than thinkable possibilities beyond the reach of realizable knowledge. But practical reason shows that with such thinkable things "the category as a mere form of thought is here not empty but obtains significance through an object which practical reason unquestionably provides through the conception of the highest good."[5] Practical reason can go where theoretical reason cannot tread. But while it can legitimately transcend "the bounds of sense," its reach cannot, with us, outrun the inherent limits of the modus operandi of the human intellect.

Chapter 4

Kant on Cognitive Systematization

1. SYSTEMATICITY IN KANT

The concept of "system" is perhaps the most portentous idea of Kant's theory of knowledge. For he saw systematization as the pivotal and determinative commitment of (pure) human reason – the quintessential instrumentality through which alone rational human inquiry can realize its key objective, the scientific knowledge of nature. Without this recourse to system, the *Critique of Pure Reason* would be like *Hamlet* without the prince.

The present discussion seeks to explicate and sustain this thesis of the centrality of system and to elucidate, largely in Kant's own words, the role of system in the Kantian scheme. Such an examination of the system-oriented aspects of his theory of knowledge is particularly worthwhile, because studies of Kant have generally failed to accord to systematization the pride of place that is its due. The fact is that the concept of system plays much the same governing role in the cognitive deliberations of Kant's *Critique of Pure Reason* that the ideas of God, freedom, and immortality play in the ethical deliberations of his *Critique of Practical Reason* or the conception of divinely instituted purposiveness in nature in the value-oriented deliberations of his *Critique of Judgment*.[1]

This chapter is a revised and expanded version of an essay entitled "Kant on the Epistemology of Scientific Questions" in Joachim Kopper and Wolfgang Marx (eds.), *200 Jahre Kritik der reinen Vernunft* (Hildesheim: Gerstenberg, 1981), pp. 313–34. Reprinted by permission of Gerstenberg Verlag.

2. WHAT A COGNITIVE SYSTEM IS

Kant maintains that the mission of systematization is the organization of knowledge, its coordination into one coherent structure under the guiding aegis of unifying principles.

> If we consider in its whole range the knowledge obtained for us by the understanding, we find that what is peculiarly distinctive of reason in its attitude to this body of knowledge, is that it prescribes and seeks to achieve its *systematization,* that is, to exhibit the connection of its parts in conformity with a single principle. This unity of reason always presupposes an idea, namely, that of the form of a whole of knowledge – a whole which is prior to the determinate knowledge of the parts and which contains the conditions that determine *a priori* for every part its position and relation to the other parts. This idea accordingly postulates a complete [organic] unity in the knowledge obtained by understanding by which this knowledge is to be not a mere contingent aggregate, but a system connected according to necessary laws. We may not say that this idea is a concept of the object, but only of the thoroughgoing unity of such concepts, in so far as that unity serves as a rule for the understanding. These concepts of reason are not derived from nature; on the contrary, we interrogate nature in accordance with these ideas, and consider our knowledge as defective so long as it is not adequate to them. (*CPuR*, A645 = B673)

The paradigm of system that lay before Kant's eyes was not that of science – of Euclid's systematization of geometry, Archimedes' systematization of statics, and Newton's systematization of celestial mechanics; his model of philosophical systematization was that of the great seventeenth-century rationalist philosophers Descartes, Spinoza, and Leibniz, as expounded by the subsequent members of Leibniz's school – especially Christian Wolff.[2]

As Kant saw it, adequate understanding can be achieved only through the systemic interrelating of facts. The mission of human reason is to furnish a basis for the rational comprehension of what we know, and this can be accomplished only by exhibiting these facts as integral parts of an organic whole. Kant develops his biological analogy of system in the following terms:

[O]nly after we have spent much time in the collection of materials in somewhat random fashion at the suggestion of an idea lying hidden in our minds, and after we have, indeed, over a long period assembled the materials in a merely technical manner, does it first become possible for us to discern the idea in a clearer light, and to devise a whole architectonically in accordance with the ends of reason Systems seem to be formed in the manner of lowly organisms, through a *generatio aequivoca* from the mere confluence of assembled concepts, at first imperfect, and only gradually attaining to completeness, although they one and all have had their schema, as an original germ, in the sheer self-development of reason. Hence, not only is each system articulated in accordance with an idea, but they are one and all organically united in a system of human knowledge, as members of one whole. (*CPuR*, A834 = B862)

The nature of systematization is accordingly explained by Kant along the lines of a fundamentally biological analogy:

In accordance with reason's legislative prescriptions, our diverse modes of knowledge must not be permitted to be a mere rhapsody, but must form a system. Only so can they further the essential ends of reason. By a system I understand the unity of the manifold modes of knowledge under one idea. This idea is the concept, provided by reason, of the form of a whole . . . [which] determines *a priori* not only the scope of its manifold content, but also the positions which the parts occupy relatively to one another. The scientific concept of reason contains, therefore, the end and the form of that whole which is congruent with this requirement. The unity of the end to which all the parts relate and in the idea of which they all stand in relation to one another, makes it possible for us to determine from our knowledge of the other parts whether any part be missing, and to prevent any arbitrary addition, or in respect of its completeness [to discover] any indeterminateness that does not conform to the limits which are thus determined *a priori*. The whole is thus an organised unity [*articulatio*], and not an aggregate [*coacervatio*]. It may grow from within [*per intussusceptionem*], but not by external addition [*per appositionem*]. It is thus like an animal body. (*CPuR*, A832–33 = B860–61)

A system is thus a whole organized on principles of organic interlinkage, completeness, and self-sufficiency, and a body of knowledge is a system when its articulation is characterized by such unity and comprehensiveness. As Kant sees it, the systemic unity of knowledge is fundamentally akin to the functional integrity of an organism.

Science as a whole is a system, and every part of the system that is science as a whole must serve in the role of a contributory subsystem, an organ of the overall organism. To be sure, the realization of such a cognitive system is far from easy:

> [W]e must not explain and determine them [sc. the sciences] according to the description which their founder gives of them, but in conformity with the idea which, out of the natural unity of the parts that we have assembled, we find to be grounded in reason itself. For we shall then find that its founder, and often even his latest successors, are groping for an idea which they have never succeeded in making clear to themselves, and that consequently they have not been in a position to determine the proper content, the articulation (systematic unity), and the limits of the science. (*CPuR*, A834 = B862)

3. SCIENTIFIC SYSTEMATIZATION AS THE CHARACTERISTIC WORK OF REASON

Only gradually, by dint of demanding cognitive labors, can the plan that underlies the various branches of knowledge and organizes their materials into increasingly integrated organic wholes be brought to light. He writes:

> Human reason is by nature architectonic. That is to say, it regards all our knowledge as belonging to one possible system, and therefore allows only such principles as do not at any rate make it impossible for any knowledge that we may attain to combine into a system with other knowledge. (*CPuR*, A474 = B502)

And again:

> Not only is each system articulated in accordance with an idea, but they are one and all organically united in a system of human knowledge, as members of one whole, and so as admitting of an architectonic of all human knowledge, which, at the present time, in view of the great amount of material that has been

collected, or which can be obtained from the ruins of ancient systems, is not only possible, but would not indeed be difficult. (*CPuR*, A835 = B863)

The mission of reason is to synthesize the deliverance of the human understanding so as to instill systemic unity into its deliverances:

[Throughout its deliberations] reason endeavors to reduce the varied and manifold knowledge obtained through the understanding to the smallest number of principles (universal conditions) and thereby to achieve in it the highest possible unity. (*CPuR* A305 = B361)

Kant insists that "in accordance with reason's legislative prescriptions, our diverse modes of knowledge must not be permitted to be a mere rhapsody, but must form a system" (ibid.). Reason accordingly endeavors to answer its questions in the framework of an articulated science, and science, to qualify as such, must be an organic system and achieve a certain self-sustaining completeness:

Every science is in itself a system, and it is not enough in it to build in accordance with principles and thus to employ a technical procedure, but we must go to work with it architectonically, as a building subsisting for itself; we must not treat it as an additional wing or part of another building, but as a whole in itself, although we may subsequently make a passage from it into that other or conversely. (*CJ*, sect. 68m, near start; p. 381, Akad.)

Its having a place alongside the rest within the all-inclusive *systema systemarum* that constitutes "the encyclopedia of all the sciences" is in fact what marks a discipline as constituting a science:

Every science must have its definite place in the encyclopedia of all the sciences . . . [Moreover] no science belongs to the transition from one to the other, because this transition only marks the articulation or organization of the system, and not a place in it. (*CJ*, sect. 79, at start; p. 416. Akad.)

The achievement of system to undergird our grasp on the unity and necessity of knowledge is the supreme governing goal of human reason:

[T]he expectation of bringing some day into one view the unity of the entire pure rational faculty (both theoretical and practical) and of being able to derive everything from one principle [is the great object of our reason]. The latter is an unavoidable need of human reason, as it can find complete satisfaction only in a perfectly systematic unity of its cognitions. (*CPrR*, p. 91, Akad.)

Reason's drive to system takes two forms. At the descriptive level, reason strives toward a taxonomic manifold of classificatory divisions that organize all features of nature into one great Porphyric tree.[3] And at the explanatory level, reason strives for a systematic unity of our scientific laws of the world under the aegis of general – and indeed mathematically formulable – principles that form an axiomatic structure which itself has an underpinning in qualitative, philosophically articulable "first principles," exactly as in the Leibnizian philosophy.[4] Accordingly, we must not only coordinate phenomena under laws, but subsume the diversified complex of laws within one coherent, orderly, organizing framework:

Particular empirical laws . . . must be considered in accordance with such a unity as they would have if an understanding (although not our understanding) had furnished them to our cognitive faculties, so as to make possible a system of experience according to particular laws of nature . . . That is, nature is represented by means of this concept as if an understanding contained the ground of the unity of the variety of its empirical laws. (*CJ*, sect. 4, nr. end; p. 180, Akad.)

The determination of the structure of a cognitive system, of its "table of contents," so to speak, is a difficult task.

The deduction of the division of a system, i.e., the proof of its completeness as well as of its continuity, namely, that the transition from the concept being divided to each member of the division in the whole series of subdivision takes place without any gaps [divisio per altum], is one of the most difficult conditions for the constructor of a system to fulfill. (*The Metaphysics of Morals*, p. 218n, Akad.)

Nevertheless, the architectonic of natural science is something we can and should eventually realize in full, even though completion of the system itself lies (as will be seen) quite beyond our human power.

In giving up this goal, reason would be untrue to itself and would no longer deserve our trust:

> Pure reason is, indeed, so perfect a unity that if its principle were insufficient for the solution of even a single one of all the questions to which it itself gives birth we should have no alternative but to reject the principle, since we should then no longer be able to place implicit reliance upon it in dealing with any one of the other questions. (*CPuR*, Axiii)

Three items, separable in theory, are inseparable in Kant's thought: (1) the systematic aspect of the phenomena as representing organized substances (i.e., perceptual [sensible, "aesthetic"] systematicity under the aegis of the transcendental unity of apperception); (2) the systematic unity of nature – the systematicity of the whole realm of experience under the aegis of natural laws, as revealed to our understanding, and (3) the teleological unity of natural laws in a comprehensive system that affords the ideal of reason. Sensibility provides the materials of knowledge, understanding endows it with its microscopic structure, but reason alone assures the harmonious overall orderliness of our knowledge – it is, in a deep sense, the architect of these as inseparable because, as he sees it, systematicity is simply indivisible – full systematicity at any cognitive level requires systematicity at every level. We cannot have a true system that is not all-comprehensive – that does not carry the pyramidal structure of systematic knowledge to its completion in the apex of one ultimate, all-unifying principle. The same regulative injunction to rational unification projects its impetus through all sectors of the cognitive stirring of the human mind. And reason stands committed to the idea of a systematic unity of nature under explanatory principles by whose means every facet of natural reality can be integrated explanatorily within one single overarching framework of scientific understanding. Systemic unity, science, and intelligibility stand as an inextricably interlocked coordination.

Accordingly, systematization is in a position to afford us a grasp on the element of necessity in our knowledge.

> By a critical elucidation of a science (or of one of its portions which is a system by itself), I understand that investigation and justification of the fact that it must have precisely the systematic form it does have and no other, when compared with another system which has as its basis a similar cognitive faculty. (*CPuR*, p. 89, Akad.)

It is by systematizing facts that we come to grasp why – in certain respects – they must be as they are.

4. THE SYSTEMATICITY OF NATURE NOT A PRODUCT BUT A PRESUPPOSITION OF RATIONAL INQUIRY – NOT A FACT BUT A REGULATIVE IDEAL

How do we know prior to the completion of natural science that our knowledge of nature will be comprehensively systematic? After all, our science is not yet, as it stands, a perfected and completed system. How, then, can we be sure that this is its destiny?

The answer Kant offers is that the systematicity of our knowledge of the world is not something that rational inquiry discovers through the deliverances of our experience, but something that it presupposes from the very outset – not, to be sure, as an established fact, but merely as a feasible goal. This systematizing impetus at work in our understanding of the operating principles of the natural world is crucial to the very possibility of a fully coherent "experience" of nature:

> Nature does indeed impose upon the understanding the exacting task of always seeking the origin of events ever higher in the series of causes, their causality being always conditioned. But in compensation it holds out the promise of thoroughgoing unity of experience in accordance with laws. [Any breach in the fabric of causality] abrogates those rules through which alone a completely coherent experience is possible. (*CPuR*, A442 = B475)

That our knowledge of the world can, in the end, be exhaustively and smoothly systematized – that a proper science of nature is actually achievable – is not something that we carry away from our study of nature as a thing of its own devising – a precondition that it imposes a priori on any accumulation of answers to questions that it is prepared to recognize as ultimately adequate:

> [Reason requires and] postulates a complete unity in the knowledge obtained for it by the understanding, by which this knowledge is to be not a mere contingent aggregate, but a system according to necessary laws . . . These concepts of reason are not derived from nature, on the contrary, we interrogate nature in accordance with these ideas, and consider our knowledge defective as long as it is not adequate to them. (*CPuR* A645 = B673)

The matter of just *how* nature is a system is something empirical, a product of scientific inquiry (*CPuR*, B165), but *that* nature is a system is determined a priori as an inherent feature of the conception of a nature accessible to empirical inquiry. Only by systematizing the answer it gives to questions can reason assure itself of their adequacy.

That the world of our experience is actually part of a truly systemic whole is not, and never will be, a certifiable fact. It is no more than a postulate, an operative presumption, a datum weaker than knowledge though stronger than a mere working hypothesis.

For Kant, the impetus to systematization in our knowledge of the world represents an operational principle of reason, a procedural or methodological rule built into the very workings of those faculties through which our knowledge of the world is constituted:

> We may not say this idea [of system] is a concept of the object [the world system, as it were], but only of the thoroughgoing unity of such concepts, in so far as that unity serves as a rule for the understanding. (*CPuR*, A645 = B673)

The systemic aspect of things – their simplicity and unity and cohesion, and so forth – are, as Kant puts it, "only the schema of this regulative principle" (*CPuR*, A683 = B711) which enjoins the human mind to conjoin its scattered experiences into coordinated wholes.

Our reason is enmeshed in an insuperable methodological commitment to the systematicity of nature:

> The hypothetical employment of reason . . . [in implementing the idea of system] is not, properly speaking, *constitutive*, that

is, it is not of such a character that, judging in all strictness, we can regard it as proving the truth of the universal rule which we have adopted as hypothesis. For how are we to know all the possible consequences which as actually following from the adopted principle, *prove* its universality? The hypothetical employment of reason is regulative only; its sole aim is, so far as may be possible, to bring unity into the body of our detailed knowledge, and thereby to *approximate* the rule to universality. The hypothetical employment of reason has, therefore, as its aim the systematic unity of the knowledge of understanding, and this unity is the *criterion of the truth* of its rules. The systematic unity (as a mere idea) is, however, only a *projected* unity, to be regarded not as given in itself, but as a problem only. This unity aids us in discovering a principle for the understanding in its manifold and special modes of employment, directing its attention to cases which are not given, and thus rendering it more coherent. But the only conclusion which we are justified in drawing from these considerations is that the systematic unity of the manifold knowledge of understanding, as prescribed by reason, is a *methodological* principle. Its function is to assist the understanding by means of ideas, in those cases in which the understanding cannot by itself establish rules, and at the same time to give to the numerous and diverse rules of the understanding unity or system under a single principle, and thus to secure coherence in every possible way. But to say that the constitution of the objects or the nature of the understanding which knows them as such, is in itself determined to systematic unity, and that we can in a certain measure postulate this unity *a priori*, without reference to any such special interest of reason, and that we are therefore in a position to maintain that knowledge of the understanding in all its possible modes (including empirical knowledge) has the unity required by reason, and stands under common principles from which all its various modes can, in spite of their diversity, be deduced – that would . . . make the systematic unity necessary, not only subjectively and regulatively, but constitutively also. (*CPuR*, A647–48 = B675–76)

Systematicity is the objectified correlate of a regulative rule of procedure, an injunction always to seek to impart systematic unity to our contentions about empirical reality. As Kant puts it,

> [T]his [systemic] unity of reason is purely hypothetical. We do not assert that such a . . . [requirement of reason] must necessarily be met with, but rather that we must seek it in the interest of reason, that is, of establishing certain principles for the manifold rules which experience may supply to us. We must endeavor, whenever possible, to bring in this way systematic unity into our knowledge. (*CPuR*, A649–50 = B677–78)

The injunction to systematization is a categorical imperative of pure theoretical (cognitive) reason governing the intellect in rational inquiry in much the same manner that the injunction to morality is a categorical imperative or pure practical reason governing the will in rational action.

Though Kant begins by telling us that a transcendent deduction to legitimate systematicity as an idea of reason is not possible (*CPuR*, A663–64 = B691–92), he goes on to explain, a few pages later, that this only means that one cannot give "the *kind* of deduction that is possible in the case of the categories" (*CPuR*, A669 = B697; italics added). His ensuing argumentation is claimed to establish

> that it is a necessary maxim of reason to proceed always in accordance with such ideas. This, indeed is the transcendental deduction of all ideas of speculative reason, not as *constitutive* principles for the extension of our knowledge to more objects than experience can give, but as *regulative* principles of the systemic unity of the manifold of empirical knowledge in general, whereby this empirical knowledge is more adequately secured within its own limits and more effectively improved than would be possible, in the absence of such ideas, through the employment merely of the principles of the understanding. (*CPuR*, A671 = B699)

Accordingly, systematicity is not a descriptive (or constitutive) feature of nature – something discovered or discoverable through inquiry – but is an inherent feature of the methodology of reason in dealing with the deliverances of experience, a guiding idea of reason without which it cannot accomplish its essential mission.

5. SYSTEM AS ASPIRATION: WE CANNOT EXPECT ACTUALLY TO ACHIEVE A PERFECTED SYSTEMATIZATION OF NATURE

The systematicity of nature represents a procedural rule – a methodological maxim of cognitive procedure. It is not an established fact and cannot, indeed, ever be realized as a fait accompli:

> The idea of systematic unity should be used only as a regulative principle to guide us in seeking for such unity in the connection of things, according to universal laws of nature; and we ought, therefore, to believe that we have approximated to completeness in the employment of the principle only in proportion as we are in a position to verify such unity in empirical fashion – a completeness which is never, of course, attainable. (*CPuR*, A692 = B720)

The cruel fact is that reason's quest for cognitive wholeness is foredoomed to failure. The questions of natural science cannot be resolved by us in any definitive or comprehensive way:

> In natural science, on the other hand, there is endless conjecture, and certainty is not to be counted upon. For the natural appearances are objects which are given to us independently of our concepts, and the key to them lies not in us and our pure thinking, but outside us and therefore in many cases, since the key is not to be found, an assured solution is not to be expected. (*CPuR* A480–81 = B508–9)

The goal of completed systematization of scientific knowledge is the El Dorado, the Promised Land, the destination the hope of whose attainment is reason's compensation for the Sisyphean task that nature has imposed upon it. For its very design as an operative faculty commits reason to embarking on a journey it cannot finish, to striving for a goal it cannot realize – the attainment of knowledge that cannot in the final analysis be attained:

> [Ideas of reason, such as the systematicity of nature] are even further removed from objective reality than are categories, for no appearance can be found in which they can be represented *in concreto*. They contain a certain completeness to which no

possible empirical knowledge ever attains. In them reason aims only at a systematic unity, to which it seeks to approximate the unity that is empirically possible, without ever completely reaching it. (*CPuR*, A567–68 = B595–96)

The character of nature, as best we can grasp it, is such that the labor of systematizing reason can never be accomplished:

[Empirical knowledge] demands an endless progress in the specification of our concepts, and an advance to yet other remaining differences, from which we have made abstraction in the concept of the species, and still more so in that of the genus. [Reason] . . . leads us to seek always for further differences, and to suspect their existence even when the senses are unable to disclose them. That absorbent earths are of different kinds (chalk and muriatic earths), is a discovery that was possible only under the guidance of an antecedent rule of reason – reason proceeding on the assumption that nature is so richly diversified that we may presume the presence of such differences, and therefore prescribing to the understanding the task of searching for them. (*CPuR*, A656–57 = B684–85)

Reason strives for a completeness it can never attain, it yearns for a satisfaction that must always elude its grasp; its quest for wholeness is foredoomed to failure:

[R]eason can never satisfy itself. The empirical use to which reason limits the pure understanding does not fully satisfy the proper calling of reason. Every single experience is only a part of the whole sphere of its domain, but the absolute totality of all possible experience is itself not experience. Yet it is a necessary problem for reason. (*Prolegomena*, sect. 40; pp. 327–28, Akad.)

And again:

Human reason is by nature architectonic. That is to say, it regards all our knowledge as belonging to a possible system, and therefore allows only such principles as do not at any rate make it impossible for any knowledge that we may attain to combine into a system with other knowledge. Nevertheless, . . . the completion of the edifice of knowledge [is] quite impossible . . . Thus the architectonic interest of reason – the demand not for empirical but for pure *a priori* unity of reason – forms a natural [commitment]. (*CPuR*, A474 = B502)

It thus emerges that the systematization of our knowledge of nature is a demand imposed by our reason that cannot ultimately be satisfied. The project of inquiry into nature is one that we cannot ever hope to bring to perfected completion. The systematicity of nature is a principle that governs our knowledge regulatively as an idea, but it is not itself in any way something that we know as a fact that characterizes the reality we know.

The "world system" is not a fact, an accomplished reality, but an idealization, a useful device of thought, a guide and goad to inquiry:

> I accordingly maintain that transcendental ideas never allow of any constitutive employment . . . On the other hand, they have an excellent, and indeed indispensably necessary, regulative employment, namely, that of directing the understanding towards a certain goal upon which the routes marked out by all its rules converge, as upon their point of intersection. This point is indeed a mere idea, a *focus imaginarius*, from which, since it lies quite outside the bounds of possible experience, the concepts of the understanding do not in reality proceed; none the less it serves to give to these concepts the greatest [possible] unity combined with the greatest [possible] extension. Hence arises the illusion that the lines have their source in a real object lying outside the field of empirically possible knowledge – just as objects reflected in a mirror are seen as behind it. Nevertheless this illusion (which need not, however, be allowed to deceive us) is indispensably necessary if we are to direct the understanding beyond every given experience (as part of the sum of possible experience), and thereby to secure its greatest possible extension, just as in the case of mirror-vision, the illusion involved is indispensably necessary . . . (*CPuR*, A644–45 = B672–73)

And again:

> The remarkable feature of these [idealized] principles, and what in them alone concerns us, is that they seem to be transcendental, and that although they contain mere ideas for the guidance of the empirical employment of reason – ideas which reason

follows only as it were asymptotically, *i.e.*, ever more closely without ever reaching them – they yet possess, as synthetic *a priori* propositions, objective but indeterminate validity, and serve as rules for possible experience. They can also be employed with great advantage in the elaboration of experience, as heuristic principles. (*CPuR*, A663 = B691)

In postulating such ideals as the systematicity of nature,

we do not really extend our knowledge beyond the objects of possible experience; we extend only the empirical unity of such experience, by means of the systematic unity for which the schema is provided by the idea – an idea which has therefore no claim to be a constitutive, but only a regulative principle. For to allow that we posit a thing, a something, a real being, corresponding to the idea, is not to say that we profess to extend our knowledge of things by means of transcendental concepts. For this being is posited only in the idea and not in itself; and therefore only as expressing the systematic unity which is to serve as a rule for the empirical employment of reason. It decides nothing in regard to the ground of this unity or as to what may be the inner character of the being on which as cause the unity depends. (*CPuR*, A674–75 = B702–3)

The bearing of ideas lies in the practical/methodological rather than in the theoretical/cognitive order.

6. THE SYSTEMATICITY OF NATURE IS NOT AN ONTOLOGICAL (CONSTRUCTIVE) FACT, BUT THE OBJECTIFICATION OF A METHODOLOGICAL (REGULATIVE) PRINCIPLE

Kant insists that it is one thing to make the substantive, constitutive, and ontological assertion "Nature is a rationally designed system," and something vastly and profoundly different to make the methodological, regulative, and epistemological assertion "We should – and indeed are by the very constitution of our mental faculties compelled to – view nature as a rationally designed system." This distinction is critical for him, and he is very emphatic about it. It is we who are ourselves the sources of system, order, and design in nature by insisting upon imputing this feature to it in the course of developing our knowledge of the world:

> It is then one thing to say, "the production of certain things of nature or that of collective nature is only possible through a cause which determines itself to action according to design," and quite another to say, "I can, *according to the peculiar constitution of my cognitive faculties,* judge concerning the possibility of these things and their production in not other fashion than by conceiving for this a cause working according to design, i.e., a Being which is productive in a way analogous to the causality of an intelligence." In the former case I wish to establish something concerning the object and am bound to establish the objective reality of an assumed concept; in the latter, reason only determines the use of my cognitive faculties, conformably to their peculiarities and to the essential conditions of their range and their limits. Thus the former principle is an objective proposition for the determinant judgment, the latter merely a subjective proposition for the reflective judgment, i.e., a maxim which reason prescribes to it. (*CJ*, sect. 75, at start; pp. 397–98, Akad.)

The systematicity of nature is therefore not a fact, but an embodiment of a methodological principle: Always strive to render your knowledge of nature systematic. It is not a product of our study of nature, but an input into it:

> For the regulative law of systematic unity prescribes that we should study nature *as if* systematic and purposive unity, combined with the greatest possible manifoldness, were everywhere to be met with *in infinitum*. For although we may succeed in discovering but little of this perfection of the world, it is nevertheless required by the legislation of our reason that we must always search for and surmise it; and it must always be beneficial and can never be harmful, to direct our investigations into nature in accordance with this principle. (*CPuR*, A700–1 = B728–29)

In the order of knowledge, the systematicity of nature is always a destination, never a point of arrival.

Thus we cannot say substantively (constitutively and descriptively) that the world is a system – that, after all, presupposes what we are trying to establish in inquiry and prejudges the outcome of our scientific investigations in an unconscionable way. But we can and should proceed to labor in the hope and expectation that we can in due course systematize our knowledge of it.

The ultimate foundation of the systematicity of nature is accordingly mind correlative. It is founded in the determination of the human mind to systematize the products of our experience into a unified whole before we are even prepared to count such experiences as parts of an objective world order (rather than as a delusion of illusion, or whatever dismissive label we attach to those erratic experiences that do not fit the orderly structure we insist on to qualify something as "objectively real"). System is the controlling idea for reason in its endeavor to grasp reality:

> The unity of reason is the unity of system; and this systematic unity does not serve objectively as a principle that extends the application of reason to objects, but subjectively as a maxim that extends its application to all possible empirical knowledge of objects. (*CPuR*, A680 = B708)

The foundation of systematicity is regulative and methodological, but its bearing is not merely thus: it has a status of bearing a priori on the materials of our experience that endows it also with a claim to "objective validity" (in Kant's characteristic and somewhat peculiar sense of this term). For the idea of system has a perfectly appropriate application to the world of experience, whose "objects," after all, are objects-for-us:

> It is the business of reason to render the unity of all possible empirical acts of the understanding systematic . . . But although we are unable to find in *intuition* a schema for the complete systematic unity of all concepts of the understanding, an *analogon* of such a schema must necessarily allow of being given. This analogon is the idea of the *maximum* in the division and unification of the knowledge of the understanding under one principle. For what is greatest and absolutely complete can be determinately thought, all restricting conditions, which give rise to an indeterminate manifoldness, being left aside. Thus the idea of reason is an analogon of a schema of sensibility; but with this difference, that the application of the concepts of the understanding to the schema of reason does not yield knowledge of the object itself (as is the case in the application of categories to their sensible schemata), but only a rule of principle

for the systematic unity of all employment of the understanding. Now since every principle which prescribes *a priori* to the understanding thoroughgoing unity in its employment, also holds, although only indirectly, of the object of experience, the principles of pure reason must also have objective reality in respect of that object, not however, in order to *determine* anything in it, but only in order to indicate the procedure whereby the empirical and determinate employment of the understanding can be brought into complete harmony with itself. This is achieved by bringing its employment, so far as may be possible, into connection with the principle of thoroughgoing unity, and by determining its procedure in the light of this principle. (*CPuR*, A605–6 = B693–94)

The systematicity of nature is objective, but with an objectivity that has a critical element of ideality in its makeup.

The systematicity of nature is the objectification of the regulative stance which counts as part of physical reality only those things that fit appropriately into the systematic structure of our "knowledge of the real world." Our methodological commitment to system is naturally objectified by our reason into an aspect of the real – indeed a definitive aspect of it:

It is, indeed, difficult to understand how there can be a methodological principle by which reason prescribes the unity of rules, unless we also presuppose a transcendental principle whereby such a systematic unity is *a priori* assumed to be necessarily inherent in the objects. For with what right can reason, in its methodological employment, call upon us to treat the multiplicity of powers exhibited in nature as simply a disguised unity, and to derive this unity, so far as may be possible, from a fundamental power – how can reason do this, if it be free to admit as equally possible that all powers may be heterogeneous, and that such systematic unity of derivation may not be in conformity with nature? Reason would then run counter to its own vocation, proposing as its aim an idea quite inconsistent with the natural order of things. Nor can we say that reason, while proceeding in accordance with its own principles, has based knowledge of this unity on the accidental constitution of nature. The law of reason which requires us to seek for this unity, is a necessary law, since without it we should have not reason at all, and without reason no coherent employment of the understanding, and in the absence of this no sufficient criterion of empirical truth. In order, therefore, to secure an empirical criterion we must presuppose the systematic unity of nature as objectively valid and necessary. (*CPuR*, A650–51 = B678–79)

The systematicity of nature is thus a perfectly "objective fact" not because we are in a position to claim to have discovered that nature as such is inherently systematic, but because nature as we can possibly come to know it must inevitably be thought of (by us, at any rate) as constituting a system. We could not count as part of "the true picture of nature" a seeming fact that did not fit within the best system of nature we can devise.

In Kant, we must distinguish between objective validity and descriptive facticity: between what the mind "must think" about the world in a regulative mode and what it can come to know constitutively about the world – between what it can establish through the inner authority of its own recourses and what it must base on the external authority of actual experience. The systematicity of nature is emphatically of the former sort: a mind-originated commitment, and not an externally grounded, independently based and experientially apprehended fact. It is a creature of thought, not an aspect of extra-mental reality, and has its basis in the nature of mind, not that of things.

7. ANSWERS TO SOME OBJECTIONS

But why should Kant feel compelled to maintain that the human mind is committed to insisting (from the very outset, a priori) that our knowledge of the world can be systematized? Why should he not simply proceed in the experimental spirit of the working hypothesis "Let's try to systematize our knowledge and see how far we get"? Why presuppose the systematicity of nature, rather than leave the issue for ex post facto resolution as a matter of contingent fact?

The answer is that Kant views this as altogether unsatisfactory, because such a contingency-accepting approach cannot provide a basis for the regulative principle at issue. If, despite our best efforts, we find our knowledge unsystematic, we would then just have to leave it at that. We would not feel the compulsion to push farther unless we stood committed to the systematicity of nature as something necessary.

One commentator tells us that by the time of his *Critique of Judgment* Kant had abandoned the idea that our mind sees system as an authentic aspect of reality and instead placed it on a wholly methodological foundation:

> In the third *Critique* the [Kantian] position is very different. Systematization of knowledge is here said to have its source in the faculty of Judgment, and it is thus made plain, from the start, that no reference to anything sense-transcendent is intended, and that in conceiving of experience as a system, we have no other aim than that of being provided with a reliable guide for our investigations into natural phenomena.[5]

Nothing could be farther from the truth. Kant continues to insist in the third *Critique* that

> By the constitution and the principles of our cognitive faculty, we can think of nature, its [systemic and] purposive arrangements which have become known to us, in no other way than as a [deliberately designed and ordered] product of an understanding to which it is subject. (*CJ*, sect. 85, nr. end; p. 441, Akad.)

Kant's position in the two *Critiques* is in fact wholly uniform in this regard. On the one hand, the systematicity of the real is something objective, built into the very modus operandi of rational thought about the phenomena of our experience; on the other hand, the underlying aegis for this commitment to systematicity is not a descriptively constitutive fact about the character of the real, but a cognitively regulative fact about the procedures of the mind's thought about the real. In both masterworks alike, Kant is perfectly explicit that the systematic unity of nature is no more (but also no less) than a projected unity, to be regarded not as given in itself, but as a problem only. The two aspects of objectivity and productivity are deliberately balanced, and the nature of this balance does not change as between the two *Critiques*.

8. THE DANGERS OF HYPOSTATIZATION

Regulatively (methodologically), systematicity is perfectly objective; constitutively (substantively), it is a mere fiction – an "as if" convenience of our human intelligence. The objects of ideas such as the systematicity of nature, Kant insists,

> ought not to be assumed as existing in themselves, but only as having the reality of a schema – the schema of the regulative principle of the systematic unity of all knowledge of nature. They should be regarded only as analogs of real things, not as in themselves real things. (*CPuR*, A674 = B702)

Moreover,

> the idea of reason is an analogon of a schema of sensibility; but with this difference, that the application of the concepts of the understanding to the schema of reason does not yield knowledge of the object (as is the case in the application of categories to their sensible schemata), but only a rule of principle for the systematic unity of all employment of the understanding. (*CPuR*, A665 = B693)

Accordingly the status of such ideas is one of objectivity in the methodological rather than in the substantive, existential order.

Properly understood, the systematicity of nature represents a regulative idea – a useful instrumentality of method that facilitates the proper work of reason: but a worm lurks in the woodwork. For the mind inclines to slip into the error of regarding this useful methodological principle as a problematic ontological doctrine.

Kant maintains that the human mind by its inherent makeup functions in such a way as to insist on thingifying systematicity, projecting its own working requirements into the object of its inquiries – the world – as an objective, ontological feature thereof.

> [R]eason cannot think this systematic unity otherwise than by giving to the ideal of this unity an object; and since experience can never give an example of complete systematic unity, the object which we have to assign to the idea is not such as experience can ever supply. [Properly speaking, then,] this object, as thus entertained by reason [*ens rationis ratiocinatae*], is a mere idea;

84

it is not assumed as a something that is real absolutely and *in itself,* but is postulated only problematically (since we cannot reach it through any of the concepts of the understanding) in order that we may view all connection of the things of the world of sense *as if* they had their ground in such a being . . . We misapprehend the meaning of this idea if we regard it as the assertion or even as the assumption of a real thing, to which we may proceed to ascribe the ground of the systematic order of the world. On the contrary, what this ground which eludes our concepts may be in its own inherent constitution is left entirely undetermined; the idea is posited only as being the point of view from which alone that unity, which is so essential to reason and so beneficial to the understanding, can be further extended. In short this transcendental thing is only the schema of the regulative principle by which reason, so far as lies in its power, extends systematic unity over the whole field of experience. (*CPuR*, A681–82 = B709–10)

As Kant sees it, our reason has a virtually insuperable inherent tendency to extend the knowledge yielded by the understanding to its farthest possible limit and then to make unwarranted assumptions about these extensions. Only with the greatest difficulty can reason master its own characteristic "optical illusion" – the mistaking of its own inherent demands for features of things in themselves, and its projection of its own demands into the real world. We must ever be on our guard "to prevent what otherwise, through a transcendental subreption, inevitably takes place, namely, the ascribing of objective reality to an idea that serves merely as a rule" (*CPuR*, A509 = B537).

Cosmological ideas like that of nature's purposively systemic unity must be handled with care:

[W]e are not justified in introducing thought-entities which transcend all our concepts, though without contradicting them, as being real and determinate objects, merely on the authority of a speculative reason that is bent upon completing the tasks which it has set itself. They ought not to be assumed as existing in themselves, but only as having the reality of a schema – the schema of the regulative principle of the systematic unity of all knowledge of nature. They should be regarded only as analoga of real things, not as in themselves real things. We remove from

85

the object of the idea the conditions which limit the concept provided by our understanding, but which also alone make it possible for us to have a determinate concept of anything. (*CPuR*, A673–74 = B701–2)

To speak of nature as a system, hypostatizing this into a descriptive (constitutive) feature of the real, would be to make an illicit ontologicization of a methodological principle.

[S]ince the systematic unity of nature cannot be prescribed as a principle for the empirical employment of our reason, except in so far as we [regulatively] presuppose the idea of an *ens realissimum* as the supreme cause, it is quite natural that this latter idea should be represented as an actual object, which in its character of supreme condition, is also necessary – thus changing a *regulative* into a *constitutive* principle . . . However, the concept of necessity is only to be found in our reason, as a formal condition of thought; it does not allow of being hypostatised as a material condition of existence. (*CPuR*, A619–20 = B647–48)

To take such a step of reification would be to impede the mission of reason. If the systematicity of nature were a given fact (rather than the systematization of our knowledge of it a given task), reason would be hindered in its cognitive work:

To take the regulative principle of the systematic unity of nature as being a constitutive principle, and to hypostatise, and presuppose as a cause, that which serves, merely in idea, as the ground of the consistent employment of reason, is simply to confound reason. The investigation of nature must take its own independent course, keeping to the chain of natural causes in conformity with their universal laws. It does indeed, in so doing, proceed in accordance with the idea of an Author of the universe, but not in order to deduce therefrom the purposiveness for which it is ever on the watch . . . Whether this latter enterprise succeed or not the idea [of a divinely instituted purpose in nature] remains always true in itself, and justified in its use, provided it be restricted to the conditions of a merely regulative principle. (*CPuR*, A694 = B722)

In its endeavor to systematize the concepts of the understanding, reason extends them beyond the limits of their legitimate sphere of operation – the realm of possible experience. It reifeis what is at bottom a merely methodological resource, and populates the real world with creatures of its own devising. Yet this is not a mere delusion – an idle, pointless fancy. It is something our reason can no more avoid than our sensibility can avoid spatiotemporality or our understanding the categories. Systematicity is perfectly objective in its regulative, methodological foundation – an inherently necessary (albeit merely presupposed) feature of our empirical world. But we must not project it onto the world as such.

In reifying the systematicity of nature – changing its basis from a methodological commitment into a substance fact about the world – we relapse into dogmatic metaphysics of the sort from which Kant's Copernican Revolution was designed to free us. And given the linkage between systematicity and purposiveness, this reification would lead straightway to transcendental doctrines of the more far-reaching and rationally dangerous sort. For as Kant sees it, a far-reaching disaster lies down this road of system hypostatization. We are not, and never will be in a position to say "Nature is a system"; we can only work to endow our own cognitive commitments with more and more systematic completeness and cohesion. A fully realized science of nature is something toward which we must ever strive but that we will never be able to claim to have attained.

To reify the systematicity of nature – that is, to mistake the injunction to work toward a systematic knowledge of nature for the thesis that nature is actually a system – is to deflect the proper course of reason into unprofitable and self-defeating channels:

> The regulative principle prescribes that systematic unity as a *unity in nature*, which is not known merely empirically but is presupposed *a priori* (although in an indeterminate manner), be presupposed absolutely, and consequently as following from the essence of things. If, however, I begin with a supreme purposive being as the ground of all things, the unity of nature is really surrendered . . . There then arises a vicious circle; we are assuming just that very point which is mainly in dispute. (*CPuR*, A693 = B721)

The systematicity of nature is a goal to guide us in our inquiries, and not a fact they deliver into our hands as available for explanatory use.

9. INQUIRY AS A PRAXIS SUBJECT TO AN IDEAL OF ITS OWN

The perfect system governed by teleological principles is an ideal of reason, representing the conception of an ultimately intelligible world – an ideal akin to a Platonic idea, of which Kant says that

> [i]deas are even further removed from objective reality than are [strictly cognitive] categories, for no appearance can be found in which they can be represented *in concreto.* They contain a certain completeness to which no possible empirical knowledge ever attains. In them reason aims only at a systematic unity, to which it seeks to approximate the unity that is empirically possible, without ever completely reaching it. (*CPuR*, A567–68 = B595–96)

Kant insists that reason in its very nature sets up a demand for finality (in both of its senses – purposiveness and definitiveness) that the resources of the human intellect are incapable of satisfying. We can never hope to realize actual knowledge of systematicity in the natural order of things. Nevertheless, the conception of a perfected system functioning under the aegis of teleological principles operates as an ideal of reason, in line with reason's commitment to the conception of an ultimately intelligible world. Theoretical reason, geared as it is to actual cognition, cannot attain to it, but practical reasons, geared to the demands of what is highest in human nature, calls insistently for its postulation. The dispensable governing principle of the practical dimension of inquiry is a venture of human practice. And so practical reason comes not to violate but to fulfill the inherent demands of theoretical reason.

Human inquiry is a practical endeavor: the production of theoretical ("speculative") knowledge is itself a praxis governed by maxims of its own – strictly analogous with those of the second *Critique:*

I entitle all subjective principles which are derived, not from the constitution of an object but from the interest of reason in respect of a certain possible perfection of the knowledge of the object, *maxims* of reason. There are therefore maxims of speculative reason, which rest entirely on its speculative interest, although they may seem to be objective principles. When merely regulative principles are treated as constitutive, and are therefore employed as objective principles, they may come into conflict with one another. But when they are treated merely as *maxims*, there is not real conflict, but merely those differences in the interest of reason that give rise to differing modes of thought. (*CPuR*, A666–67 = B694–95)

The exercise of human reason in the enlargement, development, and systematization of knowledge is an activity – a mode of praxis – and as such governed by exactly the same practical precepts that prevail in the *Critique of Practical Reason:* the impetus to completeness, autonomy, progress, etc. And here, as elsewhere in Kant, the demands of praxis come to fill the gaps of theory – those crucial hopes regulative of human endeavor which the offerings of merely theoretical cognition are unable to fill. Inquiry, like morality, stands in need of governance by guiding ideas that can direct the never-ending efforts of man's intellect precisely because perfection in these domains is not finally attainable:

Perfection [is something] of which no rational being in the world of sense is at any time capable. But since it is required as a practical necessity, it can be found only in an endless progress of that complete fitness. On principles of pure practical reason, it is necessary to assume such a practical progress as the real object of our will. (*CPrR*, p. 122, Akad.)

For Kant, the venture of seeking and producing knowledge of nature is a praxis – an essentially intellectual praxis. Speculative – that is to say, theoretical and inquiring – reason also has its practical side. And the role played by the Kantian trio of God, freedom, and immortality as governing ideals and regulative guideposts for our praxis as moral agents is exactly paralleled by the idea of a rational and intelligible system in relation to our praxis as inquiring agents.

Interesting conclusions emerge in this light when inquiry (i.e., knowledge acquisition and validation) is considered on the basis of Kant's theory of praxis. For the acceptance of cognitive claims now emerges as a mode of action – a matter of practical reasoning subject to volitionally based constraints. And this means that in cognitive regards too – where acceptance of these claims about the world is at issue – the will is in a position to assert its demand. From this standpoint, the entire noumenal dimension of the first *Critique* takes on a practical guise. That mystery of mysteries – why we do and must say that appearances are appearances *of something* – is simply an a priori requirement of the inquiry pragmatics of the human mind. And the ideals of inquiring reason – system and purpose – emerge as practically grounded instrumentalities of human theorizing. The symmetry is perfect – system and purpose are practical, regulative constraints for the practice of theoretical inquiry, even as freedom, God, and immortality are practical, regulative constraints for the practice of morality.

In this sense, then, practical reason reaches farther than theoretical. For theoretical inquiry is itself a mode of practice which, like any other, is subject to certain characteristic demands of the practical sector. Indeed, as Kant himself says, "[Practical reason cannot be held subordinate to theoretical] because *every* interest is ultimately practical, even that of speculative reason being only conditional and reaching perfection only in its practical use" (*CPrR*, p. 121, Akad.). This fact that cognitive (theoretical, "speculative") inquiry is itself a mode of praxis means that the interests of the former are incorporated within those of the latter. And it is this fact that ultimately ensures a greater reach for practical than for theoretical reason.

Kant sees that inquiry is itself a component of human praxis, and that the goal it sets itself – the discovery of an intelligible world order – is a perfectly proper postulate of practical reason.

> [T]he intention to promote the practically possible highest good at least presupposes that the latter is possible. Otherwise it would be practically impossible to strive for the object of a concept, which, at bottom, would be empty and without an object . . . This command of reason has its ground objectively in the char-

acter of things as they must be universally judged by pure reason . . . This is, therefore, an absolutely necessary need and justifies its presupposition not merely as an allowable hypothesis
but as a practical postulate. (*CPrR*, pp. 142–43, Akad.)

But Kant does insist that we are here dealing with a matter of
regulative incentive, not one of establishable descriptive (constitutive) fact.

10. BEYOND THE LIMITS

Human reason is generally unwilling – and indeed ultimately
unable – to come to terms altogether with the fact of its cognitive
limitations. Our intelligence is easily misled regarding its own
capacity to resolve the questions that confront it:

[T]he understanding in its empirical employment cannot distinguish whether certain questions lie within its horizon or
not, [and so] it can never be assured of its claims or of its possessions, but must be prepared for many a humiliating disillu-
sionment, whenever, as must unavoidably and constantly happen, it oversteps the limits of its own domain, and loses itself in
opinions that are baseless and misleading. (*CPuR*, A238 = B297)

And so, reason is impelled by the tendencies of its own nature to
overstep the limits that condition its proper workings:

[H]uman reason has a natural tendency to transgress these limits . . . [producing] what, thought a mere illusion, is none the less
irresistible, and the harmful influence of which we can scarcely
succeed in neutralizing even by means of the severest criticism.
(*CPuR* A642 = B670)

On this basis, reason finds itself impelled to operate in a dark
and profitless sphere where no useful or stable result lies within
its reach:

[Q]uestions never ceasing – its [reason's] work must always remain incomplete; and it therefore finds itself compelled to resort
to principles which overstep all possible empirical employment,
and which yet seem so unobjectionable that even ordinary consciousness readily accepts them. But by this procedure human

reason precipitates itself into darkness and contradictions; and while it may indeed conjecture that these must be in some way due to concealed errors, it is not in a position to be able to detect them. (*CPuR*, Aviii)

But reason is not content to rest satisfied with negative delimitations of its scope. It inclines to treat ne plus ultra as a provocation rather than a warning. "[F]rom the nature of universal human reason . . . questions arise which [defeat] all attempts which have hitherto been made to answer these natural questions – for instance, whether the world has a beginning or is from eternity" (*CPuR*, B22). Such science-defeating questions are all subject to the limiting restraint of the conditioned incompleteness of experience. To step beyond this realm into the transscientific is at once illegitimate and overwhelmingly tempting. The questions that crop up here are questions that arise *out of* science, but these are not questions *of* science. They pose issues of substantive metaphysics. Though it cannot avoid confronting such questions, the human mind can attain no definitive and satisfactory resolution of them. And so our reason stands in need of a chastening critique that steadfastly reminds it of its own limitations:

> [W]here the limits of our possible knowledge are very narrow, where the temptation to judge is great, where the illusion that besets us is very deceptive and the harm that results from the error is considerable, there the *negative* instruction, which serves solely to guard us from errors, has even more importance than many a piece of positive information by which our knowledge is increased. (*CPuR*, A709–37)

It is of the nature of our reason to strive for the unattainable: to yearn for a completeness and unconditionality we cannot achieve, but yet in whose absence we cannot rest satisfied; to insist upon forcing an entry into a sphere where – for us, at any rate – no prospect of secure knowledge remains.

When our questioning penetrates into this sphere – that of traditional ("dogmatic") metaphysics – it courts disaster. And so serious inquiry must abandon this arena:

> I have not evaded . . . [metaphysical] questions by pleading the insufficiency of human reason. On the contrary, I have specified

these questions exhaustively, according to principles; and after locating the point at which, through misunderstanding, reason comes into conflict with itself, I have solved them to its complete satisfaction. The answer to these questions has not, indeed, been such as a dogmatic and visionary insistence upon knowledge might lead us to expect – that can be catered for only through magical devices, in which I am no adept. Such ways of answering them are, indeed, not within the intention of the natural constitution of our reason; and inasmuch as they have their source in misunderstanding, it is the duty of philosophy to counteract their deceptive influence, no matter what prized and cherished dreams may have to be disowned. (*CPuR*, Axiii)

Indeed, the prime aim of Kant's critical philosophy is to show just why and how such questions transgress beyond the limits of legitimacy:

But since all attempts which have hitherto been made to answer these natural questions – for instance, whether the world has a beginning or is from eternity – have already met with unavoidable contradictions, we cannot rest satisfied with the mere natural disposition to metaphysics, that is, with the pure faculty of reason itself, from which, indeed, some sort of metaphysics (be it what it may) always arises. It must be possible for reason to attain to certainty whether we know or do not know the objects of metaphysics, that is, to come to a decision either in regard to the objects of its enquiries or in regard to the capacity or incapacity of reason to pass any judgment upon them, so that we may either with confidence extend our pure reason or set to it sure and determinate limits. (*CPuR*, B22)

Beyond the range of insoluble questions lies that of illegitimate questions. And if we insist on pushing into this range, our reason encounters a decisive check. It meets not with mere *insolubilia* – situations where there are no answers – but with paradoxes, situations where there are too many but conflicting answers. And the defect here lies not in the shortcomings of our reason, but in the defects of the questions that we constrain it to answer:

[W]e cannot, therefore, escape by complaints of the narrow limits of our reason, and by confessing, under the pretext of a humility based on self-knowledge, that it is beyond the power of our reason to determine whether the world exists from eternity or has a beginning; whether cosmical space is filled with beings to infinitude, or is enclosed within certain limits; whether anything in the world is simple, or everything such as to be infinitely divisible; whether there is generation and production through freedom, or whether everything depends on the chain of events in the natural order; and finally whether there exists any being completely unconditioned and necessary in itself, or whether everything is conditioned in its existence and therefore dependent on external things and itself contingent. All these questions refer to an object which can be found nowhere save in our thoughts, namely, to the absolutely unconditioned totality of the synthesis of appearances. If from our own concepts we are unable to assert and determine anything certain, we must not throw the blame upon the object as concealing itself from us. Since such an object is nowhere to be met with outside our idea, it is not possible for it to be given. The cause of failure we must seek in our idea itself. For so long as we obstinately persist in assuming that there is an actual object corresponding to the idea, the problem, as thus viewed, allows of no solution. A clear exposition of the dialectic which lies within our concept itself would soon yield us complete certainty how we ought to judge in reference to such a question. (*CPuR*, A481–82 = B509–10)

If we persist in endeavoring to answer actually illegitimate questions, we are plunged into antinomy.

11. THE UNREALIZABILITY OF SYSTEMIC PERFECTION IS A GOOD THING

The preceding account of the frustration of reason offers only part of the story. The negativities it contemplates also have their positive aspect. For Kant, the tragedy of reason is also in a way the glory of reason; its undoing is its making as well.

For the circumstance of the insatiability of reason – of the endlessness of the why–because cycle of fact and ground – is the basis for constituting man as the sort of creature he is, as *Homo quaerens*, the questioning animal.

Man's project of question answering – of rational inquiry into the ways of nature – is an inherently worthy enterprise. And the fact that it cannot be brought to an end is rather a benefit than a source of appropriate regret. A realization of this incompleteability ought, however, to serve as a stimulus rather than a deterrent to inquiry, for "[t]he consciousness of my ignorance . . . instead of ending my inquiries, ought rather to be itself the reason for entering upon them" (*CPuR*, A758 = B786).

The natural philosopher would rightly lament the ending of man's intellectual struggle with nature. The termination of science as an inventive venture – its falling once and for all into the hands of schoolmasters and expositors – would surely spell its doom rather than its victory. The work of intellect would be reduced to the handing over from generation to generation of a finished and final body of doctrine. As Kant sees it, the old dictum holds with respect to inquiry: it is better to travel than to arrive; the limitations of theoretical reason make way for the demands of practical rationality.

Science – man's systematizing inquiry into nature – is a human project which, as such, has an inherently practical dimension and is accordingly governed by exactly the same ethical precepts that prevail in the *Critique of Practical Reason:* the impetus to completeness, autonomy, progress, etc. And here, as elsewhere in Kant, the demands of praxis come to fill the gaps of theory – those crucial hopes regulative of human endeavor, which the offerings of merely theoretical cognition are unable to fill.

The unity of rational system is like the Holy Grail whose vision in the mind's eye draws the weary seeker ever farther along the toilsome albeit rewarding quest of rational inquiry. The fact that reason can never actually rest satisfied – can never reach its destination of an achieved *systema naturae* – is the stimulus that impels us with ever-renewed vigor along the road of inquiry. Only under the goad of reason that is never content as long as any problems remain unresolved can science develop satisfactorily:

> If a science is to be advanced, all difficulties must be exposed, and those which lie hidden in its way must even be sought out, for each of them calls forth a remedy without which means cannot be found to advance the science, whether in scope or in accuracy. In this way even obstacles will be means for furthering the thoroughness of the science. (*CPrR*, p. 103, Akad.)

And here it is essential that the idea of a fully realized system of nature must never be seen as an existing reality: it must never be used ontologically (constitutively), but can only function methodologically (regulatively). Otherwise we would succumb to "the error of lazy reason [*ignava ratio*]," yielding to the temptation "to regard our investigation into nature, on any subject, as absolutely complete, disposing reason to cease from further inquiry, as it had entirely succeeded in the task it had set itself" (*CPuR*, A689–90 = B717–18). If the systematicity of nature were a realized reality rather than an ever-continuing task or project, then substantial damage would be done. For the systematic unity of nature will, once mistakenly seen as actually in hand, abort the work of reason rather than encourage it. To take this line is not to use the systematic ideal, but to abuse it.

Were our knowledge of nature completeable – were we able to comprehend the world totally as one finished and ultimately adequate system – our intellectual posture would indeed be Godlike. But this circumstance could occasion nothing but distress for a creature whose inherent nature is, after all, not divine but human.

> [T]he critique of pure speculative reason demonstrates the utter insufficiency of speculative reason to solve the most weighty problems which are presented to it in a way satisfactory to its end; but that critique did not ignore the natural and unmistakable hints of the same reason or the great steps that it can take in approaching this great goal which is set before it but which it can never of itself reach even with the aid of the greatest knowledge of nature. Thus nature here seems to have provided us only in a stepmotherly fashion with a faculty needed for our end.
>
> Now assuming that it had here indulged our wish and had provided us with that power of insight or enlightenment which we would like to possess or which some erroneously believe they do possess, what would be the consequence so far as we can discern it? [Then] . . . instead of the conflict which now the moral disposition has to wage with inclinations and in which, after some defeats, moral strength of mind may gradually be won, God and eternity in their awful majesty would stand unceasingly before our eyes (for that which we can completely prove is as certain as that which we can ascertain by sight) . . .

The conduct of man, so long as his nature remained as it now is, would be changed into mere mechanism, where, as in a puppet show, everything would gesticulate well but no life would be found in the figures.

But it is quite otherwise with us. With all the exertion of our reason we have only a very obscure and ambiguous view into the future; the Governor of the world . . . allows us to view into the realm of the supersensuous, though only a glimpse. Thus only can there be a truly moral character dedicated directly to the law and the rational creature become worthy of participating in the highest good corresponding to the moral worth of his person and not merely to his actions. (*CPrR*, pp. 146–47, Akad.)

What Kant here says with respect to our moral strivings holds also with respect to our cognitive strivings when inquiry is viewed in its practical aspect as a sphere of human activity. If the work of inquiring reason were completable, this would be something utterly tragic for us humans. The crucial stimulus for our intellectual striving would then be withdrawn. The day of *ignava ratio* would come, and we would fall into a slothful torpor, bereft of any incentive to bestir ourselves in ways befitting our humanly characteristic intellectual condition.

When all is said and done, it emerges that the discontent of reason is a noble discontent. Man's commitment to the ideal of reason in systematic completeness, with its unrealizable goal of all-inclusive comprehensiveness and all-integrating unity of principle, is the faithful functional equivalent – the epistemic counterpart – of our commitment to the categorical imperative which consolidates our moral ideals. It reflects a striving to realize the rational ultimates of completeness, totality, and systematic finality – a striving that, as Kant sees it, is all the more noble because it is not finally attainable. In this regard man's cognitive and ethical strivings are in much the same situation. In each case the commandment "Be ye perfect!" faces us with an unattainable but at the same time indispensably valuable goal:

[H]uman perfection lies not only in the cultivation of one's understanding but also in that of one's will (moral turn of mind), in order that the demands of duty in general be satisfied. First, it is one's duty to raise himself out of the crudity of his nature, out

97

of this animality [quoad actuam] more and more to humanity, by which alone he is capable of setting himself ends. It is his duty to supply by instruction what is lacking in his knowledge, and to correct his mistakes. He is not merely advised to do all this by technically-practical reason with a view to his other purposes (of art), but morally-practical reason absolutely commands it of him and makes this end his duty in order that he may be worthy of the humanity dwelling within him. Second, it is one's duty to push the cultivation of his will up to the purest virtuous disposition. (*Metaphysics of Morals*, p. 387, Akad.)

As Kant sees it, both cognitive and moral perfection are different sides of one selfsame coin. With respect to the moral aspirations of the human will, Kant writes:

Perfection [of the moral will is a thing] of which no rational being in the world of sense is at any time capable. But since it is required [of us] as practically necessary, it can be found only in an endless progress to that complete fitness; on principles of pure practical reason, it is necessary to assume such a practical progress as the real object of our will . . . Only endless progress from lower to higher stages of moral perfection is possible to a rational but finite being. (*CPrR*, p. 123, Akad.)

And Kant maintains that exactly the same story holds on the side of the cognitive perfecting of the human intellect. Here, governing the practical venture of inquiry, there are comparable regulative demands urging us to an ever fuller and yet ever imperfect realization of the potentialities of the human mind. In inquiry as in the moral life it is effort, not fulfillment, that matters. (Kant is a faithful adherent to the Protestant ethic.)

Chapter 5

Kant's Teleological Theology

1. PERFECTED SYSTEMATIZATION REQUIRES A RESORT TO PURPOSE

Kant holds that to understand nature properly we must understand it purposively. The human intellect, so he maintains, insists on finding a causality of purpose behind the causality of nature. The pivotal concept is that of design – in both senses of the term, order and purpose, which Kant sees as indissolubly interlocked in human thought.

Kant thus holds that the human intellect cannot rest satisfied with merely causal explanations of nature because explanations in the order of efficient causality always proceed by invoking minor premises ("conditions") that place the case at hand within the reach of a major explanatory premise. We can never bring this process to a satisfactory conclusion – can never "find for the conditioned knowledge obtained through the understanding the unconditioned whereby its unity is completed" (*CPuR*, A307 = B364). And so no matter how we string them together, something will remain left out, something in principle explicable but itself still unexplained. The process of causal explanation is inherently interminable. But in the order of teleology, questions can have a stop: the quest for purposes behind purposes can come to an end in an ultimate, unmediated purpose: the regress of questions ceases, and the human mind can rest satisfied. As Kant himself puts it, purposively governed free choice "offers a point of rest to the enquiring understanding in determining the chain of [efficient]

This chapter is a substantially revised version of a lecture presented at the University of Göttingen in July of 1980.

99

causes, conducting it to an unconditional causality which begins to act of itself" (*CPuR*, A447 = B475). To bring inquiry to a satisfactory conclusion we humans must accordingly go beyond or behind efficient causality – to purpose.

Kant is orthodoxly Leibnizian in his belief that while natural events always occur in line with mechanical laws, the makeup of these laws themselves is to be understood in teleological terms. Underlying the mass of natural laws there is – so we humans must suppose – an orderly unification of diversity into a systemic and intelligible unity that is implemented in terms of purpose:

> We must therefore think in nature, in respect of its merely empirical laws, a possibility of infinitely various empirical laws which are, as far as our insight goes, contingent (and so cannot be cognized *a priori*) and in respect of which we judge nature, according to empirical laws and the possibility of the unity of experience (as a system according to empirical laws), to be contingent. But such a unity must be necessary presupposed and assumed, for otherwise there would be no thoroughgoing connection of empirical cognition in a whole of experience. The universal laws of nature no doubt furnish such a connection of things . . . Hence the judgment must assume for its special use this principle *a priori* that what in the particular (empirical) laws of nature is from the human point of view contingent, yet contains a unity of law in the combination of its manifold into an experience possible in itself – a unity not indeed to be fathomed by us, but yet thinkable. Consequently as the unity of law in a combination, which we cognize as contingent in itself, although in conformity with the necessary design that is a need of understanding, is represented as the purposiveness of objects (here of nature), so must the judgment, which in respect of things under possible (not yet discovered) empirical laws is merely reflection, think of nature in respect of the latter according to *a principle of purposiveness* for our cognitive faculty. (*CJ*, intro., sect. V, middle; p. 183, Akad.; italics added)

As we humans do and must see it, the systematicity of natural science rests, in the final analysis, on the fundamentally teleological fact that each law and regularity in nature plays its essential contributory role within a well-designed wider unity of purposive functioning. Only a teleological resort to purpose can show us how "nature (in its particular laws) constitutes for us one sys-tem, which can be cognized" (*CJ*, sect. 78, middle; p. 406, Akad.). The human intellect insists on the systemic coordination of natu-ral law:

> But as regards the particular laws [of nature] that can only be made known to us through experience, there can be among them such great manifoldness and diversity that Judgment must pro-vide its own principle, in order to investigate and search into the phenomena of nature in accordance with law. Such a guid-ing principle is needed if we are even only to hope for an ade-quate empirical cognition according to a thoroughgoing unity of nature according to law, or even its unity according to em-pirical laws. (*CJ*, sect. 7, near start; p. 386, Akad.)

And the solution to this problem of unification under the aegis of systemically coordinated laws is provided, for Kant, by the essentially teleological conception of nature as an organism each of whose facets cooperates in its functioning to make for a unified and coordinated whole – an intelligible structure.

Its commitment to a purposive order that unifies and organizes the law structure of the world is one of the most fundamental and characteristic features of the human understanding:

> The conceived harmony of nature in the variety of its particu-lar laws with our need of finding universality of principles for it must be judged as contingent in respect of our insight, but yet at the same time as indispensable for the needs of our un-derstanding, and consequently as a purposiveness by which nature is harmonized with our design, which, however, has only knowledge for its aim. The universal laws of the under-standing, which are at the same time laws of nature, are just as necessary (although arising from spontaneity) as the material laws of motion. Their production presupposes no design on the part of our cognitive faculty, because it is only by means of them that we, in the first place, attain a concept of what the cog-nition of things (of nature) is and attribute them necessarily to nature as object or our cognition in general. But, so far as we can see, it is contingent that the order of nature according to its particular laws, in all its variety and heterogeneity possibly at least transcending our comprehension, should be actually

conformable to these [laws]. The discovery of this [order] is the business of the understanding, which is designedly borne toward a necessary purpose that the judgment must ascribe to nature. (*CJ*, intro., sect. VI, at start; pp. 186–87, Akad.)

One commentator, eager to soften a teleology-in-nature perspective that strikes the modern ear as dissonant in Kant's teaching, has written: "Another significant feature of Kant's teaching about teleology in the third *Critique* is that he considers it to be strictly limited in the field of its application. His contention is throughout that organisms are, properly speaking, the only objects in nature in reference to which the teleology principle can be legitimately used."[1] However, given Kant's emphatic insistence that we must look at the natural universe as itself constituting an organic whole, this so-called limitation does not come to much. The salient point is that, for Kant, every lawful facet of nature contributes to ("is good for") its systemic unity, and purposive orderliness is the great unifying principle of human judgment. With Kant, cosmic purposiveness and purposive order are two sides of the same coin insofar as we humans are concerned.

It is only because we see the world as the stage of a theater in whose transactions purposes are operative that we can hope to achieve a satisfactory systematization of knowledge. Accordingly, we are bound to look on nature *as if* being known by us were its purpose, so that "we . . . ascribe to nature a regard, as it were, to our cognitive faculty according to the analogy of purpose" (*CJ*, intro., sect. VIII, near start; p. 193, Akad.). It is as though "nature specifies its universal laws, according to the principle of purposiveness, for the sake of our cognitive faculty, that is, in accordance with the essential mission of the human understanding of finding a universal for the particular which perception offers it" (*CJ*, intro., sect. V, at end; p. 168, Akad.).

For Kant, then, the scientific ideal of perfected systematicity can only be implemented by us humans in the setting of a teleological world order – a systemic unification of our "world of experience" as the product of a creative and ordering intelligence that endows it with systemic unity. Only a teleological system of the world – one which explains the constitution of nature in terms of a ruling purpose – is ultimately able to satisfy the demand of the human intellect. The issue, for him, is one of explanatory adequacy: no system can fully answer to our explanatory demands that does not proceed in reason's own terms – that is, purposively.[2]

As Kant sees it, embarking on the process of rational inquiry requires the presupposition or preassumption that this inquiry can succeed, and this it cannot do unless nature is congenial to our cognitive operations and so structured as to yield to their efforts – unless, in short, we see nature as a system designed to admit cognitive penetration by humans. This, then, is something we simply presuppose:

> This harmony of nature with our cognitive faculty is presupposed *a priori* by our judgment . . . [which] ascribes it to nature as a transcendental purposiveness (in relation to the cognitive faculty of the subject). For without this presupposition we should have no order of nature in accordance with empirical laws, and consequently no guiding thread for an experience ordered by these in all their variety, or for an investigation of them. For it might easily be thought that, in spite of all the uniformity of natural things according to the universal laws, without which we should not have the form of an empirical cognition in general, the specific variety of the empirical laws of nature, including their effects, might yet be so great that it would be impossible for our understanding to detect in nature a comprehensible order; to divide its products into genera and species, so as to use the principles which explain and make intelligible one for the explanation and comprehension of another; or, out of such confused material (strictly we should say, so infinitely various and not to be measured by our faculty of comprehension) to make a connected experience . . . If, then, we say that nature specifies its universal laws according to the principles of purposiveness for our cognitive faculty . . . we thus neither prescribe to nature a law, nor do we learn one from it by observation (although such a principle may be confirmed by this means) . . . We only require that, be nature disposed as it may as regards its universal laws, investigation into its empirical laws may be carried on in accordance with that principle and the maxims founded thereon, because it is only so far as this holds that we can make

any headway with the use of our understanding in experience so as to acquire knowledge. (*CJ*, intro., sect. V, at end; pp. 185–86, Akad.)

We are thus regulatively enjoined to look on nature as though it were a self-systematizing agency purposively endeavoring to produce a modus operandi accessible to the human mind. Yet this investment of nature with the purpose of cognitive accessibility is, of course, simply a matter of *as if* – a useful fiction. It is regulative commitment rooted in the human intellect, and not a constitutive fact whose basis lies in our categorized experience.

Throughout the length and breadth of our concern with understanding nature, from particular organic being to the organization of nature as a whole, purposiveness is pervasive and unavoidable in our thinking:

> According to the constitution of the human understanding, no other than designedly working causes can be assumed for the possibility of organized beings in nature; and the mere mechanism of nature cannot be adequate to the explanation of these its products. But we do not attempt to decide anything by this fundamental proposition as to the possibility of such things themselves. (*CJ*, sect. 78, middle; p. 413, Akad.)

And again:

> We should explain all products and occurrences in nature, even the most purposive, by mechanism as far as is in our power (the limits of which we cannot give an account of in this kind of investigation). But at the same time we are not to lose sight of the fact that those things which we cannot even state for investigation, except under the concept of a purpose of reason, must in conformity with the essential constitution of our reason and notwithstanding those mechanical causes be subordinated by us finally to causality in accordance with purposes. (*CJ*, sect. 78, at end; p. 415, Akad.)

Where Spinoza and Hume see an illicit anthropomorphizing, Kant sees an inherent thought process built into the very modus operandi of the human mind because reason's inherent commitment to intelligibility enmeshes us in the idea of the world as a great purposive whole – unified into a grand system under the aegis of purposive principles.

2. PURPOSIVENESS IS MERELY A PROJECTION OF A REQUIREMENT OF THE HUMAN COGNITIVE FACULTY

The purposiveness of nature is not something we learn, but something we presuppose – not something we find, but something that we make via an inherent commitment of our mind. Its basis is not external and observationally found, but postulationally projected in an internal disposition of the human mind:

> For since we do not, properly speaking, *observe* designed purposes in nature, but only in our reflection upon its products *think* this concept as a guiding thread for our judgment, they are not given to us through the object. It is quite impossible for us *a priori* to vindicate, as capable of assumption, such a concept according to its objective reality. It remains therefore a proposition absolutely resting upon subjective conditions alone, viz. of the judgment reflecting in conformity with our cognitive faculties. . . . We cannot otherwise think and make comprehensible the purposiveness which must lie at the bottom of our cognition of the internal possibility of many natural things than by representing it and the world in general as a product of an intelligent cause. (*CJ*, sect. 75, middle; pp. 399–400, Akad.)

Only a purposive system can fully satisfy the human mind's demands. But such a system is never achieved as the product of our inquiries. It is not something we could ever *find* in the phenomenal realm, it is *postulated*. From the very start, the human intellect presumes, as a regulative principle, that a realization of purpose can ultimately be achieved in our attempts to comprehend nature as best inquiring reason reveals it to us:

> [In] so far as matter is organized . . . it necessarily carries with it the concept of a natural purpose, because this its specific form is at the same time a product of nature. But this concept leads necessarily to the idea of collective nature as a system in accordance with the rule of purposes, to which ideas all the mechanism of nature must be subordinated according to principles of

reason (at least in order to investigate natural phenomena in it). The principle of [sufficient] reason belongs to it only as a subjective principle or a maxim: viz. everything in the world is some way good for something; nothing is vain in it. By the example that nature gives us in its organic products we are justified, nay called upon, to expect of it and of its laws nothing that is not purposive on the whole. It is plain that this [principle of purposiveness] . . . is regulative and not constitutive. (*CJ*, sect. 67, middle; pp. 378–79, Akad.)

But although our mind is so endowed (or "programmed" as it were with an inclination – an instinctive and indeed insuperable tendency – to think in this teleological and purposive-oriented way, this line of thought takes us well outside the range of what we could ever come to know.

By the constitution and the principles of our cognitive faculty, we can think of nature, in its purposive arrangements which have become known to us, in no other way than as the product of an understanding to which it is subject. But this theoretical investigation of nature can never reveal to us [its basis] . . . On the contrary, with all our knowledge of nature it remains undecided whether that supreme cause is its original ground, according to a final purpose, or whether it is not rather our understanding itself, determined by the mere necessity of its nature to produce certain forms (analogy with what we call the art of instinct in animals). (*CJ*, sect. 85, nr. end; pp. 441–42, Akad.)

The purposiveness of nature is never given – is never a matter which is learned from actual experience. For experience is impotent to reveal a purposive systematicity whose realization lies quite beyond its powers:

Now experience, since it can never embrace collective nature as a system . . . , can never, even if we had the power to survey empirically the whole system as far as it concerns mere nature, raise us above nature to the purpose of its existence, and so to the determinate concept of that supreme intelligence. (*CJ*, sect. 85, middle; p. 438, Akad.)

Purposive systematicity lies outside the range of secure human knowledge, so that the teleological completeness our intellect demands can never be realized as a matter of known fact. The purposiveness of nature lies beyond knowledge – it is emphatically not something we can learn by inquiry:

> For external objects as phenomena and adequate ground related to purposes cannot be met with; this, although it lies in nature, must only be sought in the supersensible substrate of nature, from all possible insight into which we are cut off. Hence it is absolutely impossible for us to produce from nature itself grounds of explanation for purposive combinations. (*CJ*, sect. 77, at end; p. 410, Akad.)

There is no avenue by which inquiry can determine the ultimate purpose of nature, and

> [natural science] must not transgress its bounds in order to introduce into itself as a domestic principle that to whose concept no experience can be commensurate, and upon which we are only entitled to venture after the completion of natural science. (*CJ*, sect. 68, middle; p. 302, Akad.)

System and systemic purposiveness can emerge from science only at the end of the day – that is to say, never.

The purposive unity of nature is a postulate that meets a fundamental requirement of human reason, and not a discovered or established fact which this reason can come to realize about the world. It represents a regulative, procedural rule (maxim) in the way our intellect does and must deal with the data regarding the modus operandi of nature:

> This transcendental concept of a purposiveness of nature . . . ascribes nothing to the object (nature), but only represents the peculiar way in which we must proceed in reflection on the objects of nature with a view to a thoroughly connected experience, and is consequently a subjective principle or maxim of judgment. (*CJ*, intro., sect. V, middle; p. 184, Akad.)

This yields the key to Kant's resolution of the antinomy inherent in teleological reason – the seeming conflict between the omnipresence of efficient causality throughout the domain of experience, on the one hand, and our need to invoke the causality of final causes (*Endursachen*) on the other. The clash is resolved by a clear division of labor. The former causality is authentic as a matter of theoretical reason's sovereignty over the realm of phenomena (as per the Second Analogy of the first *Critique.*) The latter is a part of practical reason's problematic hypostatization of a merely procedural principle employed in man's reflective judgment as a rule for articulating and systematizing the empirical laws of nature:

> If this assumption [of purposiveness] be treated as constitutive, it goes much further than observation has thus far been able to justify; and we must therefore conclude that it is nothing more than a regulative principle of reason, to aid us in securing the highest possible systematic unity, by means of the idea of the purposive causality of the supreme cause of the world. (*CPuR*, A688 = B716)

Purposiveness, in sum, is the human intellect's schematization, under the aegis of practical reason, of theoretical reason's demand for systematicity. As Kant himself puts it,

> It is then one thing to say, "the production of certain things of nature . . . is only possible through a cause which determines itself to action according to design," and quite another to say, "I can, *according to the peculiar constitution of my cognitive faculties,* judge concerning the possibility of these things and their production in not other fashion than by conceiving for this a cause working according to design, i.e., a Being which is productive in a way analogous to the causality of an intelligence: In the former case I wish to establish something concerning the object and am required to establish the objective reality of an assumed concept; in the latter, reason merely determines the use of my cognitive faculties conformably to their peculiarities and to the essential conditions of their range and their limits. (*CJ*, sect. 75, at start; pp. 397–98, Akad.)

On this perspective, purposive systematization is an amalgam whose components have a rather different basis. Systematicity is a commitment of reason via ideals, a telos of rational agency in general. But purposiveness is a commitment of our specifically human judgment, an implementing conception for us humans, whose basis lies in the particular constitution of the human mind. Our intellect is so constituted as to require an explanation of the phenomena and not to rest satisfied until that explanation is provided in purposive terms. Its commitment to purposiveness is its characteristic way of responding to the demands of reason.

The project of systematizing our knowledge of the world under the control of purpose is not, however, one we can bring to a satisfactory conclusion.

> The idea of systematic unity [under the aegis of a cosmic purpose] should be used only as a regulative principle to guide us in seeking for such unity in the connection of things, according to universal laws of nature; and we ought, therefore, to believe that we have approximated to completeness in the employment of the principle only in proportion as we are in a position to verify such unity in empirical fashion – a completeness which is never, of course, attainable. [If] instead of this the reverse procedure is adopted [and] the reality of a principle of purposive unity is not only presupposed but hypostatised . . . , [then] we impose ends upon nature forcibly and dictatorially instead of pursuing the more reasonable course of searching for them by the path of physical investigation. And thus teleology, which is intended to aid us merely in completing the unity of nature in accordance with universal laws, not only tends to abrogate such unity, but also prevents reason from carrying out its own professed purpose, that of proving from nature, in conformity with these laws. (*CPuR*, A692–93 = B720–21)

Accordingly, we can and should use science so as to work our way up (so to speak) to teleology as a unifying expectation, but we must never pre-assume teleology and work our way down from it as a given fact available to do explanatory work.

3. WHAT JUSTIFIES OUR MAKING THIS PROJECTION

Two considerations combine to legitimate our projecting purposiveness into nature – one negative, one positive.

The negative consideration is that we get a *nihil obstat* from cognitive reason. The first *Critique*, so Kant insists, has shown that theoretical (speculative) reason is in no position to impede a postulation of nature's systemic purposiveness, seeing that it "has previously established an unavoidable ignorance of things in themselves, and has limited all that we can theoretically *know* to mere appearance" (*CPuR*, Bxxix). Cognitive reason has no alternative but to leave open the possibility of thinking a realm of purpose to underlie the nature made known to us through cognitive faculties. We are in the standard Kantian position of a jurisdictional division or separation of powers: theoretical reason cannot intrude upon the operations of practical reason or evaluative judgment.

But this goes no farther than to indicate that there is no rational obstacle to belief in the purposive systematicity of nature. It does not go to show why we should endorse such a position and adopt this belief or what justificatory considerations provide a positive legitimation for the recourse to purpose.

At this point, Kant's thinking takes a pragmatic turn. The principle of the purposiveness of nature is fundamentally regulative. The purposiveness of nature is, in the final analysis, a procedural or methodological resource to facilitate our understanding of the "organic" aspect of nature as a system of coordinated lawfulness.

> [The invocation of design and purpose] is not meant to introduce a special ground of causality, but only to assist the employment of reason by furnishing for the use of reason a mode of investigation different from that according to mechanical principles in order to supplement the inadequacy of the latter even for empirical research into all particular laws of nature. (*CJ*, sect. 68, middle; p. 383, Akad.)

What is at issue is not a constitutively factual finding ("Nature is purposive"), but a regulative maxim ("In developing your knowledge of nature proceed on the supposition that nature is purposive"). In its regulative role a presuppositional recourse to the purposive unity and systematicity of nature is thoroughly useful:

> For the regulative law of systematic unity prescribes that we should study nature *as if* systematic and purposive unity, combined with the greatest possible manifoldness, were everywhere to be met with, *in infinitum.* For although we may succeed in discovering but little of this perfection of the world, it is nevertheless required by the legislation of our reason that we must

always search for and surmise it; and it must always be beneficial, and can never be harmful, to direct our investigations
into nature in accordance with this principle. (*CPuR*, A700–1 =
B728–29)

And indeed the invocation of purpose is not only useful, but
necessary:

> We must investigate [nature's] empirical laws throughout on
> that principle [i.e., the principle that nature is purposive for our
> knowledge of it] and the maxims founded thereon, because
> only so far as that principle applies can we make any headway
> in the employment of our understanding in experience, or gain
> knowledge. (*CJ*, sect. 5, near. end; p. 186, Akad.)

As this passage indicates, nature's salient purposiveness is a
purposiveness for our knowledge of it – a yielding vulnerability
to our inquiry, with its predilection toward simplicity, uniformity,
orderliness, and so on – in short, toward system. The real is rational: accessible to reason. All other modes of purposiveness are
in the final analysis subordinate to this. (Here the Principle of
Sufficient Reason stands at the fore once again.)[3]

Purposiveness in nature thus pivots on an ideal – an idea, in
the Platonic sense of an idealization. But this ideal is one whose
justification rests on very practical and functionally oriented considerations, an ideal whose justification rests on its utility in facilitating the work of reason. For without a recourse to purposiveness we can neither properly understand nor adequately motivate
reason's search for systematicity in nature.

Of course the purposiveness of nature at issue in "nature is re-
ceptive to being known" is a metaphor. No such reification is
necessary to accommodate the facts we actually secure through
inquiry into nature. But there is no reason to think it is illicit. On
the contrary, its justification turns on its inherent pragmatic utility in encouraging our efforts in inquiry:

> [The] greatest possible empirical employment of my reason
> rests upon an idea (that of systematically complete unity, which
> I shall presently be defining more precisely). This is an idea
> which, although it can never itself be adequately exhibited in ex-
> perience, is yet indispensably necessary in order that we may

approximate to the highest degree of empirical unity. [Accordingly] I shall not only be entitled, but shall also be constrained, to realise this idea, that is to posit for it a real object. But I may posit it only as a something which I do not at all know in itself . . . solely in order, under countenance of such an original ground, to make possible systematic unity of the manifold in the universe, and thereby the greatest possible empirical employment of reason. This I do by representing all connections *as if* they were the ordinances of a supreme reason, of which our reason is but a faint copy . . . I only think to myself the relation of a being, in itself completely unknown to me, to the greatest possible systematic unity of the universe, solely for the purpose of using it as a schema of the regulative principle of the greatest possible empirical employment of my reason. (*CPuR*, A677–79 = B705–7)

Kant explains the as-if nature of this operational (regulative) principle as follows. We are to

treat nature as resting upon a purposiveness, in accordance with universal laws for which no special arrangement is exempt . . . We then have a regulative principle of the systematic unity of teleological connection . . . What we may presume to do is to pursue the physico-mechanical connection in accordance with universal laws in the hope of discovering what the teleological connection actually is. In this [motivational] way also can the principle of purposive unity always aid in extending the employment of reason in reference to experience, without being in any way prejudicial to it. (*CPuR*, A691–92 = B719–20)

Our regulative/methodological subscription to the principle of teleology – our view of nature as a purposive system, and even our acceptance of the idea of supremely rational creative intelligence – can only aid and never impede the work of inquiring reason, provided that it is used properly, that is, as an operating directive rather than a claim of substantive fact:

This highest formal unity, which rests solely on concepts of reason, is the *purposive* unity of things. The *speculative* interest of reason makes it necessary to regard all order in the world as if it has originated in the purpose of a supreme reason. Such a principle opens out to our reason, as applied in the field of experience, altogether new views as to how the things of the

world may be connected according to teleological laws, and so
enables it to arrive at their greatest systematic unity. The assumption of a supreme intelligence, as the one and only cause
of the universe, through in the idea alone, can therefore always
benefit reason and can never injure it . . . And provided we re-
strict ourselves to a merely regulative use of this principle, even
being mistaken cannot do us any harm. For the worst that can
happen would be that where we expected a teleological connection [*nexus finalis*], we find only a mechanical or physical
connection [*nexus effectivus*]. In such a case, we merely fail to
find the additional unity; we do not destroy the unity upon
which reason insists in its empirical employment. (*CPuR*, A686–
87 = B714–15)

Kept in its proper place as a mere regulative, inquiry-grounding
principle, our postulation of systemic purposiveness can only be
beneficial and never harmful.

We are thus dealing with a presuppositional interest of human
reason and not a result of human inquiry – a methodological (regulative) device, and not a substantive (constitutive) fact:

If this assumption [of the principle that a divinely established
purpose pervades nature] be treated as constitutive it goes much
further than observation has thus far been able to justify; and
we must therefore conclude that it is nothing more than a regulative principle of reason, to aid us in securing the highest
possible systematic unity, by means of the idea of the purposive
causality of the supreme cause of the world – *as if* this being, as
supreme intelligence, acting in accordance with a supremely
wise purpose, were the cause of all things. If however, we over-
look this restriction of the idea to a merely regulative use, reason is led away into mistaken paths. (*CPuR*, A688 = B716)

Teleology is a methodologically useful resource, not a descriptive fact. Teleological conceptions have no theoretical justification,
no constitutive legitimacy, no factual status: we cannot appropriately describe or explain nature by their means. But they are
infinitely useful for the conduct of inquiry because they impel us
ever onward in the quest for systematicity, allowing us no rest in
the face of incompleteness or incoherence. In this way, Kant is a
protopragmatist. He maintains, in effect, that we are entitled to

resort to teleology not because we can show it to be true, but because of its usefulness.

But beyond utility lies also the fact of inevitability. Kant insists that "we are in fact indispensably obliged to ascribe the concept of design to nature if we wish to investigate it . . . and this concept is thus an absolutely necessary maxim for the empirical use of our reason" (*CJ*, sect. 75, at start; p. 398, Akad.). And again:

> Such a [purposive unity of the empirical laws of nature] must be necessarily presupposed and assumed, as otherwise we should not have a thoroughgoing connection of empirical knowledge in a whole of experience. (*CJ*, sect. 5, middle; p. 183, Akad.)

Kant insists emphatically that the human understanding is so construed as to demand purposiveness in nature:

> And so we are able to say: Certain natural products *must, by the special constitution of our understanding, be considered by us*, in regard to their possibility, as if produced designedly and as purposes. (*CJ*, sect. 77, near start; p. 405, Akad., italics added)

And again:

> In the natural constitution of an organized being, i.e., one suitably adapted to life, we must assume as an axiom that no organ will be found for any purpose that is not the fittest and best adapted to that purpose. (*Grundlegung*, p. 395, Akad.)

Our human intelligence requires a presupposition of purpose wherever it encounters order. For us, "Nullus ordo sine ratione": order is always purposively rationalizable. An adequate understanding that can fully respond to our demands for comprehension must have recourse to purpose:

> [W]e can no doubt try all the known and yet to be discovered laws of mechanical production, and even hope to make good progress therewith, but we can never get rid of the call for a quite different ground of production for the possibility of such a product, viz. causality by means or purposes. Absolutely no human reason (in fact no finite reason like ours in quality, however much it may surpass it in degree) can hope to understand the production of even a blade of grass by mere mechanical causes. (*CJ*, sect. 77, near end; p. 409, Akad.)

The insistence on systematic purposiveness "emerges, therefore, [as] a peculiarity of *our* [human] understanding in respect of the judgment on its reflection upon the things of nature" (*CJ*, sect. 77m, near start; p. 405, Akad.). This quest for a purposively grounded rational system is an inalienable commitment of our intellect, implicit in its very nature as the cognitive resource that is at our disposal.

Kant develops this idea of a faculty-centered inevitability of purposiveness in the justification (transcendental deduction) of the "principle of purposiveness" he offers us in the introduction to the *Critique of Judgment*. He writes:

This transcendental concept of purposiveness of nature . . . only represents the peculiar way in which we must proceed in reflection upon the objects of nature in reference to a thoroughly connected experience, and is consequently a subjective principle/maxim of judgment . . . [W]e must necessarily assume that there is such a unity without our comprehending it or being able to prove it. In order to convince ourselves of the correctness of this deduction of the concept before us and the necessity of assuming it as a transcendental principle of cognition, just consider the magnitude of the problem. The problem, which lies *a priori* in our understanding, is to make a connected experience out of given perceptions of a nature containing at all events an infinite variety of empirical laws. The understanding is, no doubt, in possession *a priori* of universal laws of nature, without which nature could not be an object of experience, but it needs in addition a certain order of nature in its particular rules which can only be empirically known and which are, as regards the understanding, contingent. These rules must be thought by it as laws (i.e., as necessary), for otherwise they would not constitute an order of nature, although their necessity can never be cognized or comprehended by it. Although, therefore, the understanding can determine nothing *a priori* in respect of objects, it must, in order to trace out these empirical so-called laws, place at the basis of all reflection upon objects an *a priori* principle, viz. that a cognizable order of nature is possible in accordance with these laws . . . This harmony of nature with our cognitive faculty is presupposed *a priori* by the judgment, on behalf of its reflection upon nature in accordance with

> its empirical laws, while the understanding at the same time
> cognizes it objectively as contingent, and it is only the judgment
> that ascribes it to nature as a transcendental purposiveness
> (in relation to the cognitive faculty of the subject). (*CJ*, sect. 5,
> middle; pp. 184–85, Akad.)

On this basis, Kant is not just a pragmatist; he is a transcendental
philosopher as well.

For Kant the unification of phenomena under laws, that unification of laws into systems, and the unification of systems under
a single all-governing purpose are all to be conceived of by us
humans as part of one vast integration under the aegis of an all-
governing intelligence. Whether the matter *is* so or not (ontologically and constitutively) – heaven only knows. But woe betide us
if we do not think so (regulatively and methodologically) – as indeed we must, given the very nature of our cognitive faculties. For
if we did not do so, we would lose our road map on the journey
of the cognitive life. Here necessity and advantage join hands in
an inescapable (albeit pre-Darwinian) symbiosis.

4. THE ROAD TO TRANSCENDENTAL THEOLOGY

Systematic arrangement is, by nature, a matter of organization in
accordance with a rational plan, and – as Kant sees it – the human
mind has a virtually insuperable tendency toward the view that
intelligibility presupposes intelligence, that planning requires a
planner, design a designer. The system we seek to provide through
rational inquiry into nature must comprise an overall plan or design whose character calls for the supposition of a responsible
intelligence. The human mind is committed to viewing its experiential world as a system endowed with purposive unity by a
creative intelligence:

> By the peculiar constitution of my cognitive faculties I can judge
> of the possibility of these [natural] things and their production
> in no other way than by conceiving for this a cause working
> according to design, i.e., an agency whose productivity is anal-
> ogous to the causality of our intelligence. (*CJ*, sect. 75, near start;
> pp. 397–98, Akad.)

Accordingly, Kant holds that the ideal of perfected systematicity can only be achieved on the setting of a teleological world order – a systemic unification of our "world of experience" as the product of a creative and ordering intelligence that endows it with systematicity:

> The greatest possible systematic unity, and consequently also purposive unity, is the training school for the use of reason, and is indeed the very foundation of the possibility of its greatest possible employment. The idea of such unity is, therefore, inseparably bound up with the very nature of our reason. This same idea is on that account legislative for us; and it is therefore very natural that we should assume a corresponding legislative reason [*intellectus archetypus*], from which, as the object of our reason, all systematic unity of nature is to be derived. (*CPuR*, A694–95 = B722–23)

As Kant sees it, the slide from teleology to theology is inexorable for the human mind:

> [I]t is absolutely impossible for us to obtain from nature itself grounds of explanation for purposive combinations, and it is necessary by the constitution of the human cognitive faculties to seek the supreme ground for these combinations in an original understanding as the cause of the world. (*CJ*, sect. 77, at end; p. 410, Akad.)

Whenever we meet with organic purposiveness in nature, we are inexorably led to suppose that a guiding intelligence has been at work. And so we find Kant telling us that

> the natural things that we find possible only as purposes constitute the best proof of the contingency of the universe. To the common understanding and to the philosopher alike they are the only valid ground of proof for its dependence on an origin from an intelligent Being existing outside the world – a Being who must be intelligent on account of its own purposive form. Teleology, then, finds the consummation of its investigations only in theology. (*CJ*, sect. 75; middle, pp. 398–99, Akad.)

And again:

> [We] can form absolutely no concept of the possibility of such a world [as ours] save by thinking of a *designedly working*

117

supreme cause thereof. Objectively, we cannot therefore assert the proposition – There is an intelligent original Being; but only subjectively, for the use of our judgment in its reflection on the purposes of nature, which can be thought according to no other principle than that of a designing causality of a highest cause. (*CJ*, sect. 75, middle; p. 400, Akad.)

Nevertheless, this sort of "proof" of God does not establish his existence per se, but only as an inherent requirement of the human intellect in its attempts to project an intelligible world view. It goes no farther than establishing the inevitability of our commitment to the conception of such a being. As Kant puts it,

> If we assume a divine being, we have no concept whatsoever either of the sure possibility . . . or of the necessity of its existence; but, on the other hand, we are now in a position to give a satisfactory answer to all those questions which relate to the contingent, and to afford reason the most complete satisfaction in respect to that highest [systemic] unity after which it is seeking in its empirical employment. The fact, however, that we are unable to satisfy reason regarding this assumption itself, shows that it is the speculative *interest* of reason, and not any *discovery* which justifies it in thus starting from a point that lies so far above its sphere, endeavoring, by this device, to survey its objects as constituting a complete whole. (*CPuR*, A675–76 = B703–4)

In practical reason's postulation of God as ultimate focus and source of natural purposiveness, Kant sees the questionable (but indispensably useful) reification of a regulative operating principle. As Kant sees it, it is not the existence of God, but our commitment to the idea of him that is demonstrable.

God is certainly not a being that – as such – can be the object of knowledge:

> Hence the concept of an absolutely necessary Being is no doubt an indispensable idea of reason, but yet it is a problematic concept unattainable by the human understanding. It is indeed valid for the employment of our cognitive faculties in accordance with their peculiar constitution, but not valid of the object. Nor is it valid for every knowing being, because I cannot presuppose in every such being thought and intuition as two distinct conditions of the exercise of its cognitive faculties, and

consequently as conditions of the possibility and actuality of things . . . Here the maxim always holds that all objects whose cognition surpasses the faculty of the understanding are thought by us according to the subjective conditions of the exercise of that faculty which necessarily attach to our (human) nature. If judgments laid down in this way (and there is no other alternative in regard to transcendent concepts) cannot be constitutive principles determining the object as it is, they will remain regulative principles adapted to the human point of view, immanent in their exercise and sure. (*CJ*, sect. 76, middle; pp. 402–3, Akad.)

Accordingly, the basis of the unifying and grounding principles throughout Kant's system is not ontological ("constitutive") but regulative – it is a thing not of fact but of method, something we come to not through inquiry but by assumption.

And this holds, in particular, also for God's role as locus or purpose in the *Critique of Judgment*. As Kant sees it in this context, we do not know of God but only think of him; we do not establish the existence of God, but rather postulate him, in line with the inner demands of human reason for intelligibility in the world:

By the constitution and the principles of our cognitive faculty we can think of nature, in its purposive arrangements which have become known to us, in no other way than as the product of an understanding to which it is subject. But the theoretical investigation of nature can never reveal [this] to us . . . On the contrary, with all our knowledge of nature it remains undecided whether that supreme cause is its original ground. (*CJ*, sect. 85, near end; p. 441, Akad.)

Or again:

To prevent a misunderstanding which may easily arise, it is in the highest degree needful to remark that, in the first place, we can *think* these properties of the highest Being only according to analogy. How indeed could we investigate [directly] the nature of that to which experience can show us nothing similar? Secondly, in this way we only think the supreme Being; we cannot thereby *cognize* Him and ascribe anything theoretically to Him . . . [W]e are only concerned with the question, what concept we can form of Him, according to the constitution of our cognitive faculties, and whether we have to assume His existence in order merely to furnish practical reality to a purpose, which pure reason without any such presupposition enjoins upon us *a priori* to bring about with all our powers. (*CJ*, sect. 88, near end; pp. 456–57, Akad.)

This postulation of God as designer is a process of the same structure as his (entirely parallel) postulation of God as moral guarantor:

Now since [we stand committed to the view that] there are . . . moral laws, it must follow that if these necessarily presuppose the existence of any being as the condition of the possibility of their *obligatory* power, then this existence must be *postulated.* (*CPuR*. A634 = B662)

The invocation of God implicit in the inherent commitment of our reason points towards a "transcendental" theology (in Kant's standard sense of the term):

But this systematic unity of ends in this world of intelligences – a world which is indeed, as mere nature, a sensible world only . . . – leads inevitably also to the purposive unity of all things, which constitutes this great whole, in accordance with universal laws of nature (just as the former unity is in accordance with universal and necessary laws of morality), and thus unites the practical with the speculative reason. The world must be represented as having originated from an idea if it is to be in harmony with that employment of reason without which we should indeed hold ourselves to be unworthy of reason, namely, with the moral employment – which is founded entirely on the idea of the supreme good. In this way all investigation of nature tends to take the form of a system of ends, and its widest extension becomes a physico-theology. But this . . . connects the purposiveness of nature with grounds which must be inseparably connected *a priori* with the inner possibility of things, and so leads to a *transcendental theology* – a theology which takes the ideal of supreme ontological perfection as a principle of systematic unity. And since all things have their origin in the absolute necessity of the one primordial being, that principle connects them in accordance with universal and necessary laws of nature. (*CPuR*, A815–16 = B843–44)

We must proceed in inquiry as if we were dealing with a nature eager to meet our inquiry effort halfway, a nature so designed (in both senses of the term) as to be a willing collaborator for inquiring man, a nature whose destiny it is to be discerned by human reason, a nature designed by its maker to answer to the purpose (among others) of being known by humans. (This, in the final analysis, is Kant's answer to the Humean problem of induction.)

Note, moreover, that for Kant, God (like the purposiveness he underwrites) is justified in terms of pragmatic considerations:

> But reason cannot think this systematic unity otherwise than by giving to the idea of this unity an object; and since experience can never give an example of complete systematic unity, the object which we have to assign to the idea is not such as experience can ever supply. This object, as thus entertained by reason [*ens rationis ratiocinatae*], is a mere idea; it is not assumed as a something that is real absolutely and *in itself*, but is postulated only . . . in order that we may view all connection of the things of the world of sense *as if* they had their ground in such a being. In thus proceeding, our sole purpose is to secure that systematic unity which is indispensable to reason, and which while furthering in every way the empirical knowledge obtainable by the understanding, can never interfere to hinder or obstruct it. We misapprehend the meaning of this idea if we regard it as the assertion or even as the assumption of a real thing, to which we may proceed to ascribe the ground of the systematic order of the world. On the contrary, what this ground which eludes our concepts may be in its own inherent constitution is left entirely undetermined; the idea is posited only as being the point of view from which alone that unity, which is so essential to reason and so beneficial to the understanding, can be further extended. In short, this transcendental thing is only the schema of the regulative principle by which reason, so far as lies in its power, extends systematic unity over the whole field of experience. (*CPuR*, A681–82 = B709–10)

And again:

> [W]hat has justified us in adopting the idea of a supreme intelligence as a schema of the regulative principle is precisely this greatest possible systematic and purposive unity – a unity which

our reason has required as a regulative principle that must underlie all investigation of nature. (*CPuR*, A699 = B727)

Accordingly, our mind is led to postulate God as a creator and designer whose acceptance can motivate, encourage, and canalize inquiry into nature. But to begin with God as an established fact and to invoke this fact in explaining the phenomena would be to turn matters upside down:

> The regulative principle prescribes that systemic unity as a *unity in nature*, which is not known merely empirically but is presupposed *a priori* (although in an indeterminate manner), be presupposed absolutely, and consequently as following from the essence of things. If, however, I begin with a supreme purposive being as the ground of all things, the unity of nature is really surrendered, as being quite foreign and accidental to the nature of things, and as not capable of being known from its own universal laws. There then arises a vicious circle; we are assuming just that very point which is mainly in dispute. (*CPuR*, A693 = B721)

And again:

> The idea of systematic unity should be used only as a regulative principle to guide us in seeking for such unity in the connection of things, according to universal laws of nature; and we ought, therefore, to believe that we have approximated to completeness in the employment of the principle only in proportion as we are in a position to verify such unity in empirical fashion – a completeness which is never, of course, attainable. Instead of this the reverse procedure is sometimes adopted. The reality of a principle of purposive unity is then not only presupposed but hypostatised; and since the concept of a supreme intelligence is in itself completely beyond our powers of comprehension, we proceed to determine it in an anthropomorphic manner, and so to impose ends upon nature, forcibly and dictatorially, instead of pursuing the more reasonable course of searching for them by the path of physical investigation. And thus teleology, which is intended to aid us merely in completing the unity of nature in accordance with universal laws, not only tends to abrogate such unity, but also prevents reason from carrying out its own professed purpose, that of proving from nature, in conformity

with these laws, the existence of a supreme intelligent cause. (*CPuR*, A692–93 = B720–21)

To appeal to God's purposes as substantive principles of explanation, rather than as a regulative principle to encourage inquiry in its ongoing quest, is to baffle reason rather than apply it:

> For in this field of inquiry, if instead of looking for causes in the universal laws of material mechanism, we appeal directly to the unsearchable decree of supreme wisdom, all those ends which are exhibited in nature. . . make our investigation of the causes a very easy task, and so enable us to regard the labour of reason as completed, when, as a matter of fact, we have merely dispensed with its employment – an employment which is wholly dependent for guidance upon the order of nature and the series of its alterations, in accordance with the universal laws which they are found to exhibit. This error can be avoided, if we . . . follow out the physico-mechanical connection in accordance with universal laws, in the hope of discovering what the teleological connection actually is. In this way alone can the principle of purposive unity aid always in extending the employment of reason in reference to experience, without being in any instance prejudicial to it. (*CPuR*, A691–92 = B719–20)

The systemically purposive unity of nature is only a goal of inquiry, a *terminus ad quem*; it is never a *terminus a quo*, a something in hand from which, as given, consequences can be deduced.

The centerpiece of Kant's theory is thus not God per se, but the *idea* of God as an instrumentality of human thought. The idea of a supreme organizing and purpose-endowing intelligence is altogether legitimate when employed regulatively, as a guide and goad to the systematization of experience. But it is problematic to the point of meaninglessness to take this idea to represent an actual reality, a potentially knowable thing of some sort:

> If, however, we overlook the restriction of this Idea [of a supreme intelligence] to a merely regulative use, reason is led into mistaken paths. For it then leaves the ground of experience, which alone can contain the road-signs for its proper course, and ventures beyond into the incomprehensible and uninvestigable, rising to heights that make it dizzy because it finds itself

entirely cut off from any activity in conformity with experience. (*CPuR*, A689 = B717)

What is at issue is no more (but also no less) than the idea of God as an organizing principle of human thought. The conception of God provides a basis for the systemic unity of knowledge.

[T]he transcendental, and the only determinate, concept which the purely speculative reason gives us of God is, in the strictest sense, *deistic*; that is, reason does not determine the objective validity of such a concept, but yields only the idea of something which is the ground of the highest and necessary unity of all empirical reality. This something we cannot think otherwise than on the analogy of a real substance that, in conformity with laws of reason, is the cause of all things. This, indeed, is how we must think it . . . [To do otherwise] is, however, inconsistent with the pursuit of that complete systematic unity in our knowledge to which reason at least sets no limits. (*CPuR*, A675 = B703)

This also explains Kant's own fastidious holding aloof from all organized religion. After all, it makes no sense to worship an instrumentality of our mind's devising, a mere cognitive contrivance, a pragmatically useful "schema of a regulative principle." God, after all, is for Kant little more than a fiction fabricated (however inevitably) by one sector of mind *pour encourager les autres:*

[S]ince this idea [of God] arises entirely out of out own reason and is made by us in order, from a theoretical standpoint, to explain the purposiveness of the universe, or, for practical purposes, to serve as an incentive in our conduct, we do not hereby have before us a being *to* whom we are obligated; for the actuality of such a being would first have to be proved (disclosed) by experience. But it is a duty of man to himself to apply this idea, which offers itself unavoidably to reason . . . In this (*practical*) sense, to have religion can be asserted to be a duty of man to himself. (*The Metaphysics of Morals*, p. 444, Akad.)

Be this as it may, the demands of theoretical reason for systemic perfection as uncovered in the first *Critique* can be met in full only when the mechanisms explored in the two later *Critiques* are also in hand to provide for a teleological system with putative God as creator-designer to serve as guarantor. The perfect system is a purposive order envisioned under the ruling aegis of a supreme guiding intelligence. (To be sure, as Kant sees it, this is not an established fact but an idealization built into the modus operandi of human reason endowing it with a practical device for the regulative guidance of human cognition.)

Purpose-based system provides a broad entryway into transcendental theology from the starting point of cognitive reason even as freedom and morality are able to do from the starting point of practical reason:

> But this systematic unity of ends in this world of intelligences – a world which is indeed, as mere nature, a sensible world only . . . – leads inevitably also to the purposive unity of all things, which constitutes this great whole, in accordance with universal laws of nature (just as the former unity is in accordance with universal and necessary laws of morality), and thus unites the practical with the speculative reason. The world must be represented as having originated from an idea if it is to be in harmony with that employment of reason without which we should indeed hold ourselves to be unworthy of reason, namely, with the moral employment – which is founded entirely on the idea of the supreme good. In this way all investigation of nature tends to take the form of a system of ends, and in its widest extension becomes a physico-theology. But this . . . leads to a *transcendental theology* – a theology which takes the ideal of supreme ontological perfection as a principle of systematic unity. And since all things have their origin in the absolute necessity of the one primordial being, that principle connects them in accordance with universal and necessary laws of nature. (*CPuR*, A815–16 = B843–44)

Throughout Kant's system, the conception of God functions unavoidably in the background to provide direction of what transpires on the stage of human experience. In the *Critique of Pure Reason*, God is the *ens realissimum* that grounds our commitment to the cognitive systematicity of our knowledge of nature. In the *Critique of Practical Reason*, God is the guarantor of freedom and morality. In the *Critique of Judgment*, God is the ultimate source of the purposiveness of the natural universe, the "supreme ground of possibility for the objective purposive formations of matter"

(*CJ*, sect. 80, near end; p. 421, Akad.). From all directions of human reason (cognitive, moral, judgmentally evaluative), we are ultimately led back to the conception of God as the ultimate unifying source of the diversified phenomena.

The practical requirements of reason – be it *cognitive* ("speculative," theoretical, or inquiring reason) or *moral* (practical) reason, or *evaluative* (judgmental) reason – all point toward God as ultimate ground and unifier. In this regard all these paths (theoretical systematicity, moral autonomy, and evaluative purposiveness) lead to a common destination by a common path. All rest on regulative maxims for the conduct of the enterprise of human reason in one or another of its major departments. At this unifying point, this great *focus imaginarius*, the demands of systematic cognition, and moral reason, and of evaluative judgment all run together.

In Kant's philosophy, the Ideal in all its manifestations (cognitive system, moral autonomy, cosmic purpose) plays a role akin to the Holy Grail of the medieval questing knight. Here is something we ever seek and cannot find, a goal that conditions and shapes our activities throughout *this* world on the basis of our hopes regarding another, profoundly different (but also very problematic) realm. For Kant, the human mind is, like Parsifal, committed to the pursuit of the unattainably ideal.

We are entitled, on Kant's view, to *postulate* what is required to make good rational sense of the world, in every sense of this expression. We are entitled to take the stance that we live in a world that satisfies the deepest yearning of human beings – intellectual (system and purpose), moral (freedom and immortality), and evaluative (cosmic purpose). All these point to God as source and guarantor. But this is so not as a matter of knowledge and as an ontological fact, but as a matter of belief and practical postulation. Still, we must recognize that postulation – even rationally warranted postulation – is not actual knowledge.

5. DOES TRANSCENDENTAL THEOLOGY BELONG IN KANT'S SYSTEM?

To be sure, as Kant himself realized, this situation leaves reason in a distinctly uncomfortable and unsatisfactory position, because its recourse to this ultimate grounding in the purposive realm is something that lies altogether beyond the range of what can possibly be known by us, that is to say, established by the rational exploitation of factual data.

And so a crowd of questions press in on the post-Kantian mind. Why reify transcendental purpose? Why invoke a transcendental purpose giver? Why should Kant not simply have left the ground of cognitive systematicity, moral autonomy, and evaluative purposiveness where he actually found it, in the modus operandi of human reason? Why should he insist on an inexorable tendency in the human mind to ground these principles of unification in a causally responsible being? Even accepting Kant's fundamental thesis that human reason insists on viewing the "world of experience" as the product of a productive and ordering intelligence that endows it with systemic unity, why should he not be content to let matters rest at the point on which his own doctrine at bottom insists – namely, that this productive and ordering intelligence is simply the human mind? Why not characterize this hypostatization as a commonplace but avoidable error? As one commentator complains, "One cannot help feeling that Kant could have brought out his point of view much more satisfactorily by a clear indication from the start, that teleology requires no more than our right to entertain the idea of purposeful intelligence in quite general and indeterminate terms."[4] Why project the idea of purposiveness into a being who is its monolithic source and locus?

In part, the answer here carries us back to our earlier deliberations regarding the actual (even if only contingently actual) makeup of the human intellect. Man's commitment to the purposiveness of nature and to the existence of a purpose-instilling intelligence that lies behind nature is, as Kant sees it, simply a facet of how the human mind does and (as such) must work. If the world indeed is an organic system – a cosmos – then we must, so Kant insists, suppose that some world-external intelligence has impressed this orderliness upon it. The matter is one not of right but of necessity. On Kant's analysis, the human mind is irrepressibly thing-oriented: it simply cannot admit design without a designer. It can no more avoid projecting things to objectify functions than the human perception can avoid seeing as bent the straight stick held at an angle under water. By the very nature of our minds we are, Kant maintains, caught in the inexorable grip of transcendental thing-hypostatizing impulsion. Purposiveness, like morality, must be grounded in a being:

> We cannot therefore assume that [there is] . . . not merely a *moral ground* for admitting a final purpose of creation (as an effect), but also for admitting a *moral Being* as the original ground of creation. But we may well say that, *according to the constitution of our rational faculty*, we cannot comprehend the possibility of such a purposiveness . . . apart from an author and governor of the world, who is at the same time its moral lawgiver. (*CJ*, sect. 88, middle; pp. 455–56, Akad.)

Kant cannot give up the view of the mind as thing projective in the framework of the *Critique of Judgment* – any more than he can in the framework of the *Critique of Pure Reason* – because to do so would be to cease to be a transcendental idealist and become an idealist pure and simple. And the same sort of thing holds for purposiveness. For Kant deems a recourse to purposiveness indispensably necessary to confirm and bind us in our commitment to cognitive systematization. As Kant sees it, the human project of devising a systematic account of nature cannot be satisfactorily legitimated short of postulating a designing intelligence that endows nature with systemic organization. We are locked into the view that only ontological systematization can underwrite cognitive systematicity.

To be sure, from the angle of a post-Kantian perspective, this worthy goal can be realized without any recourse to such questionable mediation. Systematicity would then be seen as resting wholly on a methodological commitment to systematicity per se without the prop of such quasi-mythological machinery. A Kant-like position can in theory be developed that abandons this recourse to an inexorable penchant to hypostatization. But such a "purified" Kantianism would abolish one of the salient features of the master's doctrine – his insistence on the substantival bias of the human mind with its ontologically prejudicial commitment to thing postulation and reification. It would require Kant to free himself entirely from the grip of an almost two-thousand-year-old tradition of substance metaphysics.

On the basis of a radically renovated Kantianism, purpose and its congeners would lose the status of externalized projections and become domestic contrivances of reason – mere artifacts devised by human reason as pragmatic instruments for its work. What Kant sees as transcendent reifications by a human intellect committed by its very nature to such excesses would now be seen functionally – as no more than immanent products of reason in its own self-development. Now, rather than endowing purpose and its congeners with a reified grounding in a mind-external causal agency, one could ground them wholly methodologically. One could thus stop at Kant's pragmatism without moving on to his necessitarianism. Abandoning his insistence on reification, one would be content to see them in the status of working principles of our reason legitimated solely and directly (rather than productively mediated) through their functional efficacy and pragmatic utility. This sort of grounding of a pragmatic faith in the cognitive ideals would carry us forward to Peirce. But of course Kant's commitment to aprioristic necessity would now be diluted to a point near vacuity. Thus while there is no question that a "purified" Kantianism can be devised, it is clear that this was not an option that was available to Kant himself. For realizing this option would have meant abandoning his commitment to a whole host of conceptions that define his characteristic brand of transcendental idealism.

Chapter 6

Kant on the Limits
and Prospects of Philosophy

1. INTRODUCTION

With most present-day readers of the *Critique of Pure Reason*, interest flags as they pass the middle of the book. They see the action as pretty well concluded by the end of the *Dialectic*, when the limits of experiential knowledge have been established. All of those ensuing lucubrations about ideas, ideals, regulative precepts, methodology, teleology, and practical principles they regard as mere foreshadowings of the later *Critiques* that are best put aside in the interest of getting on to those books themselves. Despite Kant's own explicit insistence in the *preface* to the second edition, they have little use for the idea that this foray beyond the realm of sense experience actually represents the crux of the first *Critique*, and that the main thesis of the book is that the limits of object-oriented knowledge simply are not the limits of valid comprehension, so that rational belief can legitimately and effectively operate in regions where actual (sense-based) knowledge is unachievable. The thought that if this were not so, then those very deliberations of the critical philosophy itself would become unraveled is something that does not occur – let alone appeal – to them. It is this thought, however, that provides the guideline of the present discussion, from whose point of view the deliberations that begin with "The Ideal of Pure Reason" are not only the concluding part of the first *Critique*, but its doctrinal culmination as well.

The ultimate goal of this chapter is set by the rarely asked ques-

I am grateful to Steven Engstrom, Alexander Pruss, and an anonymous referee for constructive comments, and to Jeff Knight for editorial suggestions.

tion of just what is to be said on Kantian epistemic principles regarding the theses of Kant's own deliberations in the *Critique of Pure Reason*. The question is that of how Kant's philosophical practice can be made to square with its own principles – how the epistemic status of Kant's contentions is to be accounted for in their own terms.

In briefest outline, the position of the present deliberations is as follows:

What Kant develops in this concluding discussion is a pragmatically validated system of ideas – a system whose "objects" are not real objects "in the world," but ideal thought objects (*Gedankendinge*). What we thus find in Kant is a dualistic ontology. On the one hand, there is "the real world" – a realm of physical reality of spatiotemporal objects conceptualized by the understanding on the basis of the deliverances of sensibility. And on the other there is a realm of virtual reality, of intellectual quasi objects constructed by reason in the service of its mission of systematizing the deliverances of the understanding. Both realms qualify as perfectly objective, each in its own way: the former because its materials have objective *reality*, since they are grounded in the deliverances of the sensibility, the latter because its materials have objective *validity* (*Geltung, Gültigkeit*), since they afford the instrumentalities needed by reason for dealing adequately with the deliverances of the understanding. Accordingly, the validation of the ideas of reason is ultimately practical; it does not lie in their sensory realization within the world's space-time framework, but in their utility in facilitating the rational systematization of what we do actually encounter there.

Now in dealing with this realm of virtual reality, we do not achieve the standard sort of established *knowledge* (*Erkenntnis*) based on sensory experience, but rather a normatively legitimate *conviction* (*Überzeugung*) based on rational reflection regarding the interests and functions of reason. And this means that for Kant the reach of cognition is larger than that of knowledge in the strict sense.

Considerations of purposive pragmatics – that is, a teleology of sorts – provide the key to the reflective deliberations at issue with this rational conviction. And it is exactly such a pragmatically purposive mode of reflection that provides the cognitive process required for of the sort of philosophical insight at issue with the *Critique of Pure Reason* itself. A close examination of his deliberations both indicate and illustrate that, for Kant, philosophizing (however "theoretical" it may look) is in fact an exercise in pure practical reason.

2. LANDMARKS OF IGNORANCE MARKING THE LIMITS OF PHILOSOPHY

Kant's position is that philosophy as a rational discipline deals not in mere facts as such, but in the necessities of things.[1] However, as Kant sees it, while our knowledge of matters of fact – of what actually is so in the real (physical) world – has to be rooted in observation, our access to matters of necessity (of what must be) does and unavoidably must hinge upon the modus operandi of the mind itself. We have, in particular, three cognitive faculties: sensibility, understanding, reason. Each of these contributes, out of its own makeup and resources, certain characteristic structural aspects of our cognition – namely forms, categories, and ideas, respectively. Thus there are:

- *Forms* of sensibility: space and time
- *Categories* of understanding: substantiality, causality, etc.
- *Ideas* of reason: uniformity, continuity, economy, and other aspects of the systematicity of our knowledge

Kant maintains that it is these various mind-contributed structural aspects of cognition that constitute the bases – and the only bases – for the validation of matters of necessity.

Given this construction of what is at issue with actual knowledge of objective fact, Kant has it that the range of what we cannot possibly know is vast and impressive. In particular, reason cannot rationalize those sensory forms and conceptual categories themselves in specific detail. Take the forms of sensibility – space, for example. Here Kant could not possibly be more emphatic:

> The much-discussed question of the communion between the thinking and the extended, if we leave aside all that is merely fictitious, comes then simply to this: *how in a thinking subject an*

> *outer intuition,* namely, that of space, with its filling-in of shape
> and motion, *is at all possible.* And this is a question which no man
> can possibly answer. This gap in our knowledge can never be
> filled. (*CPuR,* A393)

And the limits of our sensibility mark the limits of our understanding as well:

> What objects may be in themselves, and apart from all this re-
> ceptivity of our sensibility, remains completely unknown to
> us. We know nothing but our mode of perceiving them – a mode
> which is peculiar to us and not necessarily shared by every be-
> ing, though certainly by every human being. With this alone
> have we any concern. (*CPuR,* A42 = B59)

We cannot grasp the reason why of those particular structural
forms of sensibility and categorical concepts of understanding,
nor yet the inner nature of things-in-themselves as apart from
their conditioning impact:

> For what is demanded here is that we should be able to know
> things, and therefore to perceive them, without senses, and there-
> fore that we should have a faculty of knowledge altogether
> different from the human, and this not only in degree but as
> regards perception likewise in kind – in other words, that we
> should be not men but beings [*Wesen*] of whom we are unable
> to say whether they are even possible, much less how they are
> constituted. Through observation and analysis of appearances
> we penetrate to nature's inner recesses, and no one can say how
> far this knowledge may in time extend. But with all this knowl-
> edge, and even if the whole of nature were revealed to us, we
> should still never be able to answer those transcendental ques-
> tions which go beyond [experienced] nature. (*CPuR,* A277–78 =
> B333–34)

As far as sensibility goes, we humans are inexorably confined to
the cognitive resources of our de facto situation. Differently constituted intelligences are – for aught we can say – abstractly possible, but there is nothing we can say about their nature. "This
mode of intuiting in space and time need not be limited to human
sensibility. It may be that all finite thinking beings necessarily
agree with man in this respect, although we are not in a position

to judge whether this is actually so" (*CPuR*, B72). What we can – and must – do is to accept the realities of our situation as final and inexplicable on any somehow "deeper" basis. To be sure, a sensibility – any sensibility – must on Kantian principles exhibit *some* formal structure and thus be subject to some forms or other: formality in general is essential for sensibility and thereby becomes something necessary. But this is emphatically *not* the case with the particular forms of the human sensibility, space and time: there is nothing necessary about *them*.

And much the same holds for the categories. Any understanding must have some categories or other. Categoricity in general is a demonstrably indispensable requisite of understanding. (It is just exactly this that the deduction of the categories establishes.) But the *particular* way in which the human understanding specifically satisfies this generic requirement is something that admits of no sort of validation on the basis of general principles.[2]

Reason, however, is in an entirely different position. For it is self-comprehending. The resources and processes of reason can always be grasped by reason itself.

For Kant, then, a priori knowledge is restricted to the realm of necessity/universality, and this has three regions: the biological (human), the physical (corporeal), and the rational. They operate as follows:

- That which characterizes every human being: every cognition-capable intelligent being of our particular biological sort. (This encompasses the forms of sensibility.)
- That which characterizes every corporeal being: every cognition-capable intelligent being that is physically embodied. (This encompasses having forms of sensibility of some sort or other, and the categories of understanding as they specifically stand.)
- That which characterizes any rational being: every cognition-capable intelligent being possessed of reason. This encompasses categoricity (having categories of some sort or other) and the ideas of reason as they specifically stand.

The forms of sensibility are contingent through and through for us humans. However, formality *in abstracto* can be explained at the next level – that of understanding – since corporeal beings must somehow get in touch with the world in order to acquire information about it. And similarly at the next stage. The categories of understanding are contingent for embodied intelligences. But categoricity *in abstracto* can be explained at the next level (that of reason) – that is, can be rationalized – because objective knowledge is impossible without an appreciative unity. Only at the third level – that of reason itself – are the specific resources of a cognitive level rationally validatable (i.e., "deducible") *at that level itself.* Only here can a rational accounting actually be effected, and only here, with the ideas, does reason come into its own.

With Kant, the limits of sensory experience just are the limits of objective knowledge as such. But this is only the beginning of the Kantian story, and certainly not its end. For the concept of a noumenon exists to demarcate these limits, seeing that it "is only a boundary concept serving to limit the pretensions of sensibility, and thus is only of negative use" (*CPuR*, A255 = B311). But to say even this about noumena is to say *something* about them – and mercifully the limits of *knowledge* do not constitute those of cognition in a larger sense. In particular, the *ideas* of reason introduce an entirely different perspective here. Here reason comes into its own, and its ideas come to play a determinative role. The ideas are not only crucial *in* the philosophy of Kant; they are also crucial *for* the philosophy of Kant as well. For without employing materials available only within a framework of idealization we would not possibly determine the scope and limits of pure reason's capabilities, so that the project of philosophizing would be blocked from the outset.

The ideas of reason accordingly lie in a realm different from that of the forms and categories in point of rationalizability because (1) they are items that relate to the resources of reason itself, namely (2) resources which are the products of reason itself and thus matters that the mind makes rather than finds. But how can such mind-produced artifacts acquire objective validity? How can they yield information that is not actually knowledge?

3. MOTIVATIONAL INTERLUDE

Does the equator really exist? Can the North Pole actually be discovered? Is there such a thing as the international date line? Is the continental divide really there?

A sensible reply to such questions would proceed in roughly the following terms. These items are not part of the earth's physical makeup. They are not, like the Himalayas or the Great Salt Lake of Utah, material configurations that can be encountered "in the flesh." Their reality, such as it is, involves the element of idealization. They are not observable objects accessible to the senses, to touch and sight, but rather thought objects – fictions, if you will. But they are not mere fictions, idle fancies issuing from a playful imagination. They play a serious role in our cognitive endeavors and make an essential contribution to our comprehension of the world. For while they do not have the objective reality of the world's physical furnishings, these products of subjectivity – of human thought – nevertheless secure an objective legitimacy through their essential role in helping us to organize and coordinate our knowledge about those real features of the world. It is through this instrumental utility for the organization of our knowledge that such thought constructions secure a claim to objectivity and cognitive legitimacy.

The textbook illustration of a parrot does not depict something that actually exists in reality, nor does the specification of "the average breakfast" describe a particular item of reality – a meal that someone sometime actually eats. But while such items do not constitute observable realities, they are nevertheless productively effective resources for our cognitive representation of reality at large. For they are mind-devised ("subjective") instrumentalities that nevertheless serve to indicate perfectly objective aspects of the real. It is along these utilitarian lines that the ideas secure their objective relevancy.

And so while we cannot validate such thought objects in the mode of sense experience – cannot achieve knowledge of them through actual observational encounters – we can nevertheless come to comprehend them in a different mode of cognition. They are items of cognitive artifice (mental projections or postulations, if you will) whose validation lies in the realm of thought experience rather than sense experience. Their status is thus not real but rather ideal, and our "knowledge" of them is not a matter of experiential cognition but rather the point of the reflective systematization of what we do actually encounter in this confrontational mode. They are creatures of theory, thought instrumentalities that serve to enhance our understanding of the world's literal realities. Like lines of latitude and longitude, the equator or the North Pole, their utility for characterizing reality has larger consequences. It means that while they may not literally describe reality, they are nevertheless serviceable for the work of its description. In Kantian terms, they may lack *objective reality* (*Realität*) but nevertheless have *objective validity* (*Güttigkeit*) as cognitively useful creations of reason – a validity which they thus obtain in the practical rather than the strictly comparative/theoretical sector of our mental operations.[3]

With Kant, the ideas indicate that a scientifically systematic comprehension of actual reality calls for viewing the real in terms and against the background of an organizing framework of virtual reality. And only by mapping what we know into a framework accessible solely through idealization can we comprehend the character and the extent of the terra incognita that lies beyond the borders of secured knowledge. In epistemology as in geography we will not be able to say in advance of the fact what that terra incognita contains, but we can indeed say something about where it lies and how much of it there is. And this is something which in both cases alike we can know only on the basis of idealizations (such as the spherical representation of the earth or its Mercator projection).[4]

The prime task of these deliberations will be to show that it is exactly this contrast between the physically real and the products of mental artifice that we employ for its rationally adequate comprehension that elucidates that pivot for Kant's treatment of what he terms ideas of reason and provides the key to his understanding of the nature of philosophizing.

4. KANT'S EPISTEMIC DUALISM OF KNOW VS. THINK AND THE ROLE OF A RATIONAL CONVICTION

As already indicated, Kant is emphatically insistent that various important and interesting questions lead outside the range of attainable human knowledge. However, the realm of what we can warrantedly believe is different from that of what we can properly know. Our beliefs can achieve objective validity even where objective applicability lies beyond them:

> All possible speculative (theoretical) knowledge of reason is limited to mere objects of *experience*. But our further contention must also be duly borne in mind, namely, that though we cannot *know* these objects as things in themselves, we must yet be in position at least to *think* them as things in themselves . . . [Footnote: To *know* an object I must be able to prove its possibility, either from its actuality as attested by experience, or *a priori* by means of reason. But I can *think* whatever I please, provided only that I do not contradict myself . . . Yet something more is required before I can ascribe to such a concept objective validity, that is, real possibility; the former possibility is merely logical. This something more need not, however, be sought in the theoretical source of knowledge; it may lie in those that are practical.] (*CPuR*, Bxxvi)

Thus knowledge in matters of objectivity is one thing in Kant's view, and rational conviction – objectively valid thought – is something else again. This has far-reaching implications for his philosophy.

In Kant's epistemology there are two modes of "knowledge," somewhat in line with the Latin duality of *cognoscere/sapere*, reflected in such Romance-language distinctions as those between *connaitre/savoir* (French) and *conocer/saber* (Spanish). The one mode, called *Erkenntnis* by Kant, represents what is at issue in our observation-derived information about the objective furniture of the natural world about us. This observationally rooted knowledge we shall here characterize as actual knowledge. It is "objective" in the sense of being object directed, that is, in dealing with the real world's existing frameworkings and their modus operandi. The second mode of cognition, called *conviction (Überzeugung)* by Kant, represents what is at issue in our reflection-derived rational conviction regarding the operation of our own intellectual processes. Kant maps out the relevant sector of epistemology in the following terms:

> I cannot assert something, that is, declare it as a judgment necessarily valid for everyone, except that which gives rise to

conviction. [Mere] persuasion I can have on my own account, when it so suits me, but I cannot, and ought not, to make this telling for others. The holding of a thing to be true, or the subjective validity of the judgment, in its relation to conviction (which is at the same time objectively valid), has the following three levels: *opining, believing,* and *knowing. Opining* is to be true when this is holding of a judgment consciously insufficient, not only objectively, but also subjectively. If our holding of the judgment be only subjectively sufficient, and is at the same time taken as being objectively insufficient, then this is termed *believing.* Lastly, the holding of a thing to be true that is both subjectively and objectively sufficient, is called *knowledge.* The subjective sufficiency is termed *conviction* (for myself), the objective sufficiency is termed *certainty* (for everyone). (*CPuR,* A821–22 = B849–50)

When the mind is turned "reflectively" inward upon itself to consider aspects of its own modus operandi, then what we learn is a matter of conviction. It is thus not "objective," in the sense of dealing with mind-external objects, but subjective, in the sense of mental inner directiveness. However, its "subjectivity" emphatically does not obtain in the currently popular sense of being person variable and idiosyncratic. On the contrary, it bears upon the workings of the human mind in general – that is, on human subjectivity – and its appropriate rulings are universal and hold for everyone alike. The lessons we learn relate to the operation of "the [human] mind," and not to the idiosyncrasies of "my [own] mind." This reflective mode of knowledge, which is "subjective" in a decidedly technical sense, might be designated as *rational conviction* (*Überzeugung*) or *rational belief* (*Glaube*). (To translate *Glaube* as "faith" in a Kantian context is deeply problematic in its mistaken suggestion that a matter of religion or of personal ideology must be at issue.)

Kant's epistemology turns on the thesis that there is a world of difference between knowledge and rationally justified belief. For him, the scope of cognition is far broader than the region of experience-bound knowledge exactly because it also encompasses this latter domain:

The limitations of our purely speculative reason arise from the very nature of reason itself, and must therefore have their own good use and purpose, which ought not to be disdained. Why has Providence placed many things which are closely bound up with our highest interests so far beyond our reach that we are only permitted to apprehend them in a manner lacking in clearness and subject to doubt – in such fashion that our inquiring gaze is more excited than satisfied? . . . Reason is benefited by the consideration of its object from both sides [of its power and of its incapacity], and its judgment is corrected in being thus limited. What is here in dispute is not substance but style [*nicht die Sache, sondern der Ton*]. For although we have to surrender the language of *knowledge,* we still have sufficient ground to employ, in the presence of the most exacting reason, the quite legitimate language of a firmly grounded *belief.* (*CPuR,* A743–45 = B771–73)

It is in this light, then – and with a view in particular to the factor of appropriate justificatory warrant – that we must read the important passage of the preface to the second edition:

One could not even *assume* God, freedom, and immortality at the behest of the necessary employment of practical reason unless at the same time speculative reason were deprived of its pretensions to transcendent insights. For to arrive at them it must make use of principles which actually extend only to objects of possible experience, and which, if also applied to what cannot be an object of experience, actually always change this into appearance, thus rendering all *practical extensions* of pure reason impossible. I have therefore found it necessary to set *knowledge* aside to make room for *belief.* (*CPuR,* Bxxx)

The crux is that both objective knowledge (*Erkenntnis*) and subjectively legitimate rational belief (*Überzeugung*) are modes of cognition broadly understood – of appropriately thinking something to be so. Each offers a valid and appropriate basis for well-grounded acceptance-as-true (*fürwahrhalten*), and each represents a perfectly legitimate and proper route to information regarding what is so. To reemphasize, for Kant (unlike John Dewey), justified belief is emphatically not knowledge. Those "practical extensions of pure reason" are modes of cognition quite different from knowledge narrowly construed.

Kant emphatically does *not* endorse the thesis that (to paraphrase Wittgenstein) "what you can't know you can't know – and you can't whistle it either." For Kant thinks that you *can* whistle it. With him, rationally warranted conviction is just exactly such whistling, able to provide for rationally warranted assertion in the face of an absence of *knowledge* strictly understood. It would be a great service to English-language students of Kant if *Erkenntnis* were translated as "*perceptual* knowledge," and the unqualified term "knowledge" left available to characterize cognition in general, with perceptual knowledge and rationally warranted conviction or belief both included. Only thus could we avert the anomaly of having to say that all sorts of things can appropriately be thought, said, and believed about matters regarding which "we have no knowledge [i.e., *Erkenntnis*] whatsoever."

Kant is concerned to stress the limited range of objective knowledge regarding matters of necessity. And he is also concerned to establish the need for and legitimacy of a range of reflective conviction that provides for rationally justified belief and thereby embraces what might called "quasi knowledge." He dedicates so much space, effort, and emphasis to the former project that many readers are tempted to lose sight of the latter. But it is the latter that is in fact pivotal for Kant; his elaborate insistence on the limits of sense-bound knowledge proper exists simply to make room for the quasi knowledge of rationally warranted conviction (in the practical order of warrant).

Kant, in sum, is an epistemic dualist. For him there are two fundamentally distinct epistemic processes: *inquiry*, which is unavoidably the empirical work of experience (of sensibility and understanding), and *reflection*, which is unavoidably the work of reason.

And there is a plausible explanation why this should be so. For Kant, of course, sees his own critical deliberations as depicting a range of necessary fact. He thus has to be prepared to answer the question of the status of his own contentions – given that they clearly do not fit into the boundaries that he himself sets to a priori synthetic knowledge regarding matters of necessity. Without an epistemic doctrine to provide him with a supplementation to objective – and thus experience-bound – *knowledge,* Kant would have no way to make room for his own philosophical deliberations within his own cognitive framework. His own doctrine would fall victim to the old refutation of skepticism inherent in the challenge "If knowledge is impossible, then what becomes of your own skeptical contentions to this effect?" The resource of reflection is thus indispensable for Kant.

Sense-bound experience, after all, is not the whole story. For not only "can I think whatever I please, provided only that I do not contradict myself," but I am even entitled to "ascribe to such an [object] concept objective validity [note: *not* objective reality!]" subject to the presence of a "something more [that] need not, however, be sought in the theoretical sources of knowledge [but] may lie in those that are practical" (*CPuR*, Bxxvi – note). And in this respect the *utility* of certain object conceptualizations in the realm of ideas and ideals is a matter not of knowledge grounded by experience or observation, but rather one of rational *reflection*. As Kant puts it,

> *Reflection* [*Überlegung, reflexio*] . . . does not concern itself with objects themselves with a view to deriving concepts from them directly, but . . . is that state of mind in which we first set ourselves to discover the subjective conditions under which [alone] we are able to arrive at concepts. It is the consciousness of the relation of given representations to our different sources of knowledge; and only by way of such consciousness can the relation of the sources of knowledge to one another be rightly determined. *Transcendental reflection* . . . on the other hand, . . . since it bears on the objects themselves, contains the ground of the possibility of the objective comparison of representations with each other . . . and is therefore altogether different from the former type of reflection. Indeed they do not even belong to the same faculty of knowledge . . . This transcendental consideration is a duty from which no one is exempt who wishes to make any *a priori* judgments about things. (*CPuR*, A260–63 = B316–19)

It is a fundamental idea of Kant's epistemology that the limits of what can be objectively known do not constitute the limits of what can responsibly be believed or accepted – that there is a mode of intellectual comprehension that is not governed by the strictly cognitive principles of sense-based knowledge, and thereby of passive theoretical cognition, but rather emerges through an active agency of the mind itself, an agency that is productive in its spontaneous operations and capable of apprehending the materials it itself produces. Appropriate "thinking-to-be-so" *conviction* stands opposed to perceptual *knowing* through ostensive confrontation.

Kant accordingly operates a double-access theory of rational acceptance, namely *sense-evidentiated knowledge* with respect to objective (physical) facts and *reflection-based rational conviction* with respect to the immaterial thought entities of reason that have objective *validity* rather than the objective *reality* correlative with the existence as objects. On the one side lies the theoretical domain of the cognition at issue with sense-based knowledge; on the other lies the practical domain of the cognition at issue with rational conviction grounded in the requisites of praxis (broadly construed – with inquiry included). The former deals in sense-based *objective knowledge* of objects based on experience, the latter in *objectively valid conviction* grounded in considerations of practical reason based in reflection. Neither has absolute precedence or priority: each is supreme in its own particular jurisdiction but remains powerless in the jurisdiction of the other.

And this brings us to the role of ideas.

5. IDEAS AS REGULATIVE GUIDEPOSTS TOWARD UNITY – THEIR *FUNCTIONAL* (METHODOLOGICAL) STATUS: REGULATIVE VS. CONSTITUTIVE

Ideas are cognitive products of practical reason – not fruits of observational knowledge, but artifacts of reason whose validation lies in the productive guidance of the development of such knowledge. Their objectivity is not a matter of direct apprehension, but only indirect through their capacity to facilitate the work of reason. After all, the proper work of reason is not to project objects, but to provide the materials of sensory-based understanding with principles of unity – to systematize the deliverances of understanding by endowing them with a comprehensive unity:

> Reason is never in immediate relation to an object, but only to the understanding; and it is only through the understanding that it has its own empirical employment. It does not, therefore, *create* concepts (of objects) but only *orders* them and gives them

that unity which they can achieve only in their widest possible application, that is, in relation to the totality of the [experiential] series. The understanding does not address this totality, but only that connection through which, in accordance with *concepts*, such *series* of conditions *come into being*. Reason has, therefore, as its sole object, the understanding and its effective application. Just as the understanding unifies the manifold in the object by means of concepts, so reason unifies the manifold of concepts by means of ideas, positing a certain collective unity as the goal of the activities of the understanding, which otherwise are concerned solely with distributive unity. (*CPuR*, A642–44 = B670–72)

The unity of reason represented by the ideas is thus in the final analysis not a factual discovery, but a methodological principle, not an output or product of inquiry, but its controlling prerequisite, as it were:

We [cannot] say that reason, while proceeding in accordance with its own principles, has arrived at knowledge of this unity through observation of the accidental constitution of nature. The law of reason, which requires us to seek for this unity, is a necessary law [of ultimately practical import] since without it we should have no reason at all, and without reason no coherent employment of the understanding, and in the absence of this no sufficient criterion of empirical truth. In order, therefore, to secure an empirical criterion we have no option save to presuppose the systematic unity of nature as objectively valid and necessary. (*CPuR*, A651 = B679)

Note here again the crucial difference between objective reality and objective validity in relation to such ideas as that of the unity of nature.

To study nature in the manner of the natural sciences presupposes that nature indeed has an orderly structure – that it is sufficiently regular and stable for the application to it of fixed descriptive classifications to make sense. But of course "Nature is orderly" is not something that we discover; it is something we presuppose in projecting the a priori idealized view of "a lawful nature" that the sciences are presumed to investigate and – increasingly – to depict:

The idea of systematic unity should be used only as a regulative principle to guide us in seeking for systematic unity in the connection of things, according to universal laws of nature; and we ought, therefore, to believe that we have approximated to completeness in the employment of the principle only in proportion as we are in a position to verify such unity in empirical fashion – a completeness which is never, of course, attainable. Instead of this the reverse procedure is [erroneously] adopted. (*CPuR*, A692 = B720)

The ideas of reason are so closely coordinated with methodological principles of cognitive procedure that they themselves, to all intents and purposes, represent maxims (i.e., procedural principles) for inquiring reason. They thus are, in effect, regulative principles of operation.

Transcendental ideas never allow of any constitutive employment. When regarded in that mistaken manner, as supplying concepts of certain actual objects, they are but pseudo-rational, merely dialectical concepts. On the other hand, they have an excellent, and indeed indispensably necessary, regulative employment, namely, that of directing the understanding towards a certain goal upon which the routes marked out by all its rules converge, as upon their point of intersection. This point is indeed a mere idea, a *focus imaginarius,* from which, since it lies quite outside the bounds of possible experience, the concepts of the understanding do not in reality proceed; none the less it serves to give to these concepts the greatest [possible] unity combined with the greatest [possible] extension. Hence arises the illusion that the lines have their source in a real object lying outside the field of empirically possible knowledge just as objects reflected in a mirror are seen as behind it. Nevertheless this illusion (which need not, however, be allowed to deceive us) is indispensably necessary if we are to direct the understanding beyond every given experience (as part of the sum of possible experience), and thereby to secure its greatest possible extension. (*CPuR*, A644–45 = B672–73)

Accordingly, the unity of reason is thus not an accomplished fact, but an ongoing project, a work in progress. Its result is not a discovered result ("The world as we know it is a unified system"), but rather a project, a methodological objective corresponding to the instruction "Render your knowledge of the world systematic":

> The *unity of reason* is in itself *undetermined* as regards the conditions under which, and the extent to which the understanding ought to combine its concepts in systematic fashion. But although we are unable to find in *intuition* a schema for the complete systematic unity of all concepts of the understanding, an *analogon* of such a schema must necessarily allow of being given . . . [Now] the idea of reason is an analogon of a schema of sensibility; but with this difference, that the application of the concepts of the understanding to the schema of reason does not yield knowledge of the object itself (as is the case in the application of categories to their sensible schemata), but only a rule or principle for the systematic unity of all employment of the understanding. Now since every principle which prescribes *a priori* to the understanding thoroughgoing unity in its employment, also holds, although only indirectly, of the object of experience, the principles of pure reason must also have objective reality in respect to that object, not, however, in order to *determine* anything in it, but only in order to indicate the procedure whereby the empirical and determinate employment of the understanding can be brought into complete harmony with itself. This is achieved by bringing its employment, so far as may be possible, into connection with the principle of thoroughgoing unity, and by determining its procedure in the light of this principle. (*CPuR*, A665–66 = B693–94)

Against this background it becomes clear that the ideas do not represent constitutive parts of the real. They are not substantively descriptive. Rather, they reflect operational (functional) methodology with reference to which our constitutive picture of the world is itself developed.

> The hypothetical employment of reason, based upon ideas viewed as problematic concepts, is not, properly speaking, *constitutive*, that is, it is not of such a character that, judging in all strictness, we can regard it as proving the truth of the universal rule which we have adopted as hypothesis . . . The hypothetical employment of reason is regulative only; its sole aim

is, so far as may be possible, to bring unity into the body of our detailed knowledge, and thereby to *approximate* the rule to universality. The hypothetical employment of reason has, therefore, as its aim the systematic unity of the knowledge of understanding, and this unity is the *criterion of the truth* of its rules. The systematic unity (as a mere idea) is, however, on a *projected* unity, to be regarded not as given in itself, but as a problem only. This unity aids us in discovering a principle for the understanding in its manifold and special modes of employment, directing its attention to cases which are not given, and thus rendering it more coherent. But the only conclusion which we are justified in drawing from these considerations is that the systematic unity of the manifold knowledge of understanding, as prescribed by reason, is a *logical* principle. Its function is to assist the understanding by means of ideas [to contribute to the work of cognitive systematization]. (*CPuR*, A647–48 = B675–76)

As this talk of maxims indicates, the crux here lies in the distinction between a regulative (methodologically procedural) principle on the one hand and a constitutive (reality-descriptive) fact on the other:

Pure reason, which at first seemed to promise nothing less than the extension of knowledge beyond all limits of experience, contains, if properly understood, nothing but regulative principles, which, while indeed prescribing greater unity than the empirical employment of understanding can achieve, yet still, by the very fact that they place the goal of its endeavors at so great a distance, carry its agreement with itself by means of systematic unity to the highest possible degree. But if, on the other hand, they be misunderstood, and be treated as constitutive principles of transcendent knowledge, they give rise, by a dazzling and deceptive illusion, to persuasion and a merely fictitious knowledge, and therewith to contradictions and eternal disputes. (*CPuR*, A701–2 = B729–30)

Accordingly, the ideas which encapsulate the unity of reason do not relate to objects of secured knowledge, but rather to procedural principles:

The unity of reason is the unity of system; and this systematic unity does not serve objectively as a principle that extends the application of reason to objects, but subjectively as a maxim that extends its application to all possible empirical knowledge of objects. Nevertheless, since the systematic connection which reason can give to the empirical employment of the understanding not only furthers its extension, but also guarantees its correctness, the principle of such systematic unity is so far also objective, but in an indeterminate manner [*principium vagum*]. It is not a constitutive principle that enables us to determine anything in respect of its direct object, but only a merely regulative principle and maxim, to further and strengthen *in infinitum* [indeterminately] the empirical employment of reason – never in any way proceeding counter to the laws of its empirical employment, and yet at the same time opening out new paths which are not within the cognisance of the understanding. (*CPuR*, A680 = B708)

We are not entitled to say categorically and substantially that we have determined that the world is a system and so are able to reason: "*Since* the world is a system, we can conclude *P*." Instead, our stance is methodological: "Supposing the world to be a system, we will have to proceed *P*-wise if an adequate account of it is to be provided." What is at issue is a procedural stance, a matter of proceeding *as if*:

[We can safely venture] to assume confidently, and with general approval, that everything in an animal has its use, and subserves some good purpose. If this assumption be treated as constitutive it goes much further than observation has thus far been able to justify; and we must therefore conclude that it is nothing more than a regulative principle of reason, to aid us in securing the highest possible systematic unity, by means of the idea of the purposive causality of the supreme cause of the world – *as if* this being, as supreme intelligence, acting in accordance with a supremely wise purpose, were the cause of all things. (*CPuR*, A688 = B716; cf. A673–74 = B701–2)

And again:

There is a great difference between something being given, to my reason as an *object outright*, or merely as an *object in the idea*. In the former case our concepts serve to determine the object; in the latter case there is in fact only a schema for which no object, not even a hypothetical one, is *directly* given but which only enables us to represent to ourselves other objects in an indirect manner, namely in their systematic unity, by means of their relation to this idea. Thus I say that the concept of a highest intelligence is a mere idea . . . (that is to say, it lacks the objective reality of pertaining directly to an object, for in that sense we should not be able to justify its objective validity). It is . . . only a schema constructed in accordance with the conditions of the greatest possible unity of reason – the schema of the concept of a thing in general, which serves only to secure the greatest possible systematic unity in the empirical employment of our reason. We then, as it were, derive the object of experience from the supposed object of this idea, viewed as the ground or cause of the object of experience. We declare, for instance, that the things of the world must be viewed *as if* they received their existence from a highest intelligence. The idea is thus really only a heuristic, not an ostensive concept . . . [The transcendental ideas,] although they do not directly apply to, or determine, any object corresponding to them, none the less, as rules of the empirical employment of reason, lead us to systematic unity, under the presupposition of such an *object in the idea;* and they thus contribute to the extension of empirical knowledge, without ever being in a position to run counter to it. We may conclude that it is a necessary maxim of reason to proceed always in accordance with such ideas of speculative reason, not as *constitutive* principles for the extension of our knowledge to more objects than experience can give, but as *regulative* principles of the systematic unity of the manifold of empirical knowledge in general, whereby this empirical knowledge is more adequately secured within its own limits and more effectively improved than would be possible, in the absence of such ideas, through the employment merely of the principles of the understanding. (*CPuR,* A670–71 = B198–99)

Of course such procedural principles in the modality of *as if* cannot be objectified; they cannot be transmogrified into existing things:

> We are not justified in introducing mere thought-entities [*Gedankenwesen*] which transcend all our concepts – though without contradicting them – as being real and determinate objects, merely

149

on the authority of a speculative reason that is bent upon completing the tasks which it has set itself. They ought not to be assumed as existing in themselves, but only as having the reality of a schema – the schema of the regulative principle of the systematic unity of all knowledge of nature. They should be regarded only as analoga of real things, not as in themselves real things . . . If, in this manner, we assume such ideal beings, we do not really extend our knowledge beyond the objects of possible experience; we extend only the empirical unity of such experience, by means of the systematic unity for which the schema is provided by the idea – an idea which has therefore no claim to be a constitutive, but only a regulative principle. (*CPuR*, A673–74 = B701–2)

We must always bear in mind that the use of an operationally effective organizing principle is one sort of thing and the discovery of substantive fact another. One is a matter of process, the other of product. Conflation of the two would be a fateful error – that of reifying a procedural device. (Think again of the equator!)

6. ARE IDEAS MEANINGLESS?

The fact that ideas are sense detached and lack objective reality means that they fall outside the realm of the Kantian categories. With respect to the ideas, all the usual conceptualizing bets are off. And so, inappropriateness invariably arises "when I think of as existing a being to correspond to a mere and only transcendental idea, since I can never assume the existence of such a thing itself, because no concepts suffice through which I could think in a determinate way of a particular object" (*CPuR*, A676–77 = B704–5). And this insistence means that when we venture wholly outside the field of the senses with the ideas of reason, then "there are no concepts available [for objective knowledge] . . . and even the concepts of reality, substance, causality, nay even that of necessity in existence lose all applicability and are empty titles to concepts themselves entirely without [referential] content" (*CPuR*, A679 = B707). But such contentions have to be construed with care. It is certainly not the case that we are here in the sphere of unintelligible gibberish and deal with what is literally senseless. Just as in

Kant *knowledge* (*Erkenntnis*) is actually *perceptual* knowledge and must be distinguished from cognition in general, so with Kant a *concept* (*Begriff*) is actually an *experiential* (i.e., sense-based) concept, and must be distinguished from what is intelligible (*verständlich*) broadly speaking. After all, his very reason for distinguishing between applicable concepts and imputable ideas is to distinguish the strictly conceptualizable from the broadly intelligible. The point is that ideas are distinctively extraconceptual intellectual tools – thought instrumentalities which, from the conceptual point of view, are no more than schematic glimmerings that just cannot be passed off as concrete objects. But to say that we have no categorical concept for the understanding is emphatically not to say on Kantian grounds that we have no idea – no "conception" broadly understood. We are emphatically still within the sphere of intellection. Thus when Kant says that the ideas "lose all their meaning" we have to realize that "meaning" is here subject to something like the Fregean distinctions between *Sinn* (sense, intelligibility) and *Bedeutung* (reference, applicability). The ideas do indeed lack a "meaning" in the way of having no reference to concrete things-in-the-world, but this is not to say that they have no meaning in the way of having no sense – that they represent what we would ordinarily dismiss as "meaningless nonsense."

With Kant, ideas function appropriately at the level of the sort of *virtual* reality that preoccupies reason. They are inappropriate only insofar as we become so careless as to envision them to function at the level of observational (i.e., physical) reality. To expect to find them manifest here would be as futile as looking for the dot of black paint depicting the *focus imaginarius* of a painting.

"But a Kantian idea is a mere fiction – a product of mind. Surely that fact blocks its claim to reality or objectivity of any sort." Not at all! On Kantian principles *all* objects are mind established, seeing that space, time, and the categories are all mind provided. Kant's fundamental point, after all, is that we can have no cognitive dealings with mind-inaccessible "things-in-themselves." The difference between physical objects and ideas is not that of mental versus nonmental, but simply turns on the issue of which department of mind is involved – namely, sensibility-cum-understanding or reason. Only the former, real-world objects have objectivity in the sense of objective reality, but the latter have it in the sense of objective validity. And so Kant would certainly not agree that terms like "fact" and "objection" and "reality" are applicable in the former sphere alone and should be withheld in the sphere of ideas.

7. ARE IDEAS ILLUSORY?

No doubt the most serious disability of ideas is that they do not fall under the categories, so that the concepts by which we standardly conceptualize real things are not applicable to ideas. But this of course only means that reason requires thought machinery over and above the conceptual tools of the understanding. This, after all, is the very point of introducing the ideas of reason – to indicate that reason has resources of its own so that the conceptual knowledge provided by the understanding in working on the deliverances of sensibility does not exhaust the realm of meaningful thought. After all, if rational thought's resources were not greater than the concept scheme of sense-based understanding, then a philosophical enterprise like that of the *Critique* itself would become impossible. (This last point is critically important, and we shall have to return to it later.)

Ideas are certainly not a matter of mere illusion, although Kant sometimes seems to encourage the thought. He writes:

> Transcendental illusion . . . does not cease even after it has been detected and its invalidity clearly revealed by transcendental criticism (e.g., the illusion in the proposition: The world must have a beginning in time). The cause of this is that there are fundamental rules and maxims for the employment of our reason (subjectively regarded as a faculty of human knowledge), that have all the appearance of being objective principles. We therefore take the subjective necessity of a connection of our concepts, which is to the advantage of the understanding, for an objective necessity in the determination of things in themselves. This is an *illusion* which can no more be prevented than we can prevent the sea appearing higher at the horizon than at the shore, since we see it through higher light rays; or to cite a still better example, than the astronomer can prevent the moon from appearing larger at its rising, although he is not deceived by this illusion . . . Here

> we have to do with a *natural* and inevitable *illusion*, which rests on subjective principles, and foists them upon us as objective . . . [Such illusion, which is] inseparable from human reason, and which, even after its deceptiveness has been exposed, will not cease to play tricks with reason and continually entrap it into momentary aberrations ever and again calling for correction. (*CPuR*, A297–98 = B353–54)

It is thus clear, at any rate, that this so-called illusion is not a *delusion* at all, but something natural, inevitable, and in fact unavoidably serviceable for reason's accomplishment of its definitive task in the systematization of knowledge.

The reality of it is that that *illusion* is as unavoidable for our minds as optical illusions are for our eyes:

> This illusion, which can certainly be prevented from actually distracting us, is indeed actually necessary if we are to direct the understanding to its greatest and largest extension so as to reach beyond any actually available experience. (*CPuR*, A645 = B673)

However, this need not prove harmful, and need not issue in an outright *delusion,* as long as we are mindful of the need to avoid hypostatization's leap to actual objectification – to claiming objective reality where there is only the objective validity that is secured by applicative efficacy and utility. The illusion produces actual error when (but only when) we mistake – as we are naturally inclined to do – a commitment to an aim for acceptance of an actually existing object in which the achievement of this aim is embodied or even pre-assured. This is the cart-before-the-horse fallacy that Kant dismisses as "lazy reason," *ignava ratio* (*CPuR*, A689 = B717). Regrettably, this fallacy is only too tempting for us humans.

The crux, however, is that illusion can have different aspects. The statement "There is no such thing as an *X*" is clearly equivocal, since it can either be construed to deny the reality of *X*'s or their thinghood. Now, with ideas, it is the second possibility that is at issue. The *focus imaginarius* of a picture, or the equator of the earth, are not illusions in the manner of mirages or hallucinations. They are "really there." But they are not part of the physical furnishing of the world. Their bearing on physical reality is oblique through being instrumental and pragmatic: they function as though devices, mind creations that serve to organize our thought about the real in an effective way – a feature that endows them with objective validity rather than objective reality. The focus is not literally part of the picture nor the equator one of the earth's physical features. Such ideas occupy a status of intermediation between objecthood and pure delusion – which is exactly what Kant's distinction between objective reality and objective validity is intended to convey. Those "illusions" are indeed delusive if mistaken for objects, but are in fact authentic and indeed indispensably serviceable in their role as mind-coordinate organizers. It is not that they *are* illusions (flat out), but that they *can* be illusory if misunderstood through being mistaken for objects of the sensorially accessible sort at issue with nature's physical – and ipso facto observable – furnishings.[5]

And so, what we have here is not inconsistency but two-sidedness. On the one hand, the ideas do not define objects, do not present observable reality, do not somehow supplement or supplant the reality-descriptive categories. On the other hand, they do define a virtual reality that relates to actual objects in a way indispensable to their cognitive rationalization. In emphasizing each of these two sides, Kant does not mean to deny the other.

With Kant, then, the items at issue with ideas are not observed; they are not encountered in sensory experience. Experience – the work of sensibility and understanding – has nothing to do with them. They are creatures of reason (*Verstandeswesen*). They are not cognized (*erkannt*) but thought (*erdacht*) – projected by the mind by way of positing or postulation. But all the same, there is nothing arbitrary about them. They may not be objects, but they are objective – that is, objectively valid. They represent useful, indeed indispensable instruments for the intellect's adequate development of objective knowledge. They may (in a sense) be illusions, but they are not delusions – not idle, haphazard, inappropriate fancies. They may be just as "unreal" as the North Pole or the equator, but not a scintilla more so.

Accordingly, despite their lack of objective reality, ideas have an objective validity that renders their application in the setting of cognitive transactions not only useful, but even necessary if reason's work is to be effectively pursued. The systematic unity of reason upon which all the ideas pivot is as real and significant an element of our cognitive resources as any. And while Kant rejects the ideas as inappropriate delusions if (mis-)construed substantively as characterizations of objects, he accepts them with enthusiastic endorsement as appropriate and indeed essential if construed functionally as reason-impressed hallmarks of the systematicity of the real.[6] This duality of the issue comes to the fore with force and vivacity when one considers more closely Kant's commitment to the centrality of the interests of reason.

8. THE INTERESTS OF REASON

While the ideal entities of reason do not represent objects real in space-time, they are nevertheless such that reason's commitment to them is emphatic and absolute because they are inseparably bound up with reason's capacity to accomplish its definitive mission:

> Reason is impelled by a tendency of its nature to go out beyond the field of its empirical employment, and to venture in a pure employment, by means of ideas alone, to the utmost limits of all knowledge, and not to be satisfied save through the completion of its course in [the apprehension of] a self-subsistent systematic whole ... [We must regard this impetus] as having its source exclusively in the practical interests of reason. (*CPuR*, A797 = B825)

On this basis, the ideas represent what in effect are practical maxims of reason:

> I entitle all subjective principles which are derived, not from the constitution of an object but from the interest of reason in respect of a certain possible perfection of the knowledge of the object, *maxims* of reason. There are therefore maxims of speculative reason, which rest entirely on its speculative interest, although they may seem to be objective principles. (*CPuR*, A666 = B694)

And these maxims have a rationale. For the fact of the matter is that the ideas of reason, unlike the forms of sensibility and categories of understanding, are rationalizable, explicable. Fundamentally, they are as they are because reason legislates (postulates) them in the service of a certain characteristically rational interest, namely the systematic articulation of knowledge.

Seen in this light it is clear that ideas are not products of *cognitive* (or speculative/theoretical) reason, but rather products of *practical* reasoning. Kant himself develops this point in such teleological and even theological terms as the following:

> This highest formal unity, which rests solely on concepts of reason [i.e., on ideas], is the *purposive* unity of things. The *speculative* interest of reason makes it necessary to regard all order in the world as if it had originated in the purpose [*Absicht*] of a supreme reason. Such a principle opens out to our reason, as applied in the field of experience, altogether new views as to how the things of the world may be connected according to teleological laws, and so enables it to arrive at their greatest systematic unity. The assumption – albeit only in the idea – of a supreme intelligence as the one and only originator of the universe can therefore always benefit reason and can never injure it. (*CPuR*, A686–87 = B714–15)

Exactly this circumstance, that even theoretical/speculative reason has its interests, lies at the basis of the validation of ideas.

> To posit something as a real being corresponding to the idea is not to say we can extend our knowledge of [actual] things by means of transcendental concepts. For this being is based only on the idea and not itself; and thus serves only to express the systematic unity which affords a rule for the empirical employment of reason. It settles nothing about the ground of this unity or what might be the inner character of the being on which it depends as cause . . . This consideration shows that it is the speculative *interest* of reason, and not its *insight,* that justifies it in starting from a point that lies so far above its sphere in order to survey its objects as constituting a complete whole. We here encounter a distinction regarding the procedure of thought in dealing with one and the same assumption, a distinction which is somewhat subtle, but of great importance in transcendental philosophy. I may have sufficient ground to assume something in a relative sense (by *suppositio relativa* [i.e., as real *if* reality is rational]), and yet have no right to assume it absolutely (*suppositio absoluta* [i.e., as real *since* reality is (known to be) rational]). (*CPuR*, A674–76 = B702–4)

What is thus crucial for the justificatory reasoning that validates the ideas is that it does not involve inferences consequent upon what is known, but rather looks to the antecedent conditions requisite for the realization of adequate knowledge. The whole argumentation accordingly pivots on matters of aim, purpose, and goal, and thereby assumes a profoundly teleological cast with reference to reason's commitment to systematicity.

The long and short of it is that the *quid juris* question of reason's entitlement to project or postulate the ideas lies in its, reason's, irrationalizable dedication to its own interests – the pursuit of its characteristic mission of systematizing knowledge, an enterprise in which "we have no option save to presuppose the systematic unity of nature as objectively valid and necessary" (*CPuR*, A650–51 = B678–79). Kant's validation of the ideas of reason (their "deduction," in his terminology) thus rests in the final analysis on the consideration of their indispensability as practical instruments that effectively serve the interests of reason. This aspect of the matter requires and deserves a closer look.

9. THE VALIDATION OF IDEAS AS PRACTICAL INSTRUMENTS: THE "TRANSCENDENTAL DEDUCTION" OF IDEAS AND THE DISTINCTION BETWEEN OBJECTIVE VALIDITY AND OBJECTIVE REALITY

Reason for Kant is two-sided. On the one side there is theoretical/ cognitive reason, concerned to address the issues of experiential reality – the realm of what exists at a level where actual observation is possible. And on the other side there is practical reason, whose concern is with the normative realm of what ought to be. However, reasoning is an activity, and the actual exercise of reason – even of theoretical/cognitive reason – is unavoidably a matter of praxis. Our empirical inquiries dedicated to the development of objective knowledge are therefore themselves governed by various procedural – and thus practical – methodological or operational norms. Accordingly, the demands of praxis pervade and superimpose themselves upon the operations of theoretical cognition as well. The methodological, or as Kant simply calls it, logical, realm is governed by principles of practical reason even where matters of empirical cognition – of knowledge development – are concerned.

Now in this context it is clear that the work of the ideas of reason is not descriptive but functional. Their task is to provide for "complete unity in the knowledge obtained by the understanding, by which their knowledge is to be not a merely contingent aggregate, but a system connected according to necessary laws" (*CPuR*, A645 = B673). Kant sees reasoning as itself being a goal-directed praxis which, as such, has an aim or purpose: the systematizing of knowledge. And any rational purposive activity is geared to interests – that is, to pursuing the realization of some appropriate aim of ours. And this is the basis on which a validation of its productive activities in the projection of ideas must ultimately be based:

> There must, however, be some source of positive cognitions that belong to the domain of pure reason, and which perhaps lead to error only through being misunderstood, and in actual fact form the goal of reason's efforts. For how else could one explain our inextinguishable desire to find firm footing somewhere beyond the limits of experience? Reason has a presentiment of objects which possess a great interest for it. When it follows the path of pure speculation [i.e., of purely theoretical inquiry] in order to approach them, they fly before it, but perhaps it may look for better fortune in the only other path open to it, that of its *practical* employment. (*CPuR*, A795–96 = B823–24)

Substantiating reason's postulation of the transcendental ideas therefore can and should proceed on this basis as a practical validation:

> Reason has, in respect of its *practical employment*, the right to postulate what in the field of mere speculation it can have no kind of right to assume without sufficient proof. For while all such assumptions do violence to [the principle of] completeness of speculation, that is a principle with which the practical interest is not at all concerned. In the practical sphere reason has rights of possession, for which it does not require further proof. (*CPuR*, A776 = B804)

Reason both has the right to postulate the ideas and is right in doing so.

The greatest apparent threat to the present favorable interpretation of the Kantian ideas comes from such passages as this:

> If, however, we overlook this restriction of the idea to a merely regulative use, reason is led away into mistaken paths. For if they leave the ground of experience, which alone can contain the signs that mark out its proper course, and venture out beyond it to the incomprehensible and unsearchable, rising to dizzy heights where it finds itself entirely cut off from all possible action in conformity with experience. (*CPuR*, A688–89 = B716–17)

But two remarks are in order here: (1) the misled "reason" at issue in this passage and its congeners is of course specifically cognitive (i.e., theoretical/speculative) reason. It is indeed crucial for Kant that cognitive reason cannot reach beyond "the ground of [sensory] experience." But of course it is no less crucial for him that practical reason can go where cognitive, inquiring reason cannot tread. It must be recognized that the "reason" of such passages as the one just quoted is not reason at large but specifically the cognitive reason that is crucially dependent on experiential materials. Moreover: (2) there is a crucial difference between the following two positions:

(i) X should not be viewed as a being at all; it is no entity but a mere practical contrivance, a mere thought devise.

(ii) X can indeed be viewed as a being (though not, of course, as an object), although the justification for doing so is one which, in the nature of the case, must proceed on grounds of practical rationality relating to effective methodology and procedure. *Entia rationis* are actual *entia* (entities, beings of sorts), even though not knowable objects.

It should by now be clear that, on the present construal of the Kantian ideas, it is (ii) and it alone that is to be endorsed.[7]

With Kant, the legitimation of any structural feature of our knowledge will have to proceed by way of a process for establishing the validity of a cognitive resource of the genre that he calls a "transcendental deduction." And he insists that just as the forms of sensibility and the categories of understanding need and admit of such a validation, so it must also be with the ideas of reason. However, very different sorts of transcendental deductions are at work in the cases of objective knowledge and rational belief.

Regarding the transcendental ideas, Kant indeed says: "A transcendental deduction of them cannot, however, be effected; in the case of ideas . . . such a deduction is never possible" (*CPuR*, A664 = B692). However, he does not mean this literally, for what he sees as unrealizable is not a transcendental deduction as such, but only a transcendental deduction of the sort previously encountered with the concepts of understanding. His position is that in the present case this by now familiar sort of transcendental deduction must be replaced by something similar and yet different:

> We cannot employ an *a priori* concept with any security without having first given a transcendental deduction of it. The ideas of pure reason do not, indeed, admit of the same sort of deduction as the categories. But if they are to have any objective validity at all, however indeterminate, and not to represent mere empty thought-entities (*Gedankendinge; entia rationis ratiocinatis*), then a deduction of them must be possible, even though (as we admit) it may differ substantially from that which one can give for the categories. (*CPuR*, A669–70 = B697–98)

The situation is as follows: The "deduction" of forms of sensibility and categories of understanding must show how such items constitute *necessary conditions* for an experiential knowledge of objects on the part of any finite intellect. By contrast, the deduction of the transcendental ideas consists in an argument that shows in specific how these several ideas are *functionally conducive* to reason's accomplishment of its proper work. With a knowledge deduction of the sort encountered with the categories, we have as the pivot point a *necessary condition* (nescon) for the realization of a certain cognitive end result. It is a matter of "conditions under which alone" something can be known. However, with a belief deduction of the sort encountered with the ideas of reason we have to deal with an optimality condition (optcon) for the realization of a certain endresult. The pivot here is the functional objective of optimizing the efficiency and effectiveness with which the result in view can be achieved. And so, while the first sort of justifying deduction is presuppositional, the second is pragmatic (or practical). It relates to those things which must be posited (stipulated or presupposed) to facilitate maximally the realization of that positive end result. Accordingly, Kant's deduction of the ideas runs as follows:

> It is, indeed, difficult to understand how there can be a logical principle by which reason prescribes the unity of rules, unless we also presuppose a transcendent principle whereby such a systematic unity is *a priori* assumed to be necessarily inherent in the objects. For with what right can reason, in its [methodo-]logical employment, call upon us to treat the multiplicity of powers exhibited in nature as simply a disguised unity and to derive this unity, so far as may be possible, from a fundamental power – how can reason do this, if it be free to admit as likewise possible that all powers may be heterogeneous, and that such systematic unity of derivation may not be in conformity with nature? Reason would then run counter to its own vocation, proposing as its aim an idea quite inconsistent with the constitution of nature. Nor can we say that reason, while proceeding in accordance with its own principles, has arrived at knowledge of this unity through observation of the accidental constitution of nature. The law of reason which requires us to seek for this unity, is a necessary law, since without it we should have no reason at all, and without reason no coherent employment of the understanding, and in the absence of this no sufficient criterion of empirical truth. In order, therefore, to secure an empirical criterion we have no option save to presuppose the systematic unity of nature as objectively valid and necessary. (*CPuR*, A650–51 = B68–79)

In sum, the methodological praxis by which actual reason can pursue the definitive aims of its cognitive mission requires it to presuppose or to postulate the machinery of the ideas.

P. F. Strawson has maintained that "[i]t is an essential characteristic of an idea of reason [for Kant] that it arises inevitably in the course of empirical inquiry."[8] This makes it seem as though *products* of inquiry were at issue. But the matter is actually one of *process*, and specifically of the conditions under which alone an effective process is possible in the cognitive domain. Strawson's way of putting it overlooks the presently operative distinction between two types of Kantian validation, namely that between (1) *a condition for being* that is conceptually essential and is thus *logically inevitable*, and (2) a *condition for proceeding* that is operationally optimal and is thus *practically requisite*. With a *theoretical* transcendental deduction we deal with the conditions under which alone a certain state of affairs is possible, while with a *practical* transcendental deduction we deal with the conditions requisite for the pursuit of a certain end to be efficiently and effectively practicable.

And so, the authentication of ideas looks not to a theoretical and objective, but rather to a pragmatic mode of validation, seeing that ideas do not represent experiential objects, but procedural functions:

> The ultimate aim to which the speculation of reason in its transcendental employment is directed concerns three objects: the freedom of the will, the immortality of the soul, and the existence of God. In respect of all three the merely speculative interest of reason is very small; and for its sake alone we should hardly have undertaken the demanding labor of transcendental investigation in the face of endless obstacles, since whatever discoveries might be made here should be inapplicable *in concreto*, that is, in the study of nature . . . If, then, these three cardinal propositions are not at all necessary for [objective] *knowledge*, and yet are urgently recommended by our reason, then their importance must be regarded as concerning only the *practical*. (*CPuR*, A798–800 = B826–28)

On this basis, then, ideas are validated not as constitutive elements of knowledge formulation, but as providing instruments for knowledge development. As Kant sees it, reason's acceptance of a realm of *entia rationis* is inherent in its commitment to the effective prosecution of its own proper characteristic mission. For, as he insists time and again, the ideas are practical instruments serving the larger interests of reason in the systematization of knowledge:

> If . . . we assume such ideal beings, we do not really extend our knowledge beyond the objects of possible experience; we extend only the empirical unity of such experience, by means of

the systematic unity for which the schema is provided by the idea – an idea which has therefore no claim to be constitutive, but only a regulative principle. For to allow that we posit a thing, a something, a real being, corresponding to the idea, is not to say that we profess to extend our knowledge of things by means of transcendental concepts. For this being is posited only in the idea and not in itself; and therefore only as expressing the systematic unity which is to serve as a rule for the empirical employment of reason. (*CPuR*, A673–74 = B701–2)

Accordingly, it is the interests of reason that constitute the hinge on which the transcendental deduction of ideas pivots. The ideas are not products of inquiry, but serve as tools for its rational development and systematization. And reason has no real choice but to postulate the availability that renders its work not only theoretically possible, but operationally practicable.

Kant's position here is essentially as follows: The project of scientific inquiry is committed to order in nature and is feasible only on its basis. The existence of such order is a presupposition – albeit one that is practical and regulative, representing a condition that must be satisfied if the project is to be pursued successfully. And, given the principle of sufficient reason, there must – so we are committed to think – be a ground of this order.[9] Now while this particular segment of order can be grounded in that particular segment, order in general can be rationally grounded only in a supreme orderer, an order-external being who institutes a system of order in a purposive way. The project of seeking to endow our knowledge of nature with the maximum of systematic unity thus requires us to think of all elements of order "as if they were the advances of a supreme reason of which our reason is but a feeble copy" (*CPuR*, A678–B706). The ideas, in sum, are pivotal requisites if reason is to accomplish its characteristic work of systematizing knowledge in the deductive (and ultimately syllogistic) mode characteristic of Euclidean geometry and Newtonian physics. And such a justification of the ideas of reason brings to the fore a realization that the "objectivity" of such ideas is not a matter of their applicability to objects (their reference to actual objects), but rather one of their utility – their functional efficacy in the development of objective knowledge.

It would, however, be a grave error of hypostatization to insist upon an existent object as the objective correlate of such a methodological idea:

> [Error ensues] when the reality of a principle of purposive unity is not only presupposed but hypostatised. Since the concept of a supreme intelligence is in itself completely beyond our powers of comprehension, we then erroneously proceed to determine it in an anthropomorphic manner, and so to impose ends upon nature, forcibly and dictatorially, instead of pursuing the more reasonable course of searching for them by the path of physical investigation. And thus teleology, which is intended to aid us merely in completing the unity of nature in accordance with universal laws, not only tends to abrogate such unity, but also prevents reason from carrying out its own [proper work]. (*CPuR*, A692–93 = B720–21)

The thought things we encounter in the ideal domain are emphatically not actual, experientially encounterable objects but rather methodologically serviceable quasi objects whose status is that of mind-projected *entitia rationis*. Their status is not objective as such, but rather what might be called "objectivity facilitative" (or even "objectivity enhancing"); they are not objectively real but only objectively valid, and their basis is not theoretical/cognitive but rather practical/procedural.

Those principles of unity that pervade the domain of reason are certainly not experientially learned facts – nothing universal and necessary could be obtained on this basis. They are supplied by reason itself – as Kant's Copernican inversion insists they must be. They are projections or postulations of reason as essential conditions not for the *a tergo* possibility, but for the *a fronte* teleology of reason's work. Kant accordingly insists on their hypothetical character:

> The hypothetical employment of reason has . . . as its aim the systematic unity of the knowledge of understanding, and this . . . systematic unity (as a mere idea) is, however, only a *projected* unity, to be regarded not as given in itself, but as a problem only. This unity aids us in discovering a principle for the understanding in its manifold and special modes of employment, directing its attention to cases which are not given, and thus rendering it

more coherent. But the only conclusion which we are justified in drawing from these considerations is that the systematic unity of the manifold knowledge of understanding, as prescribed by reason, is a *logical* principle. Its function is to assist the understanding by means of ideas, in those cases in which the understanding cannot by itself establish rules. (*CPuR*, A647–48 = B675–76)

Their function in relation to the work of reason validates the ideas as *pure* because they are not something that we *derive* from our experience, but something that we bring to it. For Kant, the salient features of a rationally based belief or practical conviction (*Überzeugung*) lies in its being the product not of a passive fact recognition, but of the active spontaneity of a projection of information. The unity of reason is not something given in or derived from rational inquiry – it is merely projected or posited by reason as an operating principle. And the validity – indeed *objective* validity – of such postulations is to be established on the basis of practical considerations. For their appropriateness lies in their essentially methodological serviceability in furthering the defining interests of our cognitive project – namely, to secure systematically comprehensive and coherent answers to our questions about the whys and wherefores of things:

> No *objective deduction*, such as we have been able to give of the categories, is, strictly speaking, possible in the case of these transcendental ideas. Just because they are only ideas they have, in fact, no relation to say [knowable] object that could be given as coinciding with them. We can, indeed, undertake a subjective derivation of them from the nature of our reason; and this has been provided in the present chapter. [For reason demands] absolute completeness *on the side of the conditioned*. For the former alone is required in order to presuppose the whole series of the conditions, and to present it *a priori* to the understanding. Once we are given a complete (and unconditioned) condition, no concept of reason is required for the continuation of the series; for every step in the forward direction from the condition to the conditioned is carried through by the understanding itself. The transcendental ideas thus serve only for *ascending*, in the series of conditions, to the unconditioned, that is, to principles. As

regards the *descending* to the conditioned, reason does, indeed, make a very extensive [methodo-]logical employment of the laws of understanding, but no kind of transcendental employment; and if we form an idea of the absolute totality of such a synthesis (of the *progressus*), as, for instance, of the whole series of all *future* alterations in the world, this is a creation of the mind [*ens rationis*] which is only arbitrarily thought, and not a necessary presupposition of reason. For the possibility of the conditioned presuppose the totality of its conditions, but not of its consequences. Such a concept is not, therefore, one of the transcendental ideas; and it is with these alone that we have here to deal. (A336–37 = B393–94)

What is pivotal for the "deduction" of the ideas is thus an interest-serving endorsement made on general principles of rational practice in pursuit of the inherent goals of reason. And such ratifications do not, of course, represent propositions that we learn through observation, but they nevertheless are propositions that we accept on rationally cogent grounds – albeit grounds that lie in the practical order of reason.

One commentator has it that for Kant "we are fully justified in resorting to the idea of design as long as one important matter is borne in mind: our appeal to a designer ought not to be taken as signifying an actual being beyond nature."[10] Two points warrant emphasis here. (1) That phrase "ought not to be taken" is exactly the wrong phrase to use here. Taking, supposing, or postulating is just exactly what *is* in order here. What is *not* in order is seeing that designer as a world-internal object, the focus of a claim to perception-based knowledge. Moreover: (2) That phrase "actual being beyond nature" is also not the right expression. It erroneously prejudices the question of whether for Kant nature (physical reality), which is indeed the realm beyond which no objects of perceptual knowledge can be found, is thereby also the realm of everything that exists, has reality, is a being. Not only does Kant never say this; he emphatically insists that the contention that spatiotemporal empirical reality is all there is represents a claim to which our (scientific) knowledge cannot reach, and which for that very reason we are entitled and authorized to reject on practical grounds with a view to what is required in the service of the interests of reason. Thus what should have been said is that the appeal to a designer can indeed be taken on *practical* grounds as referring to a being[11] which, for this very reason, has to be viewed as altogether detached from observable nature.

10. THE PROBLEM OF HARMONIZATION: CAN RATIONAL CONVICTION CONFLICT WITH KNOWLEDGE? THE SIN OF HYPOSTATIZATION

Kant insists that there simply is no way in which the virtual objects at stake with practical reason's ideas and ideals can come into clash or conflict with cognitive reason's physical objects as invested by empirical inquiry. No possible way, that is, as long as we avoid mistaking those virtual objects for real ones – looking for God at the end of a telescope, so to speak, or for the equator with a looking glass. The two modes of cognition and their respective sorts of "objects" – constitutively real (physical) and regulatively virtual (ideal) – can and should be kept in harmonious collaboration:

> When merely regulative principles are treated as constitutive, and are therefore employed as objective principles, they may come into conflict with one another. But when they are treated merely as *maxims*, there is no real conflict, but merely those differences in the interest of reason that give rise to differing modes of thought. In actual fact, reason has only one single interest, and the conflict of its maxims is only a difference in, and a mutual imitation of, the methods whereby this interest endeavors to obtain satisfaction. Thus one thinker may be more particularly interested in *manifoldness* (in accordance with the principles of specification), another thinker in *unity* (in accordance with the principle of aggregation). Each believes that his judgment has been arrived at through insight into the object, whereas it really rests entirely on the greater or lesser attachment to one of the two principles. [However]. . . neither of these principles is grounded in actual objects, but solely in the interest of reason. (*CPuR*, A666–67 = B694–95)

The need for and feasibility of an avoidance of a clash here is one of the prime aims of the *Critique of Pure Reason*, with its insistence that conflict cannot possibly arise so long as the due proprieties are preserved, although it can and will arise if certain errors of confusion are committed. As Kant sees it, knowledge of actual existents and rational conviction regarding ideas belong to different intellectual jurisdictions and cannot possibly come to collision.

Kant relies heavily on just this legal analogy of different and distinct jurisdictions. His core thesis is that objective knowledge relates to experientially accessible objects existing in the real (physical) world. And in this sphere, rational belief has nothing whatever to do or to say. Thus only if there is the mistake of a Fallacy of Hypostatization – a projection of what in fact are thought instrumentalities into real-world objects – can problems arise:

> To take the regulative principle of the systematic unity of nature as being a constitutive principle, and to hypostatise, and presuppose as a cause, that which serves, merely in idea, as the ground of the consistent employment of reason, is simply to confound reason. (*CPuR*, A693 = B721)

This sort of hypostatization is a misemployment of the ideas and constitutes the greatest sort of error into which reason can fall. For as Kant sees it,

> We mistake the meaning of this idea from the very start if we regard it as the assertion or even as the assumption of an actually real thing, to which one could ascribe the ground of the systematic order of the world. Rather, whatever this ground which eludes our concepts may be in its own inherent constitution is left entirely undetermined. One only stipulates an idea as a point of view from which alone that unity, which is so essential to reason and so salutary to the understanding, can be further extended. In sum, this transcendental thing is only the schema for that regulative principle by which reason extends systematic unity over the whole for that of experience, as far as it is able to. (*CPuR*, A681–82 = B709–10; cf. *CPuR*, A669 = B697)

The basic reason why hypostatization is a fallacy that threatens to destroy any comprehension of the real is that what is at issue with ideas is not an object of experience, but a thought instrumentality for the guidance of reason:

> The question whether we may not at least think this [supreme] being, which is distinct from the world, on *analogy* with the ob-

jects of experience, then the answer is: *by all means,* but only as object in *idea* and not in reality, namely, only as being a substratum, to us unknown, of the systematic unity, order, and purposiveness of the arrangement of the world – an idea which reason must form as the regulative principle for its investigation of nature. Nay, more, we may freely, without laying ourselves open to censure, admit into this idea certain anthropomorphisms which are helpful to the principle in its regulative capacity. For it is always an idea only, which does not relate directly to a being distinct from the world, but to the regulative principle of the systematic unity of the world, and only by means of a schema of this unity, namely, through the schema of a supreme intelligence which, in originating the world, acts in accordance with wise purposes. What this primordial ground of the unity of the world may be in itself, we should not profess to have thereby decided, but only how we should use it, or rather its idea, in relation to the systematic employment of reason in considering the things of the world. But one may proceed to ask: Can we, on such grounds, assume a wise and omnipotent Author of the world? *Undoubtedly* we may; and we not only may, but *must,* do so. But do we then extend our knowledge beyond the field of possible experience? *By no means.* For all that we have done is merely to presuppose a something, a merely transcendent object, of which, as it is in itself, we have no concept whatsoever. It is only in relation to the systematic and purposive ordering of the universe, which, we must presuppose in studying nature, that we have thought this unknown *on analogy* with an intelligence (an empirical concept); that is, have . . . endowed it, in respect of the ends and the perfection which are grounded upon it, with just those properties which, in conformity with the conditions of our reason, can contain the ground of such systematic unity. This idea is thus valid only in respect of the employment of our reason *in reference to the world.* If we [mistakenly] ascribed unqualified objectivity to it, we should be forgetting that what we are thinking is merely a being in idea only. (*CPuR,* A696–98 = B724–26)

This fallacy of illicit hypostatization is encountered in particular in the domain of "rational cosmology," where experientially inaccessible thought resources such as "the universe as a whole" or "the ultimate cause of all that exists" or "the perfectly systemic order of nature" are misconstrued and projected through reification into actually real objects that conflicts can ensue – as is marked by the contradictions at issue in the Kantian "antinomies." Ideas by their very nature open the door to such abuses:

> In thinking the cause of the world, we are justified . . . in representing it in our idea not only in terms of a certain subtle anthropomorphism (without which we could not think anything whatsoever in regard to it), namely, as a being that has understanding, feelings of pleasure and displeasure, and desires and volitions corresponding to these, but also . . . in ascribing to it a perfection which, as infinite, far transcends any perfection that our empirical knowledge of the order of the world can justify us in attributing to it. For the regulative law of systematic unity prescribes that we should study nature *as if* systematic and purposive unity, combined with the greatest possible manifoldness, were everywhere to be met with, *in infinitum.* For although we may succeed in discovering but little of this perfection of the world, it is nevertheless required by the legislation of our reason that we must always search for and surmise it; and it must always be beneficial, and can never be harmful, to direct our investigations into nature in accordance with this principle . . . [To be sure,] I do not base the principle upon the existence and upon the knowledge of such a being, but upon its idea only, and I do not really derive anything from this being, but only from the idea of it – that is, from the nature of the things of the world, in accordance with such an idea. (*CPuR*, A700–1 = B728–29)

Thus consider the metaphysically crucial conception of an ultimate being, an *ens realissimum*. Here Kant says:

> If, in following up this idea of ours, we proceed to hypostatise it, we shall be able to determine the primordial being through the mere concept of the highest reality, as a being that is one, simple, all-sufficient, eternal, etc. . . . In any such use of the transcendental idea we should, however, be overstepping the limits of its purpose and validity. For *reason*, in employing it as a basis for the complete determination of things, has used it only as the concept of all reality, without requiring that all this reality be objectively given and be itself a thing. Such a thing is a mere fiction in which we combine and realize the manifold of our idea in an ideal, as an individual being. But we have no right

to do this, not even to assume the possibility of such a [reification-al] hypothesis. (*CPuR*, A580 = B608)

We should not – must not – hypostatize these thought tools into real things that form part of the order of actual existence, lest we annihilate any prospect of rational comprehension of the real. For the ideas are not objects of knowledge, but subjects of putatively objective characterizations that play a productive role in the development of objective knowledge. As such they have an instrumental status in the cognitive domain that provides them with a basis of appropriateness and validity. They possess a status of legitimation that is not objective but instrumental, and as long as hypostatization is avoided, the ideas of reason, seen as instruments of thought, are legitimate and indeed necessary.

But at this point we are brought face to face with the cardinal Kantian sin of mistaking the "subjective necessity of a connection of concepts" for an "objective necessity in the determination of things in themselves" (A297 = B253). As Kant sees it, the human mind's inherent tendency to hypostatization – the objectification of thought entities (*entia rationis*) as physically real objects – is part of the tragic reality of the human condition. This is Kant's version of the Genesis story of man's fall from the grace of the empyrean of pure reason in the quest for knowledge. Hypostatization is the original sin for Kantian philosophizing, a fatefully wrong but nevertheless humanly almost unavoidable transgression. And so, painful though it may be, we must, so Kant insists, learn to deal with the limitations of our reason itself:

All our [objective] claims that go beyond the field of possible experience are deceptive and without foundation . . . [nevertheless it transpires that] human reason has a natural tendency to transgress the limit, and that transcendental ideas are just as natural to it as the categories are to understanding – though with this difference, that while the categories lead to truth, that is, to the conformity of our concepts with the object, the ideas produce a mere though nevertheless irresistible illusion, whose deceptiveness [namely the false conviction of objective reality] even the severest criticism can hardly avert. (*CPuR*, A642 = B670)

171

The situation is particularly threatening in the case of the cosmological ideas, which in their seeming reference to natural reality come into apparent conflict – and thus potential contradiction – with the world of experienced reality as science enables us to understand it. In this case, and in this case alone, actual self–contradiction (rather than mere error) can occur:

> There is nothing whatsoever to hinder us from *assuming* these ideas to be also objective, that is, from hypostatising them – except in the case of the cosmological ideas, where reason, in so proceeding, falls into antinomy. The psychological and theological ideas contain no antinomy; and involve no contradiction. [Yet] they ought not to be assumed as existing in themselves, but only as having the reality of a schema – the schema of the regulative principle of the systematic unity of all knowledge of nature. They should be regarded only as analoga of real things, not as in themselves real things. (*CPuR*, A673–74 = B701–2)

On the one hand, Kant insists that there is a conclusive case against the endeavor to use theoretical reason for the grounding of transcendental theology. The resources of sense-based knowledge are unavailable in the theological sphere, and cognition at the level of actual science can gain no purchase here. But this, so Kant equally insists, does nothing to block the power and potential of practical reason in this domain. For Kant, practical reason can indeed go where theoretical reason cannot tread – exactly because its jurisdictional home domain is a different one.

11. THE KINSHIP OF PRACTICAL AND MORAL REASON

One must, however, resist the profoundly mistaken notion that with Kant practical reason is limited to the domain of what we would nowadays consider as such. For as its prominence in the first *Critique* indicates, practical reason is also importantly operative in specifically epistemological matters, seeing that inquiry is also a praxis, and the development of knowledge is every bit as much a matter of doing as are the actions at issue with morality.

Kant actually construes the moral realm as that of normative appropriateness at large, thus adopting a characteristically (and to us odd-soundingly) large view of this domain as effectively including the whole realm of practical reason.[12] In view of this, considerations of practical reason provide, with Kant, not only for commitments to act (imperatives of moral comportment), but also for commitment to believe (imperatives of cognitive comportment). This leads him to such claims as that "[the idea of] a moral world leads inevitably also to the purposive unity of all things, which constitute this great whole, in accordance with universal laws of nature" (*CPuR*, A816 = B844), and that "[a] *Supreme Reason*, that governs according to moral rules, [must] likewise be posited as the underlying cause of nature" (*CPuR*, A809 = B837). And it is on this basis that Kant arrives at the idea that the systematic unity of nature ultimately has a moral status:

> The systematic unity of nature cannot be proved *in accordance with speculative principles of reason*. For although reason does indeed have causality in respect of freedom in general, it does not have causality in respect of nature as a whole; and although moral principles of reason can indeed give rise to free actions, they cannot give rise to laws of nature. Accordingly it is in their practical, meaning thereby their moral, employment that the principles of pure reason have objective reality . . . The idea of a moral world has, therefore, objective reality, not as referring to an object of an intelligible intuition (we are quite unable to think any such object), but as referring to the sensible world, viewed, however, as being an object of pure reason in its practical employment, that is, as a *corpus mysticum* of the rational beings in it. (*CPuR*, A 807–8 = B835–36)

The crux is that Kant understands "morality" so broadly that (for example) the epistemic duties involved in the proper exercise of one's cognitive faculties are part and parcel of morality in general. And so, rational beings are obliged by this very fact to exercise that rationality in both practical and cognitive matters – perhaps with some difference in urgency.

The ruling practical imperative (one might even call it the "prime directive" or "supreme imperative") of Kantian philosophy inheres in the stipulation "Act as a truly rational being would in the particular circumstances that confront you: Alike in cognitive as in moral or evaluative matters conduct your business appropriately – proceed as any rational agent would and should in the circumstances."[13] The leading principle is that of generalization: to perform one's actions in particular cases as though they were to be the definitively binding precedent for a universal law of practice. And this rationality-enjoining generalization absorbs the proprieties of the cognitive enterprise into the practical domain. It renders the pursuit of cognitive adequacy and of moral appropriateness in the narrower sense (of dealing with matters of other-regarding conduct) into two aspects of one single, wider, and more inclusive enterprise. As Kant sees it, cognition too is a mode of practice – a thought practice whose rules of proper procedure inhere in the universal dictates of reason.

As such considerations indicate, the Kantian metaphysic of morals includes not only imperatives of rational behavior, but also imperatives of rational belief. And on this basis our experientially based knowledge of the world is rounded off in systemic coherence by a complex of pragmatically based convictions regarding its nature. For Kant, the demands of praxis and morality require certain convictions about the nature of the world and accordingly have extensive ramifications in the theoretical, and specifically the metaphysical, sphere.

Against this background, Kant's validation of the ideas of reason emerges as the crossroad at which themes of his three *Critiques* – namely rationality, morality/practicality, and purposiveness – come together at an intersection. The ideas are the intersection that marks the transcendental unity of Kantian philosophizing. And it is this fact which makes "The Ideal of Pure Reason" and its aftermath into the culmination of the *Critique of Pure Reason*.

This line of thought finally brings us to the issue of Kant's view of philosophy and its standing within the framework of his epistemology.

12. THE STATUS OF PHILOSOPHY

Consider such a central Kantian thesis as that of the key principle that "one cannot perceive what is outside oneself, but only what is in us, and the whole of our self-consciousness therefore yields nothing save merely our own determinations" (*CPuR*, A379). Just what can the cognitive status of this thesis about the inherent limitations of sensibility possibly be within the Kantian framework? This thesis is evidently synthetic, but on Kantian principles it can scarcely count as an item of objective knowledge about "the understanding." Or, consider the following claim: "It is only when we have thus produced synthetic unity in the manifold of intuition that we are in a position to say that we know an object. But this unity is impossible if the intuition cannot be generated in accordance with a rule by means of such a function of synthesis as makes the reproduction of the manifold *a priori* necessary, and renders possible a concept in which it is united" (*CPuR*, A105). How exactly is the cognitive status of this "ens et unum convertuntur" thesis that objectification demands identification to be conceived of on Kant's own epistemic principles? Or again, consider the pivotal Kantian Principle of the Transcendental Unity of Apperception to the effect that "unity of consciousness would be impossible if the mind in knowledge of the manifold could not become conscious of the identity of function whereby it synthetically combines it in one knowledge" (*CPuR*, A108). We come here to Kant's pivotal thesis that "[i]t must be possible for 'I think' to accompany all my representation since otherwise something would be represented in me which could not be thought at all, and this is equivalent to saying that the representation would be impossible, or at least would be nothing to me" (*CPuR*, B131–32). What can possibly be the epistemic status within the Kantian system of his crucial contention that the synthesis essential to cognition is possible only when the series of experiences relevant to the issue is united in one single consciousness? Such a claim is clearly synthetic. And it is clearly a priori. Since it roots neither in sensibility nor understanding, its source must be reason. But exactly how can this transpire?

The same fundamental problem arises throughout. How can we reconcile Kant's own philosophical claims with what he says about the modus operandi of human cognition? Can philosophy possibly deliver any synthetic a priori knowledge? On his own principles, Kant has no alternative but to answer this question negatively, since actual philosophical knowledge will have to be confined to the analytic region of the merely definitional exposition of philosophical concepts,[14] seeing that "philosophical knowledge is the knowledge given by reason from concepts" (*CPuR*, A713 = B741) and is thereby purely analytic.[15] There can be no such thing for Kant as philosophical knowledge (*Erkenntnis*) in matters reaching beyond the purely analytic: synthetic philosophical knowledge is out of the question. The putative objects of traditional philosophy – preeminently, physical reality ("the world"), the human soul, and God – are all transcendental; they are experience transcending, and with Kant knowledge of objects is available through experience alone. Beyond this mere theoretical reason cannot go, with the result that its cognitive power in this domain is decidedly limited: "The greatest and perhaps the sole use of all philosophy of [theoretical] pure reason is therefore only negative; since it serves not as an organon for the extension but as a discipline for the limitation of pure [theoretical] reason, which, instead of [here] discovering truth, has only the modest merit of guarding against error" (*CPuR*, A795 = B823). With Kant, objective knowledge is literally knowledge of objects, and there are no such things as philosophical objects.

Still, with Kant the limits of knowledge are not limits of cognition. But insofar as philosophy can deliver any synthetic lessons at all, its teachings must, on Kantian principles, proceed in the mode of a rational conviction different from knowledge *strictu sensu*. It must arise wholly from the reflective capacity of reason. In consequence, philosophical propositions clearly do not actually represent knowledge, but rather are procedurally presuppositional posits whose validation must, in consequence, lie ultimately in the practical domain. They are stipulations laid down (i.e., postulated) by human reason in the interest of making the life of the mind itself intelligible. Their status is not that of constitutive claims to knowledge, but that of regulative injunctions whose adoption facilitates an appropriate appreciation of our mental powers and an instructive explication of our mental operations. And for this reason the justificatory rationale of philosophical claims has to lie within the pragmatic realm.

Practical reason must prevail in relation to the big questions of philosophy such as God, freedom, and immortality because pure speculative reason is impotent here: "The transcendental critique, which has disclosed to me all the resources of our pure [theoretical/ speculative] reason, has completely convinced me that, just as it is incapable of arriving at affirmative assertions in this domain, it is equally and indeed even less able, to establish any negative conclusion regarding these questions" (*CPuR*, A753 = B781). Philosophy too is thus a venture in pure practical reason – at any rate insofar as it reaches beyond merely analytic (concept-clarificatory) matters. Our philosophizing must proceed in terms of what we need to suppose (i.e., postulate) in order to pursue effectively the project of rational systematization – that is, in order to succeed in effectively serving the definitive interests of reason. The only way to make sense on Kantian principles of Kant's position regarding the fundamental contentions of his own critical philosophy is to see them as representing instrumentalities of practical reason – intellectual processes whose ultimate status is regulative of the explanatory project at issue in philosophy's attempt to enable us to get a proper intellectual grasp on the cognitive and the performative sectors of the human condition.

With Kant, philosophy indeed cannot aspire to the objective knowledge that is at issue with speculative/theoretical matters – but of course the rational conviction at issue with practical reason is something else again – a matter not of objective knowledge, but of an objectively validatable stipulation that is not based in sensation but in reflection and not on factual but on practical considerations. And the conviction-authorizing processes of rational reflection required for the validation of ideals are just the same as the processes of pure reason required for the validation of philosophical principles. For Kant, philosophizing – theorizing activity though it is – is nevertheless a venture in the exercise of pure practical reason, seeing that even theoretical systematization itself is a mode of praxis.

Philosophy is thus not a system, but a praxis – an endeavor to devise a system. It represents an intellectual aspiration, one which, like the moral aspiration to perfection, is a matter of goal pursuit rather than goal attainment:

> *Philosophy* is the system of all philosophical knowledge. If we are to understand by it the archetype for the estimation of all attempts at philosophising, and if this archetype is to serve for the estimation of each subjective philosophy, the structure of which is often so diverse and liable to alteration, it must be taken objectively. Thus regarded, philosophy is a mere idea of a possible science which nowhere exists *in concreto,* but to which, by many different paths, we endeavor to approximate, until the one true path, overgrown by the products of sensibility, has at last been discovered, and the image, hitherto so abortive, has achieved likeness to the archetype, so far as this is granted to [mortal] man. Till then we cannot learn philosophy; for where is it, who is in possession of it, and how shall we recognise it? We can only learn to philosophise, that is, to exercise the talent of reason, in accordance with its universal principles, on certain actually existing attempts at philosophy, always, however, reserving the right of reason to investigate, to confirm, or to reject these principles in their very sources. (*CPuR* A837–38 = B805–6)

Philosophy, for Kant, is a matter of the practical activity of reason in the pursuit of theoretical ends.

As Kant saw it, traditional metaphysics allocated to theoretical reason that which properly belongs to the jurisdiction of practical reason. Just here, as Kant maintained, is the Achilles' heel of the fatally flawed metaphysics of the old, precritical regime. It proceeded on the idea that objective knowledge could be determined in a region where reflective thought alone can function, and it thought that the tools of theoretical/inquiry reason could be employed in a domain where only the resources of practical reason can prove of effective service.

To be sure, on Kantian principles philosophy also has no right whatever to reify or hypostatize its ideas into objects of consideration. No right, that is, within the jurisdiction limits of theoretical reason. But of course the domain of practical reason provides for a different situation:

> For the purposes of this enquiry, theoretical knowledge may be defined as knowledge of what *is,* practical knowledge as the representation [reflective consideration!] of what *ought to be.* On this definition, the theoretical employment of reason is that by

which I know *a priori* (as necessary) that something is, and the practical that by which it is known *a priori* what ought to happen . . . Now since there are practical laws that are absolutely necessary, that is, the moral laws, it will follow that if these necessarily presuppose the existence of any being as the condition of the possibility of their *obligatory* power, this existence must be *postulated;* and this for the sufficient reason that the conditioned, from which the inference is drawn to this determinate convention, is itself known *a priori* to be absolutely necessary. At some future time we shall show that the moral laws do not merely presuppose the existence of a supreme being, but also, as themselves in a different connection absolutely necessary, justify us in postulating it, though, indeed, only from a practical point of view. (*CPuR,* A633–34 = B661–62)

The main issue is not one of postulation versus mere assumption or supposition, but one of theoretical versus practical postulations. Postulation is there either way; it is just that its basis is rather different in the two cases.

The paradigm illustration here is afforded by the aforementioned principle that Kant designates as the Transcendental Unity of Apperception, which enjoins that experience can only yield objective knowledge when it belongs to a single experiencing individual as the experience of one selfsame experiencer. This principle maintains that a unity of apprehension as regards an object of knowledge demands a unified apprehender, and thus requires a unity of apprehension on the side of the knowing subjects. This means that only insofar as I accept your experience at face value – that is, treat it as being vicarious experience of my own – can I employ its data, accepting them as appertaining to an item that figures in the manifold of my knowledge. In sum, I must appropriate your experience in order to derive cognitive benefit from it. "Treat the determinable interests of others as a part of your own" is a central practical principle of Kant's moral philosophy. And similarly, "Treat the determinable objectifications of others as a part of your own" is a central practical principle of Kant's cognitive philosophy. But these are clearly practical/methodological principles of rational procedure – that is to say, ultimately practical principles. And it is exactly this that renders them valid in the a priori synthetic mode.

But how are those a priori theses that are crucial to philosophy to be validated? On Kantian principles, there are, in matters of necessity, two access ways to the validation of synthetic knowledge by a "transcendental deduction":

- Nescon based, via the preconditions for a praxis to be *feasible* – to be able to yield its intended result at all. And in the present case it proceeds via the nescons of the human faculties in the production of objective knowledge.
- Optcon based, via the preconditions for a praxis to be *efficient* – to be able to yield its result in a manner that is maximally efficient and effective. And in the present case it proceeds via the optcon of rational action throughout the domain of praxis (cognitive as well as strictly moral).

The former, knowledge–nescon approach relates to the necessary truths grounded in the operation of the sensibility and the understanding – and thus ultimately including mathematics generally and arithmetic in particular, as well as logic and the fundamental categorical principles of natural philosophy (causality, etc.). The later, praxis–optcon approach relates to the necessary truths of practical philosophy grounded in the operation of the categorical imperatives of agency – and thus ultimately including the practical principles of rational praxis in general as well as those of specifically moral praxis in the stricter sense. And it is in this region that the deliberations of philosophy are to be located whenever more than merely analytic issues are at stake. But while the nescon validations of theoretical philosophy are anthropocentric, geared to the cognitive resources of the human condition, optcon validations of practical philosophy are strictly universal, geared to the modus operandi of rational beings in general. And they are universalizable because of the inherent coordination between what is good for the part and what is good for the whole that obtains in the ideal order of things – and thus in the optimality-geared framework of thought that lies at the basis of the philosophical perspective that Kant inherited from Leibniz and Wolff.

For Kant, then, philosophy itself is the sibling of moral theory under the common parentage of praxis. The one explicates the ways and means of appropriate cognitive praxis, the other the ways and means of appropriate praxis in matters that involve the affective (i.e., noncognitive) interests of persons (ourselves included).

It is true that Kant has it that "the moral laws, and these alone, belong to the pure practical employment of reason" (*CPuR*, A800 = B828). But of course this equation of the moral with the practical indicates an enlargement of the former domain rather than a narrowing of the latter. With Kant, even the principles of the metaphysics of objective knowledge are part of the practical domain – a circumstance which renders the type of metaphysics of theoretical cognition that is exemplified by the first *Critique* itself part and parcel of the practical sphere. For Kant, knowledge development is a praxis, and the theory of this praxis is part of practical philosophy.

13. A PRAGMATIC METAPHYSIC

As Kant sees it, metaphysics is the heart and soul of philosophy. And he conceives of it as Janus faced, oriented in two directions: nature and free agency:

> The system of pure reason, that is, the science which exhibits in systematic connection the whole body of (real as well as apparent) philosophical cognition yielded by pure reason . . . is entitled *metaphysics*. This title may also, however, be given to the whole of pure philosophy, inclusive of critique, so as to encompass both the investigation of all that can ever be known *a priori* and the exposition of that which constitutes a system of the pure philosophical cognitions of this type – in distinction, therefore, from all empirical as well as all mathematical employment of reason. Metaphysics is divided into that of the *speculative* and that of the *practical* employment of pure reason, and is accordingly either *metaphysics of nature* or *metaphysics of morals*. The former contains all the principles of pure reason based on mere concepts . . . regarding the *theoretical* knowledge of all things; the latter, the principles which *a priori* determine and necessitate our actions and inactions . . . "Metaphysics," in its *strict* sense, is commonly reserved for the metaphysics of speculative

reason. But as pure moral philosophy also forms part of this special branch of human and philosophical knowledge provided by pure reason, we shall accord it also the title "metaphysics." (*CPuR*, A841–42 = B869–70)

Metaphysics accordingly combines the moral and the natural domain into one overarchingly comprehensive whole:

> The legislation of human reason [philosophy] has two objects, nature and freedom, and therefore contains not only the law of nature, but also the moral law, presenting them at first in two distinct systems, but ultimately in one single philosophical system. The philosophy of nature deals with all *that is*, the philosophy of morals with that which *ought to be*. (*CPuR*, A840 = B868)

But this bicameral whole is not exactly a union of equals. The practical has primacy. In principle, there are two ways in which the duality of nature and agency can be integrated into holistic unity: naturalistically, with agents seen as parts of nature, or idealistically, with whatever nature that can be of any concern to intelligences being at least in part the product of their own agency. Kant's way is that of the second alternative. For him, philosophy is ultimately one system, despite its apparent duality, because the philosophy of ought (moral philosophy) invades and pervades the philosophy of is (philosophy of nature). And this circumstance roots in the pivotal service of ideas and ideals provided by reason in the service of its own interests – that is, through reason's ought-based commitment to the ideal that an adequate theoretical account of nature must be systematic.

But the role of praxis is critical here, because the foci of philosophizing are not independently constituted objects that are somehow given to us. All that we have – and all that we can get – is such philosophy as is the product of our activity of philosophizing. And this activity – like any other – is a matter of human free agency that is subject (like any activity!) to those imperatives of rational action which Kant characterized as practical. And our overarching Kantian imperative "Comport thyself as any agent should and any truly rational agent would" obtains just as much in relation to our cognitive (theoretical) as in relation to our personal (practical) action: it is as relevant and as valid in inquiry as it is in morality.

And so, as Kant sees it, the purely theoretico-ontological (dogmatic) metaphysics of the precritical past simply is not a viable project. What *is* practicable is a practicalistic metaphysics whose work does not lie in the description of observable reality (the task of natural philosophy, now taken over by natural science), but in the construction of a virtual ("as if") reality. Its task is the development of thought-devised conceptions that indeed do not describe experientially encountered objects (constitutively), but rather provide methodological ("regulative") thought resources that can rationalize – and thereby facilitate and motivate – the scientific project of real-object characterizations. In the final analysis, it is involvement with and commitment to reason's thought instrumentalities that renders metaphysics a venture into the domain of practical rather than theoretical/speculative reason. It is on just this basis that Kant insists on the supremacy of metaphysics as a rational discipline:

> Metaphysics, alike of nature and or morals, and especially that criticism of our adventurous and self-reliant reason which serves as an introduction or propaedeutic to metaphysics, alone properly constitutes what may be entitled philosophy, in the strict sense of the term . . . [And] metaphysics is also the very capstone of human reason. Quite apart from its influence, as science, in connection with certain specific ends, it is an indispensable discipline. For in dealing with reason it treats of those elements and highest maxims which must form the basis of the very *possibility* of some sciences, and of the *use* of all. That, as mere speculation, it serves rather to prevent errors than to extend [objective] knowledge, does not detract from its value. On the contrary this gives it dignity and authority, through that censorship which secures general order and harmony. (*CPuR*, A850–51 = B878–79)

For Kant, then, the task of metaphysics lies in the practical order, its mission being both to keep philosophy honest (by averting its intrusion upon the work of science) and to render it productive (through encouraging and supporting the furtherance of scientific work). After all, "the rational mind" is itself an idealization, just like "the perfected system of knowledge." And so if indeed our only cognitive entryway into the realm of the idea is via practical reason, then a critical account of the operations and resources of reason will itself have to proceed in the practical order of deliberation.

Two conclusions emerge regarding the fundamentals of Kant's position. The first is that philosophizing constitutes a valid enterprise because it alone provides a systematic understanding of the resources by which we can come to comprehend and systematize our own modus operandi as investigators of the world and agents within it. The second is that it is only in the modality of the quasi knowledge represented by a praxis-mediated rational conviction that we are able to prosecute philosophy's essential work and thereby manage to serve adequately the crucial interests of reason.

14. SUMMARY

The present discussion offers a nonstandard view of Kant's position regarding metaphysics by viewing this as an essentially practical project: a metaphysic of praxis that is so amply conceived as to encompass both a metaphysic of morals and a metaphysic of cognition. The main theses of these deliberations have been as follows:

1. The range of the synthetic (nonanalytic) knowledge of necessity that can be obtained is rather narrow. And specifically it excludes all philosophical matters that go beyond the mere definition of terms.

2. Since our human nature cannot – and our rational nature ought not to – rest content with vast areas of ignorance constituting a terra incognita regarding fundamentals, we must, can, and legitimately may take recourse to the quasi knowledge represented by the rationally appropriate belief that is involved with objectively validatable conviction.

3. The rational appropriateness at issue here is a matter of what is required to serve the inherent interests of reason. And we are thus engaged in a practical project, irrespective of whether it is the theoretical/speculative concerns of inquiry reason or the propriety of action of moral reason that is at issue.

4. This practical dimension brings to the fore the idea of an optimality condition (optcon), that is, a necessary condition (nescon) for the maximally effective service of legitimate interests. For those rationally appropriate beliefs at issue with objectively

valid conviction are beliefs that cash out the optimality conditions (optcons) of rational praxis.

5. Accordingly, while we cannot lay claim to achieving objective knowledge of matters of necessity in metaphysics, we must, can, and should develop the quasi knowledge of rationally valid conviction in this domain. A metaphysics of practice is a perfectly viable project – one that yields a system closely akin to that of Leibniz and Wolff, but now seen as resting upon an entirely different basis – one that is not cognitive and objective, but ultimately inherent in the subjectivity of praxis.

As Kant saw it, metaphysics cannot touch the objective realities of the field of appearance because the contingent realities of experience – for which the operations of sensibility and understanding are determinative – indeed lie entirely outside its scope as a purely rational endeavor. Its appropriate concerns lie in the domain of reason alone, and here its proper instruments are those of specifically practical reason. Accordingly the fundamental division of labor between the practical and the theoretical/speculative domains means that a properly developed metaphysics can neither be aided nor impaired by the results of empirical inquiry. Metaphysics has nothing to hope and nothing to fear from our factual investigations, since the concerns of science belong to another jurisdiction altogether.

Anyone who thinks that Kant is a positivistically inclined thinker for whom perceptually based sense knowledge is the be-all and end-all should read attentively the final section of the first *Critique*, "The History of Pure Reason." For Kant here explicitly positions himself as an intermediary between the "mere sensualist" and the "mere intellectualists," where "Those of the former school maintained that reality is to be found solely in the objects of the senses, and that all else is fiction; while those at the latter school declared that in the senses there is nothing but illusion, and that only the intellect knows what is true" (*CPuR*, A853 = B882). A proper comprehension of the facts will, so Kant insists, call for combining the two positions. There is both a realm of real objects (i.e., the physical realities of the natural world) as the material of scientific investigation based on observation, and a realm of ideal reality as the material for intellectual reflection under the aegis of reason (in its specifically practical orientation). As Kant sees it, neither a purely experiential realism (radical empiricism) alone nor an intellectualist realism (transcendental rationalism) alone will do. What is needed is a critically judicious joining of the two, although this must be one where each is kept within the jurisdictional confines of its own proper province.

Kant is traditionally portrayed as the discoverer of a via media, a middle way mediating between the empiricism built up by British thinkers to accommodate Newtonian science and the idealism built up by German thinkers to accommodate Leibnizian metaphysics. The fact, however, is that Kant is not the discoverer of a third and different way, but an ingenious syncretist who conjoins these two enterprises, with Newtonian science prevailing at the level of empirical reality and Leibnizian metaphysics prevailing at the level of the virtual reality that is essential to the work of reason.

In closing, it is helpful to summarize the overall line of thought at issue in the development of Kant's position regarding the nature of philosophy:

- Philosophy is a work of pure reason: its ultimate concern is with the "self-development of reason" (*CPuR*, A835 = B863) – that is, with what reason can manage to contrive out of its own resources.
- The only things that pure reason generates from its own resources are ideas (which prominently include ideals).
- A "transcendental deduction" to establish the validity of ideas is possible, seeing that there are two distinct routes to objective validity – namely, objective applicability (which indispensably requires the collaboration of sensibility and understanding and thus is the work of speculative/theoretical reason), and objective utility (which is the work of practical reason). Accordingly,
- Since philosophy is pure – and thereby prescinds from theoretical reason's focus on issues of real-world applicability – it follows that the proper work of philosophy lies on the side of practical reason.
- To be sure, practical reason has two dimensions, according as it addresses our moral interests or our cognitive interests. (For theory and speculation too are matters of praxis with regard to which there are "interests of reason.") Accordingly philosophy has both moral and cognitive sectors. But the deliberations that

are at issue in either sector are both matters of practical reason, and thus ultimately of moral deliberation broadly construed.

- On this basis, philosophizing is ultimately a matter of practical rather than theoretical reason.

It was not for nothing that C. S. Peirce, the founding father of pragmatism, viewed Kant as a precursor.

As these considerations indicate, the "The Ideal of Pure Reason" chapter and its aftermath are not just the end but also the telos of Kant's book. For it is not until this culminating discussion that he "shows his hand," so to speak, regarding the status of the deliberations in which the *Critique of Pure Reason* is itself involved.

Chapter 7

On the Reach of Pure Reason in Kant's Practical Philosophy

1. THE PROBLEM: HOW CAN PRACTICAL REASON OVERREACH THEORETICAL REASON?

In the *Critique of Pure Reason,* Kant time and again puts us on notice that various substantive (nonanalytic) truths to which reason can attain on its own, a priori and independently of the empirical deliverances of the senses, are the product of the modus operandi of our specifically human intelligence and are grounded in the specific workings of our human faculty of knowledge. How other intelligences might think in such matters – minds not endowed with our particular modes of sensibility or our particular categories of understanding – is something of which we do and can know nothing. Accordingly, all of our a priori theoretical knowledge is legitimated through, but also confined to, the operation of our human intellect – and is thus restricted in validity to the sphere of how matters stand from a specifically human point of view. In the theoretical domain, man's a priori knowledge is man correlative.

However, when we turn to the practical sphere of the *Critique of Practical Reason,* matters take on a very different appearance. For Kant here tells us with great explicitness that

> [the] principle of morality, on account of the universality of its legislation . . . , is declared by reason to be a law for all rational beings in so far as they have a will . . . It is thus not limited to human beings but extends to all finite beings having reason and

This essay is a revised and enlarged version of a paper presented to the Philosophy Colloquium at the University of Rochester in February of 1979 at the invitation of Lewis White Beck.

will; indeed it includes the Infinite Being as the supreme intelligence. (*CPrR*, p. 32, Akad.)

Kant is emphatic in insisting that no explicit reference need be
made to man as such in dealing with the legitimacy of the principles of morally practical reason, since what matters here is rationality in general rather than humanity in specific:

> For its [moral] legislation it is required that reason need pre-
> suppose only itself, because a rule is objectively and universally
> valid only when it holds without any contingent subjective con-
> ditions which differentiate one rational being from another.
> (*CPrR*, pp. 20–21, Akad.)

And again:

> Thus if there is to be a supreme practical principle and a cate-
> gorical imperative for the human will, it must be . . . [grounded
> in] that which is necessarily an end for everyone because it is an
> end in itself . . . The ground of this principle is: rational nature
> exists as an end in itself. Man necessarily thinks of his own
> existence in this way . . . But every other rational being also
> thinks of its existence by means of the pure rational ground
> which holds also of myself. It is thus at the same time an ob-
> jective practical principle from which as a supreme practical
> ground, it must be possible to derive all laws of the will. (*Grund-
> legung*, pp. 428–29, Akad.)

The legislations of moral reason are to be binding for all rational
agents, without limitation or qualification.

Thus while the a priori truths known through theoretical reason are man correlative, the a priori laws validated by practical
reason in the moral sphere are man transcending and binding
upon rational beings at large. Ethical duties, laws of freedom, and
moral imperatives are accordingly radically distinct from the
nature-characterizing necessitations of the human condition that
root in our forms of sensibility and our categories of understanding. Kant maintains as emphatically as words permit that morality must not be thought to hinge on the contingent makeup of our
faculties, that "moral principles are not founded on the peculiar-
ities of human nature but must stand on themselves, a priori, and

that for such [a priori] principles practical rules for *every* rational creature . . . must be derivable" (*Grundlegung*, p. 410n, Akad.). And again:

> [It must be shown] that there is a practical law which of itself commands absolutely and without any incentives, and that obedience to this law is duty. With a view to attaining this, it is extremely important to remember that we must not let ourselves think that the reality of this principle can be derived from the particular constitution of human nature. For duty is practical unconditional necessity of action; it must, therefore, hold for all rational beings (to which alone an imperative can apply), and only for that reason can it be a law for all human wills. Whatever is derived from the particular natural situation of man as such, or from certain feelings and propensities, or even from a particular tendency of the human reason which might not hold necessarily for the will of every rational being (if such a tendency is possible), can give a maxim valid for us but not a law; that is, it can give a subjective principle by which we might act only if we have the propensity and inclination, but not an objective principle by which we would be directed to act even if all our propensity, inclination, and natural tendency were opposed to it. (*Grundlegung*, p. 425, Akad.)

The moral law and its implications must hold good for all rational agents and thus for men too, albeit merely in virtue of the fact that we count as rational agents:

> Practical principles . . . are objective, or practical *laws,* when the condition [for their determination of the will] is acknowledged as objective, that is, as *valid* [not just for us humans, but] for the will of every rational being. (*CPrR*, p. 19, Akad., italics added)

Accordingly, Kant maintains that

> [w]e cannot refuse to admit that the law of thesis concept [of morality] is of such broad significance that it holds not merely for men but for all rational beings as such . . . For with what right could we bring into unlimited respect something that might be valid only under contingent human conditions? And how could laws of the determination of our will be held to be laws of the determination of the will in general and of ourselves insofar as

we are rational beings, if they were merely empirical and did not have their origin completely a priori in pure albeit practical reason? (*Grundlegung*, p. 408, Akad., italics added)

Pure practical reason accordingly has a greater reach than pure theoretical reason because it can establish what holds for rational intelligence in general whereas pure theoretical reason is bound to the limits of the specifically human intelligence.

But how can this larger universality be established? For clearly we cannot – on Kantian principles – penetrate the veil of the noumenal realm to determine the modus operandi of rational agents in general. What, after all, would then become of the mind centrality of Kant's vaunted Copernican Revolution? Given that in the *Critique of Pure Reason* Kant insists that various a priori principles can attain this status only through their inherence in the modus operandi of our human intellect, how can he now maintain in the *Critique of Practical Reason* that certain principles (viz. moral ones) appertain to rational intelligence in general, freed of the restrictive correlativity to human capacities that elsewhere governs universality and necessity for Kant?

2. THE CONCEPTUAL TURN

One of the key theses of the *Critique of Practical Reason* runs as follows:

> If a rational being is to think its maxims to be practical universal laws, it can do so only by considering them as principles which contain the determining grounds of the will because of their form and not because of their matter. (*CPrR*, p. 27, Akad.)

We must read this *Lehrsatz* not as a flat claim as to how rational beings must think, but rather as a statement of how rational beings must (*ex hypothesi*, in virtue of their stipulated rationality) be thought to think. Kant's doctrine of morality deals with rational beings only indirectly via an inquiry into the concept of a rational being – into how rational beings must be understood to operate, given what is at issue in the very concept in question. As he himself puts it,

The question is thus: Is it necessary law for all rational beings that they should always judge their actions by such maxims as they themselves would will to serve as universal laws? If it is such a law [which, of course, is the case], then it must be connected wholly *a priori* with the concept of the will of the rational being as such. (*Grundlegung*, p. 426, Akad.)

Our commitment to the causality of freedom in rational agents bound by the moral law is inherent in the very conception of a moral agent acting through his (*ex hypothesi* available) resource of freedom of the will:

Everyone must admit that a law, if it is to hold morally, i.e., as a ground of obligation, must imply absolute necessity; he must admit that the command, "Thou shalt not lie," does not apply to men only, as if other rational beings had no need to observe it. The same is true for all other moral laws properly so called. He must concede that the ground of obligation here must not be sought in the nature of man or in the circumstances in which he is placed, but sought *a priori* solely in the concepts of pure reason, and that every other precept, . . . even a precept which is in certain respects universal, so far as it leans in the least on empirical grounds (perhaps only in regard to the motive involved), may be called a practical rule but never a moral law. (*Grundlegung*, p. 389, Akad.)

As Kant saw it, the principles of morality are universal and necessary because they represent essentially conceptual truths. But nevertheless, they are not analytic.

At this point a brief digression is necessary in order to avert possible misunderstanding about Kant's analytic–synthetic distinction. For Kant (unlike Leibniz or the later logical positivists), "analytic" bears a very narrow construction, since for him a proposition is analytically true just if it is derivable from definitions alone, without appeal to any further, nondefinitional principles. Thus if "primes" are (by definition) "integers with no divisors apart from themselves and one," and "integers (by definition) are whole, positive numbers," it follows that the statement "Primes are positive numbers" is an analytic truth. Again, if 3 is by definition 2 + 1, and 4 is by definition 3 + 1, it follows that $4 = (2 + 1) + 1$

is an analytic truth. However, $4 = 2 + 2$ is synthetic! For to establish this we require the equation $(2 + 1) + 1 = 2 + (1 + 1)$, that is to say, we need to have recourse to the principle represented by the law of the associativity of addition. And this is a principle over and above the definitions of the ideas at issue. Thus the truth in question, though assuredly demonstrable, is not demonstrable from definitions alone. And this fact of its dependence on extra-definitional principles precludes this proposition's "analyticity" in Kant's narrow sense of the term.[1]

In this way, the thesis that the moral law holds for rational agents in general, while not analytic in Kant's rigoristic sense of mere definition inherence, is nevertheless a demonstrable truth that holds in virtue of the nature of the concept of a rational agency:

> [I]t is evident that it is not only of the greatest necessity in a theoretical point of view . . . but also of the utmost practical importance to derive the concepts and the law of morals from pure reason and to present them pure and unmixed . . . without making the principles depend upon the particular nature of human reason as speculative philosophy may permit and indeed sometimes find necessary. But since moral laws should hold for every rational being as such, the principles must be derived from the universal concept of a rational being generally. (*Grundlegung*, pp. 411–12, Akad.)

It is purely and simply by unraveling the ramifications of the concept of rational agency that we are able to say that all are subject to the (everywhere uniform and identical) moral law. The truth at issue is synthetic, seeing that analyticity in Kant's technical sense fails here because the conceptual linkage is not straightforwardly definition inherent, but indirectly mediated by a nondefinitional principle, as shown by the following diagram:

free agents
(beings endowed with a will that is autonomous and free, and therefore good)

*rational
beings*

*beings subject to
practical and moral laws*

Kant develops this line of thought as follows:

> As will is a kind of causality of living beings so far as they are rational, freedom would be that property of this causality by which it can be effective independently of foreign causes determining it . . . What else, then, can the freedom of the will be but autonomy, i.e., the property of the will to be a law to itself? The proposition that the will is a law to itself in all its actions, however, only expresses the principle that we should act according to no other maxim than that which can also have itself as a universal law for its object. And this is just the formula of the categorical imperative and the principle of morality. Therefore a free will and a will under moral laws are identical. Thus if freedom of the will is presupposed, morality together with its principles follows from it by the mere analysis of its concept. But the principle is nevertheless a synthetical proposition: an absolutely good will is one whose maxim can always include itself as a universal law. It is synthetical because by analysis of the concept of an absolutely good will that property of the maxim cannot be found. Such synthetical propositions, however, are possible only by the fact that both cognitions are connected through their union with a third in which both of them are to be found. The positive concept of freedom furnishes this third cognition. (*Grundlegung*, pp. 446–47, Akad.)

The crux here is that a (synthetic) route to the a priori is available in Kant – one that works for practical truths alone – via the faculty-imprinted self-classification of rational creatures as being free agents.

However, neither empirical psychology nor metaphysical ontology provides this insight into the minds of rational agents in general, but only concept analysis, only unraveling the inner implications of the conception of rational agency. Yet what is at work here is not mere concept containment in Kant's sense of analyticity as effective tautology. Rather, all crucial linkage is here mediated through the intervention of a *tertium quid*, namely a principle of process regarding free agents and their modus operandi. Kant's Copernican Revolution is not abrogated here, but only sophisticated by the realization that conceptual reflection also affords an avenue to synthetic a priori truth.

In cognitive (speculative, theoretical) matters, synthetic a priori truth is always rooted in the special constitution of the specifically human mind. But in practical matters synthetic a priori truth roots in the self-application of the reflectively based conception of a rational agent. The conceptual crux at issue is a matter of self-classification and of the principles that govern "how we think of *ourselves*." For, of course, we see ourselves as members of both communities – that of humans and that of rational agents. We can in this respect go beyond the specifically human because in so doing we do not go beyond what we are – or rather what we take ourselves to be. We can accordingly see ourselves as both members of a natural order governed by efficient causality and members of a literally supernatural moral order governed by the causality of freedom.

Kant's overall argument is developed in the middle of the third section of the *Grundlegung,* in a paragraph under the rubric "Freedom Must Be Presupposed as the Property of the Will of All Rational Beings":

> It is not enough to ascribe freedom to our will, on any grounds whatever, if we do not also have sufficient grounds for attributing it to all rational beings. For since morality serves as a law for us only as rational beings, morality must hold valid for all rational beings, and since it must be derived exclusively from the property of freedom, freedom as the property of the will of all rational beings must be demonstrated. And it does not suffice to prove it from certain alleged experiences of human nature (which is indeed impossible, as it can be proved only a priori), but we must prove it as belonging generally to the activity of rational beings endowed with a will . . . Now I affirm that we must necessarily grant that every rational being who has a will also has the idea of freedom and that it acts only under this idea. For in such a being we think of a reason which is practical, i.e., a reason which has causality with respect to its objects. Now, we cannot conceive of a reason which consciously responds to a bidding from the outside with respect to its judgments, for then the subject would attribute the determination of its power of judgment not to reason but to an impulse. Reason must [by its very nature] regard itself as the author of its principles, independently of foreign influences; consequently, as practical

reason or as the will of a rational being, it must regard itself as free. That is to say, the will of a rational being can be a will of its own only under the idea of freedom, and therefore in a practical point of view such a will must be ascribed to all rational beings. (*Grundlegung*, pp. 447–48, Akad.)

It is the conceptual, quasi-analytic makeup of legitimate justifications in the moral domain that establishes the difference between demonstration in mathematics and in the moral domain:

For all moral proofs can as philosophical ones only be adduced by means of rational knowledge from concepts and not, as is mathematics, through the construction of concepts. Mathematics allows a plurality of proofs for one and the same proposition, because in a priori intuition there can be several determinations of the nature of an object all of which lead back to the very same ground. [But in moral theory the situation is different.] If one proof of the duty of veracity, for instance, were first drawn from the harm that a lie causes other men, and then another from the worthlessness of a liar and the violation of his self-respect, what would be proved in the first argument is a duty of benevolence and not a duty of veracity, that is to say, not the duty of which a proof was required, but another duty. (*The Metaphysics of Morals*, p. 403, Akad.)

Thus Kant is perfectly clear that in the domain of moral truths we are dealing not with existential facts but with purely conceptual relationships – not with actual moral agents as such (of which human history may very possibly contain none), but with what is involved, in virtue of the very concept at issue, in being a moral agent.

The absolutely good will, the principle of which must be a categorical imperative, is thus undetermined with reference to any objects. It contains only the form of volition in general . . . How such a synthetical practical a priori proposition is possible and why it is necessary is a problem whose solution does not lie within the boundaries of the metaphysics of morals. Moreover, we have not here affirmed its truth, and even less professed to command a proof of it. We have only shown through the development of the universally received concept of morality that autonomy of the will is unavoidably connected with it, or rather that it is its foundation. (*Grundlegung*, pp. 444–45, Akad.)

In the matter of self-conception, is and ought come together. We can, do, and must proceed on the principle inherent in the supposition that we human beings are rational free agents, and thus credit ourselves with a morally determinative causality of freedom.[2]

And so in Kant's practical philosophy the reach of pure reason exceeds that of his theoretical philosophy. The latter is subject to certain irrationalizable contingencies – to wit, the modus operandi of the faculty structure of the human mind. But the former is free from such contingencies. Its operations proceed in the realm of conceptual necessities as a matter of pure reason alone (albeit practical reason, of course). But the facts at issue are nevertheless synthetic, because more than mere definitions are at issue in their grounding – namely, principles that define our modus operandi as free rational agents.

3. ENTER THE "SPECIAL CONSTITUTION OF THE HUMAN MIND"

On this basis, there remains one absolutely crucial point at which the peculiar constitution of the human mind does indeed enter into Kant's moral philosophy. And this is at the point of the range of applicability of moral strictures.

As Kant sees the matter, moral principles are a priori – universal and necessary – on a strictly conceptual basis. But moral principles as such go no farther than to say: "Rational agents must (necessarily and universally) act such and such wise [i.e., in line with the Categorical Imperative]." Now, of course, from the fact that rational free agents must act thus, it does not follow that I (or we) must act thus, that the duty at issue is my (our) duty, unless it is premised that I (we) are rational free agents. A minor premise about me/us is needed to place our own selves within the scope of the major premise at issue. And this is something that indeed does inevitably root in the special constitution of the human mind. We humans do and cannot but regard ourselves as members of the community of rational free agents: we see ourselves as members of a natural order governed by efficient causality and as members of a literally supernatural moral order governed by the causality of freedom. That I am a rational free agent is not a deliverance of reason as such, but of my own understanding. But it is this reflective self-perception alone that renders moral laws binding on us, and this is a synthetic necessity of the standard Kantian type – one that is rooted in the special constitution of the human mind.

The "Thou shalt" or "Thou shalt not" injunctions of morality represent a synthetic truth grounded judgmentally in the application of concepts – namely in the application *to us* of the conception of a free rational agent (with all of the ramifications and consequences of analytically implicated theses).

The general principles of rational agency in general specify no more than what ought to be in the moral realm of free rational agents. But that *I* am obligated to do something – that the mandates of rational agency apply to *me* in specific – is a further distinct and emphatically nonconceptual step:

> It is clear, then, that it is owing to the subjective constitution of our practical faculty that the moral laws must be represented as commands and the actions conforming to them as duties, and that reason expresses this necessity, not by an "is" (happens), but by an "ought to be." . . . [The context of] an intelligible world in which everything would be actual merely because (as something good) it is possible, together with freedom as its formal condition, is for us a transcendent concept, not available as a constitutive principle, to determine an object and its objective reality, yet because of the constitution of our (in part sensuous) nature and faculty it is, so far as we can represent it in accordance with the constitution of our reason, for us and for all rational beings that have a connection with the world of sense, a universal *regulative principle.* This principle does not objectively determine the constitution of freedom, as a form of causality, but it makes the rule of actions according to that idea a command for everyone, with no less validity than if it did so determine it. (*CJ*, sect. 76, near end; pp. 403–4, Akad.)

Morality is necessarily binding upon all rational agents as a matter of their very constitution as such. But its application to the contingent being that I myself am in this experiential world is something whose basis is merely regulative – and thus practical. For only by taking ourselves to be rational free agents – a subjective step governed by the operational principles of the human mind – do we come within the province of the moral law.

The a prioris of theoretical and teleological reasons are inherent in the attempts of our cognitive faculties to come to grips with this world. But in the practical, and, above all, the moral domain, we leave this world behind. Here man enters into his true, world-removed home – the realm of purely rational intelligences and agents. And he thereby enters also the wider realm of the duties and obligations of a nature-separated sort of being represented by purely rational intelligences. In viewing himself as possessed of such an intelligence, man becomes "larger than life" – a member of a supernatural order that literally transcends the limitations of nature. Kant's moral philosophy is deeply theological in its insistence that, insofar as it involves rationality, the true home of the human spirit does not really lie within nature at all.

Chapter 8

On the Rationale of Kant's
Categorical Imperative

1. EQUALITY BEFORE THE (MORAL) LAW

Few issues have caused greater difficulty to expositors and students of Kant's ethical teachings than that centerpiece of his moral philosophy, the Categorical Imperative.[1] Together with the conception of moral universality on which it rests, it raises a host of issues that both demand closer scrutiny and amply deserve it.

Kant's ethics is based on the principle of equality before the moral law as inherent in the intrinsic dignity of a rational being. This equality is implemented through the idea that whatever acts are morally permissible (or impermissible or obligatory) for one person must likewise be so for another.[2]

Kant's moral theory accordingly rests on the following Generalization Principle:

- $\text{perm}(X \text{ does } A) \to \text{perm}(Y \text{ does } A)$
- $\sim\text{perm}(X \text{ does } A) \to \sim\text{perm}(Y \text{ does } A)$
- $\text{oblig}(X \text{ does } A) \to \text{oblig}(Y \text{ does } A)$

And here we need only deal with the first of these principles of universality for moral lawfulness. For the second is equivalent to it by contraposition. And the third is equivalent to these two once one accepts that obligation is tantamount to a prohibition from refraining ($\sim\text{perm}\sim$ = oblig) together with an acknowledgment that omission also counts as a kind of action.

Note moreover that a strong mode of universalization immediately follows from such principles. Take obligation. Since Y is

I am indebted to Uwe Meixner, Alexander Pruss, and an anonymous referee for helpful suggestions on a draft of this essay.

effectively a free variable in those formulas, that third principle (for example) entails that, for any X:

$$\text{oblig}(X \text{ does } A) \to (\forall y)\text{oblig}(y \text{ does } A)$$

and therefore

$$(\forall x)[\text{oblig}(x \text{ does } A) \to (\forall y)\text{oblig}(y \text{ does } A)]$$

Accordingly we have

$$(\exists x)\text{oblig}(X \text{ does } A) \to (\forall x)\text{oblig}(x \text{ does } A)$$

In this way, it becomes clear that an action is to be deemed obligatory for an agent only if everyone is obligated to do the same. With Kant, what is obligatory (permissible, etc.) for someone is thereby obligatory (permissible, etc.) for everyone. And of course there is no problem about strengthening the preceding implication to an equivalence ($\leftrightarrow$).

And the same story holds for permission. We therefore have the Generalization Principles

$$(\exists x)\text{oblig}(X \text{ does } A) \leftrightarrow (\forall x)\text{oblig}(x \text{ does } A)$$

$$(\exists x)\text{perm}(X \text{ does } A) \leftrightarrow (\forall x)\text{perm}(x \text{ does } A)$$

Where permission and obligation are concerned, the situation at once becomes general, and we have

(G/oblig) $\text{oblig}(\text{doing } A) \leftrightarrow (\forall x)\text{oblig}(x \text{ does } A)$

(G/perm) $\text{perm}(\text{doing } A) \leftrightarrow (\forall x)\text{perm}(x \text{ does } A)$

Permissibility and obligation are person indifferent; here particular individuals drop out of view. As Kant sees it, the rulings of rationality are universal, and morality's universality inheres in that of rationality itself, seeing that moralists do – and must – recognize that their deliberations have to be based on impersonal reason (dass sie notwendig rational verfahren müssen [*CPrR*, pp. 7–8, Akad.]).

2. MORAL ACCEPTABILITY

There is, however, another critically important aspect to Kant's thought about morality. It pivots on the idea that: People's doing what is morally permissible for them, issues in a morally acceptable state of affairs – one that is morally appropriate (*moralisch möglich*). It seems plausible to designate this as the Permittedness Acceptability Principle (PA). Using ACCEPT to indicate such moral acceptability, this principle may be formulated as follows:

$$(PA) \qquad \text{perm}(X \text{ does } A) \leftrightarrow \text{ACCEPT}(X \text{ does } A)$$

This Permittedness Acceptability Principle has the immediate and obvious consequence:

$$[\text{perm } (X \text{ does } A) \& \text{perm}(Y \text{ does } B)] \leftrightarrow$$
$$[\text{ACCEPT}(X \text{ does } A) \& \text{ACCEPT}(Y \text{ does } B)]$$

However, acceptability so functions in this Kantian context that what is distributively acceptable will also be jointly acceptable:

$$[\text{ACCEPT}(F) \& \text{ACCEPT}(G)] \leftrightarrow \text{ACCEPT}(F \& G)$$

In view of this, the Permittedness Acceptability Principle yields the stronger Acceptability Combination Principle (C):

$$(C) \qquad [\text{perm}(X \text{ does } A) \& \text{perm } (Y \text{ does } B)] \leftrightarrow$$
$$\text{ACCEPT}(X \text{ does } A \& Y \text{ does } B)$$

This principle – so it will emerge – has ramifications that fundamentally shape and characterize the nature of Kant's metaphysic of morals. In particular, (C) yields by generalization a Generalized Combination Principle (C*):[3]

$$(C^*) \qquad (\forall x)\text{perm}(x \text{ does } A) \leftrightarrow \text{ACCEPT}(\forall x)(x \text{ does } A)$$

And this when conjoined to the Permission Generalization Principle (G/Perm) yields the following Universalization Principle (U):

$$(U) \qquad (\exists x)\text{perm}(x \text{ does } A) \leftrightarrow \text{ACCEPT}(\forall x)(x \text{ does } A) \leftrightarrow$$
$$\text{perm}(\text{doing } A)$$

For Kant, determining the moral permissibility of an action thus lies in assessing the acceptability of the fictive condition that would result if everyone were to realize this permission. An act is permissible for someone just in case its universalization is acceptable.[4]

A further word about the sort of acceptability that is involved here is in order. It is best approached from the negative side, by considering that a state of affairs is to be deemed "unacceptable" if it is (i) logically or conceptually impossible to realize, (ii) physically impracticable or infeasible to realize, or (iii) socially obnoxious if realized.[5] In each case there results a conflict or contradiction – with the principles of logic, or of natural law, and of social order, respectively. The idea is that acceptability is tantamount to viability and unacceptability to anomaly, where the anomaly at issue consists in conflict with the norms of the logical, the natural, and the social order, respectively. Acceptability, in sum, is a matter of compatibility with an ideal moral order, and anomaly is in conflict with it. With such anomaly there thus arises what Kant calls a "contradiction" – not so much a logical (self)-contradiction as a contradiction to the demands of right reason – a conflict with the demands of a rational will.[6]

The sort of anomaly at issue with item (iii) is, in effect, a rent in the fabric of the moral order. And the "moral order" involved here is what Kant himself characterizes as "a most fruitful concept, namely, that of a kingdom [realm, *Reich*] of ends" which comprises "the systematic interconnection of rational beings through common objective laws" (*Grundlegung*, p. 433, Akad.). This sort of order arises "when we abstract from the personal differences among rational beings, and thus from all content of their [contingent] practical ends" (ibid.). It is – to reemphasize – the idealized order that is the object of a rational (rather than merely empirical) will. For, as Kant emphasized in the *Critique of Judgment*, it is only in an ideal, teleologically perfected order that reason can take real satisfaction (ibid., sect. 84).

S. Körner has objected that if the anomaly at issue is to be not a merely logical contradiction, but one that involves some sort of moral incongruity "then Kant's [universalization] test [of moral acceptability] becomes circular – or else superfluous."[7] But this overlooks Kant's ultimate reliance on rationality broadly construed.[8] What is wrong with an unproductive society or a boorish society, for example, is not that they are logically infeasible, but that they are rationally unacceptable choices, because in no case does it make rational sense to prefer something of whose opposite (a productive society, a caring society) is inherently preferable. It would thus be quite mistaken to see the Categorical Imperative as imposing a purely formal, altogether logical constraint. The nonuniversalizability at issue is a matter of the substantive anomalousness that goes with contravening the demands of reason – principally by way of conflict with the conditions under which the life of reason can flourish. The flaw of such unacceptable states of affairs is fundamentally axiological: they are incompatible with a sound moral order of the normative sort at issue in a kingdom of ends. In this regard, Kant is a consequentialist ethicist of sorts: as he sees it, acts become morally prohibited when their generalization produces unacceptable (i.e., bad) results. However much an immoral act may cater to one's wants and desires, it causes injury to the moral order that is the ultimate object of every rational aspiration.

Observe, however, that (C) has the consequence

$$\text{ACCEPT}(X \text{ does } A \text{ and } X \text{ does } B) \leftrightarrow$$
$$[\text{perm}(X \text{ does } A) \& \text{perm}(X \text{ does } B)]$$

Now if A and B are incompatible actions, and in particular when $B = \text{not-}A$, then ACCEPT(X does A & X does B) will clearly be false. So in this case we have $\sim\text{perm}(X \text{ does } A) \vee \sim\text{perm}(X \text{ does } B)$, which is to say that one of two incompatible actions will always be prohibited. In particular, this means that with any action A, either A or not-A, will be prohibited, so that in effect there are no morally indifferent actions, that is, actions of such a sort that both the act and its omission are permissible (say, giving up one's job as a grocer and becoming a watchmaker instead.) But this anomalous consequence does not actually follow on Kantian principles. Whenever (as in the example) the acts in questions are (by hypothesis) morally indifferent, nothing untoward ensues. For Kant is designing a theory for morally relevant actions, and there the principles at issue can be maintained. (A "science" cannot be expected to treat objects that fall outside of its domain: quantum physics does not address the issues of horticulture.)

So far so good. But not, alas, much farther! For it is clear that problems ensue when the Universalization Principle (U) is viewed from other perspectives.

3. OBSTACLES

Consider the following ways of acting:

- Giving all one has to the poor
- Abstaining from reproductive activity
- Prescribing medicine for an ill person

None of these inherently permissible actions is "universalizable" in the sense at issue, since the generalization of each into a universalized practice leads to a clearly unacceptable result. Upon act generalization of the sort now under contemplation, the first way of proceeding leads to self-incongruity: gifting becomes impossible when no one is prepared to have any possessions. Moreover, the second leads to catastrophe – the extinction of the race – and the third creates havoc by putting everyone into the prescribing business (even the totally untrained and incompetent). Accordingly, each of these seemingly acceptable modes of action would become morally impermissible if subjected to the aforementioned modus operandi of Kantian generalization. And exactly the same sort of thing happens with innumerable other perfectly innocuous actions. Consoling your recently widowed neighbor or admonishing her errant offspring may be all right for you, her friend, but it is hardly acceptable that everyone should do so. The envisioned construction of the Categorical Imperative has to be seen as inappropriate without drastic qualification or reinterpretation.

And the problem here roots in a difficulty that goes back right to the start – to that fundamental Permission Generalization Principle

$$\text{perm}(X \text{ does } A) \rightarrow \text{perm}(Y \text{ does } A)$$

and its cognates for obligation and prohibition. Protecting the palace is obligatory for Sgt. Gun, the guardsman, but not for Mr. Roast, the cook. Flying the plane is not permissible for Miss White, the stewardess, but is not thereby impermissible for Mr. Black, the pilot. In all such cases, the universalizability in question simply fails to hold good.

Something has clearly gone wrong with the projected interpretation of Kant's position when act generalization is construed in this sort of way. The envisioned approach to the idea of "equality before the moral law" needs to be radically modified. Condition-alization is going to be necessary if universalization is to be maintained. Kant has to come to terms with the appropriateness of the Roman dictum "Quod licet Iovi, non licet tibi, bovi": he has to come to terms with the moral relevancy of the circumstantial difference between gods and fools, between adepts and amateurs. And this is a step that he is perfectly willing to take.

4. THE NEED FOR CONDITIONALIZATION

To secure a plausible construction of Kant's position one has to go back to basics. It is clear that to have any prospect of succeeding, universalization in morality must not address itself to actions pure and simple, but rather to duly conditionalized actions. For the problem with any unqualified moral universalization rule is that there is no merely behavioral mode of acting that is always and everywhere appropriate or inappropriate irrespective of circumstances and conditions; no unqualifiedly specifiable candidate for A such that ACCEPT$(\forall x)(x$ does $A)$ can plausibly be maintained.[9] What is required for moving in the direction of universality is to qualify and conditionalize A in some suitable behavior-transcending manner. The governing idea now becomes that an action is permissible only if it admits of universalization once it is appropriately conditionalized.

In the abstract, to be sure, conditionalization can trivialize universalization: even the singular statement "Socrates is a philosopher" can be "universalized" as "All individuals identical with Socrates are philosophers." The crux is that the conditionalization must be achieved not merely formally (and so with potential triviality), but in a morally relevant way. Good sense must be used to ensure that the "conditions" have a moral relevancy (as a mere difference between individuals – Socrates versus Plato – would not).

But how is this conditionalization to be achieved? Here two possibilities present themselves. We can do so either by way of the agent-external circumstances and conditions (C) of the particular case at hand, or by way of the agent-internal rationale (R) that constitutes the agent's motive or reason for acting. We accordingly have two prime prospects here:

- Conditionalizing the act to the prevailing circumstances (C)
- Conditionalizing the act to the agent's motivating rationale (R)

As Kant sees it, both sorts of conditions have to enter into the morally relevant characterization of an act (generally in an inter-related way). For him, the morally requisite characterization of action thus involves three components: (i) the act as a generic way of acting, (ii) the circumstances operative in its performance, and (iii) the agent's motivating rationale (the "subjective ground" of the action).[10] Some examples of acts construed in the complex manner that is called for in Kant's moral theory would thus be

- To pay someone the money one owes him in order to settle the debt
- To give someone the aid she requires in order to help her

As Kant has it, then, the morally germane characterization of an act – an "action modality," as we shall here call it – thus has three constituents – act (A), circumstances (C), and rationale (R), as in the example

A: Overcharging a customer
C: When this customer happens to be an innocent (say a child or a newcomer)
R: In order to satisfy one's greed

When acts are viewed in this complexly full-bodied A:C:R man-ner, their moral acceptability can, with Kant, be determined via the question of universalization. Thus suppose that X committed a theft under the following conditions:

- He took some bread (act)
- Unauthorizedly [not, say, as a delivery man] (act-characterizing circumstance)
- In order to avoid paying for it (motivating rationale)

The act in and of itself is morally neutral; its moral status emerges only as its circumstances (duly construed)[11] and its rationale be-come known. Thus if an agent lied in that he

- Answered a question falsely
- Knowingly and deliberately
- With deceitful intent

he lied and deserves condemnation. And since it is (or should be) clear that this action modality cannot be universalized, the act in question becomes morally impermissible.

One aspect of Kant's focus upon complex action modalities rather than mere actions as such warrants note. It is repeatedly represented as a shortcoming of Kant's approach to ethics that while emphasizing intention and motivation he is insufficiently alive to the issue of the effort with which these intentions are pursued. But of course the manner of acting should enter into an act description as well: it is one thing to pursue a certain end with a degree of effort appropriate to the circumstances and something quite different to be lackadaisical about it. The shift from acts to action modalities provides Kant with the means for taking account not only of what the agent does, but how he goes about it.

The matters at issue with this idea that the moral status of acts is subject to their full characterization need closer examination.

5. UNIVERSALIZATION AND THE PRIMACY OF REASONS

On Kantian principles, moral universalizability requires that the individuals at issue must be similarly situated with respect to the act-determinative circumstances, since that which is permitted (prohibited, obligatory) for a duly circumstanced individual is then – at most and at best – also permitted (obligatory, etc.) for anyone else in the same circumstances. Thus if X, a ticket holder, is allowed to enter into the fairgrounds, then it is acceptable that [not everyone, but rather] all the other ticket holders should also enter. And if killing someone is to be permitted to Mr. Death, acting in the line of his duty as an executioner, then doing so will also be permitted to any other agent who is also in this situation.

The circumstances of an obligatory action can encompass both duty-activating circumstances (e.g., I promise to lend you the money when you shall ask for it) and duty-impeding circumstances (e.g., an unforeseeable market crash makes it impossible for me to raise the money needed to keep my promise to you). Moreover, duty-impending circumstances themselves can be of different kinds, since when I fail to do my duty (to honor my obligations) because the contextual circumstances prevent me, two sorts of circumstances can come into it, namely,

- The uncontrollable, those which lie outside the range of what I can manage and can foresee. (I have scraped together the money for repaying my debt and am robbed en route to doing it.) My inability to repay is due to "circumstances beyond my control."
- The controllable, those which fall within the range of what I can manage and/or foresee. (I fail to repay the debt because it is inconvenient for me. I spend the money needed to settle the debt on some form of self-indulgence. My inability to repay is self-engendered by drink.)

The former sort of duty-impeding circumstances are mitigating and in some way exculpatory, the latter are aggravating and reprehensible.

Kant has nothing against duty-activating circumstances as such; for him, they are an inevitable part of the moral picture. And as regards duty-impeding circumstances, he already has the machinery needed to deal with them via his emphasis on the primacy of intention. Only the uncontrollably duty-impeding circumstances create further problems for him. But here Kant's position is that they should be sidelined. For he refuses to allow exculpating circumstances to be brought into it wherever matters of moral theory are at issue. That sort of thing is a topic for casuistry, not for systematic moral theory. As far as Kant is concerned, only applied ethics – casuistry – can take cognizance of the issues of damage containment that arise when a "stepmotherly nature" confronts us with conflicts of duty or similar perplexities.[12]

Kant's strategy of universalization accordingly works itself out in a special sort of way. He is prepared to conditionalize in the interest of universality, yet not with respect to the uncontrollably contingent circumstances that he sees as morally irrelevant. His focus accordingly is on the internal motivation encompassed in the agent's rationale (or – in Kant's terminology – the "subjective ground" for acting). As far as Kant is concerned, it is the complex composite of act–circumstance–rationale – the "action modality," as we have called it here – that is the proper unit of moral appraisal. For him, the action at issue in moral evaluation is not

"Giving this sum of $100 to the plumber Smith as per the agreement made with him two days ago" but rather "Paying a workman the agreed amount in order to honor one's agreement with him." And so Kant in effect rejects the idea of morally evaluating single particular concrete actions independently of context. For him the unit of moral appraisal is the overall modality of act–circumstance together with the rationale which motivates acting on the particular occasion at hand. And he deems this focus on action modalities as necessary because for him a heavy burden of moral evaluation is borne by the rationale.

Suppose that someone (X) kills his fellow townsman (Y) – say, by beheading. In a Kantian context, the morally appraisable action is not the particular act plus circumstance ("causing the death of a tailor called Jones by beheading him with an ax"). It is at once something less ("killing someone") and something more ("killing a legally condemned person while acting in the line of duty as an executioner"). And above all, the operative rationale – the factor which Kant calls "the subjective ground of the action" – comes into it in a critical way. For the moral nexus lies in that act's being conditionalized to a rationale, a ground, a reason or motive for doing the act: "out of rage," or "for vengeance," or "to facilitate a robbery," or "in the line of one's lawful duties as executioner."

This line of approach reflects the fact that a given sort of action – such as killing someone – can figure in an endless variety of action modalities: killing someone out of rage, in line of military duty, by accident while hunting, etc. For, to reemphasize, with Kant the proper objects of moral appraisal are not bare acts (such as killing) at all, but rather generic action modalities. Thus taking one's own life because living has become tiresome or troublesome is one sort of thing, but doing so to avert the prospect of betraying one's country under torture would be something quite different. On Kantian principles, motivation is a critical factor in determining the ethical status of actions, and the morally contingent nature of acts contrasts critically with the morally determinate nature of the overall complexes that constitute action modalities.

As Kant saw it, until we know "the reason why" – the rationale of an act – we are simply unable to say whether it is permitted, obligatory, and so on – exactly because we really do not know (or know only very incompletely) just what it is that the agent actually did in the morally critical mode that incorporates the "subjective ground" of acting.

When matters are understood in this way, the Kantian universalization of permission takes the form of the following amplified construction of (U):

(U) $(\exists x)\text{perm}(x \text{ does } A{:}C{:}R) \leftrightarrow \text{ACCEPT}(\forall x)(x \text{ does } A{:}C{:}R)$

And spelling this out still more fully we obtain the reformulation

$$(\exists x)\text{perm}(x \text{ does } A{:}C{:}R) \leftrightarrow \text{ACCEPT}(\forall x)$$
$$(C \text{ obtains} \rightarrow x \text{ does } A \text{ for } R)$$

To reemphasize: with Kant, the governing idea is that if a certain way of acting – a certain action modality – is permissible for (or impermissible to or obligatory upon) someone, then not only is it similarly so for anyone, but it is morally acceptable for everyone to do so.[13]

Consider, for example, the action

- Prescribing a situationally indicated medicine in the endeavor to cure someone

This, clearly, is not permitted to everyone (e.g., not to nonphysicians). But that fact does not counterinstance universality because the act specification needs to be expanded into a full-scale act modality that encompasses A plus C plus R overall. And, by contrast, the full-scale action modality

- Prescribing situationally indicated medications in the course of providing authorized medical services

is indeed incumbent on everyone. (Even of the nonphysician it holds that if he were a physician then this is what he would have to do.) As such examples indicate, Kantian ethics has it that moral status appertains not to bare acts, but to motivation-coordinate ways of acting in appropriate circumstances – that is, to full-scale modalities of action. And it is on this basis of a complex conditionalization that moral status comes to be universalizable.[14]

The pivotal role of the rationale of an action (its motive or "subjective ground") in Kant's ethics reflects (1) his insistence on the centrality of good will as a motive of actions; (2) his insistence that "good works" are morally creditable only if they issue from a morally worthy motive, such as a disinterested concern for the welfare of others, and not from "inclination"; (3) the paramount impact of acting from a recognition that so doing is the morally right thing to do – that is, acting in an acknowledgment of duty; and (4) that the crux of moral merit lies in the demands of "a will which of itself conforms to right reason" (*Grundlegung*, p. 415, Akad.) or "the will of a rational being as such" (ibid., p. 426).

Onora O'Neill has objected to Kant's Categorical Imperative that "It seems easy enough to formulate *some* principle of action for any act . . . which can meet the criterion of any universality test, whatever the act. Notoriously some Nazi war criminals claimed that they were only 'doing their jobs' or only 'obeying orders' – which are, after all, not apparently morally unworthy activities."[15] But this objection is not fair to Kant. For him, it is not the bare act as such, but the action modality, the act in its full-fledged conditionalization, that is the focus of moral appraisal: not "imprisoning someone in performance of duty" or "killing someone under orders," but "imprisoning someone illegally simply to obey orders, no questions asked" or "killing someone out of racial hatred." And motivation in its full explicitness becomes decisive here. To judge that Nazi bully's action on Kantian universalization principles we must look beyond the act to the motive as well – and then things clearly do not look favorable.

His emphasis upon the rationales of action also explains why Kant dismisses moral dilemmas and refuses to worry about them. Such dilemmas arise when the concrete circumstances render it impossible to discharge all one's obligations. In honoring obligation no. 1 one is circumstantially constrained to violate obligation no. 2. You cannot give your clients the time you must now dedicate to your ailing child. Particular circumstances can create conflicts with particular obligation actions. You owe $5.00 to X and $5.00 to Y. But you only have $5.00 in all, because your other funds were stolen. So doing the right thing by X means, in these contingently agent-impeding circumstances, dishonoring your obligation to Y (and conversely). There is a pull in different directions.

But with full-fledged action modalities the problem evaporates.

No moral stain attaches to "failure to honor an obligation by act-ing so as to minimize the damage that must be done when uncon-trollable circumstances create an incapacity." And all is well if you give $2.50 to each creditor (on the rationality principle of "Treat like cases alike!") with the full intention of doing the best that can be done to honor your obligation in the circumstances that an un-cooperative fate has brought to pass. In this sort of indirect way – that is, through their entry into the rationales of action – Kant is indeed willing and able to take an agent's circumstances into account. Since with Kant the burden of moral evaluation is borne by the rationale, it is here – through the role it plays in relation to the operative rationale – that circumstantiality can and must come into it insofar as it has a valid role in moral appraisal.

6. THE ROLE OF MAXIMS

Kant's emphasis on the rationale of action led him to move in a somewhat idiosyncratic direction and to shift from the moral ac-ceptability of acts as such to the viability of the maxims (or pre-cepts) that characterize modalities of action. A Kantian maxim is closely bound up with what we have called the "modality" of action. It involves three component elements: an act or action type, a rationale (reason, motive, ground) for performing the ac-tion, and an injunction or instruction that this is to be done as a general rule in appropriate circumstances. It is a procedural law (rule) of practice – that is, action – which also incorporates the rationale ("subjective ground") of the action. A maxim thus takes the form of the inherently general instruction "Under conditions C, do A subject to the rationale $R!$" where A represents a suitably construed way of acting, C its morally relevant conditions, and R a justifactory rationale for its performance, that is, a specific mo-tive or reason for it. But the heart and core of a Kantian maxim is the motivational "subjective principle of volition" that it incorpo-rates (*Grundlegung*, p. 400n, Akad.).

At this point, generalization comes upon the scene. A maxim (M) is universalizable if its being followed in general – by everyone – is a morally appropriate state of affairs. Since maxims take the form "Do $A:C$ subject to the rationale R," such universalizability comes down to the moral acceptability of $(\forall x)(C \rightarrow\_x$ does A subject to $R)$. And when this is so, maxims represent "moral laws." Accordingly, maxims are then only moral laws when they are "objective" in the sense of being valid for every rational being (*CPrR*, p. 19, Akad.).

Let us consider the situation somewhat more formally. Maxims are characterized as "universalizable" if the state of affairs of their being universally honored – actually always being followed – is acceptable:

$$\text{UNIV}(M) \leftrightarrow \text{ACCEPT}(\forall x)(x \text{ does what } M \text{ stipulates})$$

Since a maxim takes the form "Do $A{:}C{:}R!$" this Maxim Universalization Principle can be reformulated as what is, in effect, a definition of maxim universalizability (U-MAX):

$$(\text{U-Max}) \quad \text{UNIV}(\text{do } A{:}C{:}R!) \leftrightarrow \text{ACCEPT}(\forall x)(x \text{ does } A{:}C{:}R)$$

And this can be spelled out more fully as

$$\text{UNIV}(\text{do } A{:}C{:}R!) \leftrightarrow \text{ACCEPT}(\forall x)(C \text{ obtains} \rightarrow x \text{ does } A \text{ subject to } R)$$

Accordingly, as Kant sees it, maxim universalizability comes down to the acceptability of a rule-correlative generalization. For example, the maxim "Keep your promises as a matter of honesty!" is universalizable because everyone's keeping their word and honoring their promises (in suitable circumstances) is an acceptable (and indeed desirable) state of affairs.[16] By contrast, consider the maxim "For reasons of sheer personal convenience, refrain from troubling yourself to work to develop your talents and abilities." Here generalization would issue in a world of incompetent sloths – a condition of things that is clearly unacceptable to rational people on grounds of social negativity.

However, maxims, so understood, enjoin not just acts, but action modalities: acts subject to specified circumstances and rationales. And this is crucial to their universality. Consider a legal analogy. The law requires that attorneys act in their clients' best interest or that doctors exercise due care for the well-being of their patients. The relevant laws *hold* for everyone, but of course *apply* only to some (viz. attorneys or doctors). The injunctions at issue are universal – "When functioning as an attorney (or a doctor), then . . . " – although the universal principles at issue only come into occasional and limited operation. It is in just this manner that the maxims of morality are universal while nevertheless their bearing may be rangewise limited to doctors, lawyers, spouses, or kings. No one is exempt from the principle that when functioning as a physician one should honor the Hippocratic oath for reasons of professional integrity; it is just that the principle comes into play only with doctors. It operatively applies only to some but holds good for everyone.

To be sure, actually specifying the maxim at issue in the concrete case of a particular person's particular performance of a certain act could prove to be somewhere between difficult and impossible. In actual practice we may never really know the rationale (the "subjective ground") of a concrete action – indeed, not even one of our own. The capacity to see accurately into the heads and minds of people – ourselves included – to discern their actuating motives is somewhere between limited and unavailable. In actual practice, we may well never really be able correctly to determine what led someone to act as he did. But this practical difficulty does not stand in the way of developing a systematic theory of morals.

7. THE CATEGORICAL IMPERATIVE

Kant's various statements of the Categorical Imperative (CI) are given in Display 1. Here we must construe "act" as: You must so act, it is obligatory.

Henceforward boldface letters will here be used to indicate that the "actions" at issue are full-fledged Kantian *A:C:R*–style action modalities that are accordingly rationale encompassing (i.e., are of the type ""killing an enemy for vengeance" or "repaying a debtee to honor an agreement" rather than an unqualified "killing" or "repaying"). On this basis, maxim universalizability is a necessary and sufficient condition of moral permittedness: permitted acts are exactly those which are suitably maxim universalizable:

$$\sim\text{univ}(\text{do } \mathbf{A}!) \leftrightarrow \sim\text{perm (doing } \mathbf{A})$$

Display 1. *Formulas for the Categorical Imperative (CI)*

CI-1 Law-Willing Formula:
"Act only on the maxim through which you can concurrently will that it should become a universal law." (*Grundlegung*, p. 421, Akad.; cf. pp. 402 and 426)

CI-2 Law-Transmuting Formula:
"Act on the maxim which could thereby become a universal law." (Ibid., pp. 436–37)

CI-3 Universal Legislation Formula:
"So act that your will can regard itself as concurrently legislating universally." (Ibid., p. 434)

CI-4 Universal Law of Nature Formula:
"Act as if the maxim of your action were to become through your will a universal law of nature." (Ibid., p. 421; cf. p. 437)

CI-5 Kingdom of Ends Formula:
"So act as if you were always through your maxim a legislator [i.e., law-maker] in a universal kingdom of ends." (Ibid., p. 438)

CI-6 End-in-Itself Formula:
"So act as to use humanity, both in your own person and in the person of every other, always and at the same time as an end, and never simply as a means." (Ibid., p. 429)

We accordingly have

$$\text{(CI)} \qquad \text{perm(doing } \mathbf{A}) \leftrightarrow \textsc{univ}(\text{do } \mathbf{A}!),$$

recalling that throughout

$$\textsc{univ}(\text{do } \mathbf{A}!) \leftrightarrow \textsc{accept}(\forall x)(x \text{ does } \mathbf{A}).$$

The burden of Kant's Categorical Imperative is thus that maxim universalization is the touchstone of permittedness.

To illustrate the workings of the Categorical Imperative, Kant instances four impermissible action types:

- Committing suicide
- Promising falsely
- Neglecting one's talents
- Being indifferent to the interests of others

It is clear that in each case universalizing the act would indeed produce an anomalous result, as follows:

- Depopulation
- Demise of promising as a practice

- An unproductive society
- A boorish society

None of these represents a state of affairs that a rational person would or could see as desirable. In all of these cases we can therefore deploy the Categorical Imperative so as to establish the impermissibility of the acts in question on grounds of the nonuniversalizability of the corresponding maxim. Exactly the same uniform strategy of argumentation is operative throughout such examples. In each case it is argued that unacceptability of universalizing a certain mode of action indicates its impermissibility.

A different way of looking at the matter is available by substituting not-**A** for **A** in the preceding formula. We then have

$$\sim\text{univ(omit }\mathbf{A}!) \leftrightarrow \sim\text{perm(doing not-}\mathbf{A})$$

or equivalently

$$\text{(O)} \quad \sim\text{univ(omit }\mathbf{A}!) \leftrightarrow \text{oblig(doing }\mathbf{A})$$

This is simply an equivalent reformulation of the Categorical Imperative.

8. DEMONSTRATION OF THE CATEGORICAL IMPERATIVE

In a Kantian perspective, the Categorical Imperative emerges as a straightforward consequence of first principles. This is readily demonstrable as follows:

Proof:
    (1) perm(doing **A**) $\leftrightarrow$ ($\forall x$)perm(x does **A**)   by (G/perm)
    (2) ($\forall x$)perm(x does **A**) $\leftrightarrow$ ACCEPT($\forall x$)(x does **A**)   by (C*)
    (3) ACCEPT($\forall x$)x does **A** $\leftrightarrow$ UNIV(do **A**!)   by (U-max)
    (4) perm(doing **A**) $\leftrightarrow$ UNIV(do **A**!)   from (1)–(3), Q.E.D.

Kant's Categorical Imperative is, in effect, a straightforward consequence of a commitment to certain basic principles of deontic reasoning that underlie his position in ethical theory.

At this point we do, however, have something of a paradox. For Kant is very explicit in characterizing the Categorical Imperative as the highest or supreme principle of morality, the "oberstes Prinzip der Moralität." How, then, is one to reconcile this with our present approach which sees such generalization principles as (G/perm) as still more fundamental?

The sensible response here will (as is usual in philosophy) proceed via a distinction. For it is inappropriate to distinguish between priority and fundamentality in the order of grounding or substantiation on the one hand and in the order of importance for operative utilization on the other. On Kantian principles, the Categorical Imperative can and indeed will be the supreme principle of procedure in moral evaluation, even though there is reason to think that in the context of moral systematization other principles may play a more fundamental role.

9. KANT AS A QUASI DEONTOLOGIST

Kant is generally seen as the very model of a deontologist. And this makes perfectly good sense, since for him a benign action is always morally meritorious when done from a sense of duty. But it deserves note that the preceding considerations actually represent Kant as also a consequentialist, seeing that for him duties themselves follow from the contemplation of consequences. For on Kant's approach obligation obtains when the result of universalizing an omission is unacceptable.

(1) $\text{oblig(doing } \mathbf{A}) \leftrightarrow \sim\text{UNIV(omit } \mathbf{A}!)$ by (G/oblig)

(2) $\sim\text{UNIV(omit } \mathbf{A}!) \leftrightarrow \sim\text{ACCEPT}(\forall x)x \text{ omits } \mathbf{A}$ by (U-max)

(3) $\text{oblig(doing } \mathbf{A}) \leftrightarrow \sim\text{ACCEPT}(\forall x)x \text{ omits } \mathbf{A}$ from (1)–(2)

This result clearly makes Kant into a consequentialist of sorts, seeing that for him the questions "What would happen on universalizing an omission? Would this yield something acceptable or not?" become pivotal for the assessment of moral obligation. With Kant, the issue of individual permissions and obligations comes down to the acceptability of certain general modes of comportment – that is, to the question of the acceptability of what would happen if everyone conformed to the maxims at issue. Accordingly, Kant's moral theory takes the form of a hypothetical consequentialism by pivoting the moral status of actions (i.e., of action

modalities) upon the question of whether the result of rule generalizing this way of acting would be acceptable or not. The issue here
is thus not one of deontology versus consequentialism, because
Kant's deontology is itself axiologically consequentialistic.

10. IDEAL- VS. REAL-WORLD MORALITY:
CASUISTRY VS. "SCIENTIFIC" MORAL THEORY

To be sure, Kant's way of articulating his ethical theory is not without its complications and difficulties. In particular, the problem
with the Combination Principle

$$(C) \qquad [\text{perm}(X \text{ does } \mathbf{A}) \text{ \& perm } (Y \text{ does } \mathbf{B})] \rightarrow$$
$$\text{ACCEPT}(X \text{ does } \mathbf{A} \text{ \& } Y \text{ does } \mathbf{B})$$

is that the conjunctivity it claims is to all surface appearances quite
unrealistic. For while it may be permissible for X to administer a
certain dose of a lifesaving drug to Z, and also for Y to do so, problems of overdosage may arise when they both do so.

Kant, however, simply abstracts from complications of this sort.
For his focus is on compatibility with an ideal moral order. And
the characteristic feature of such an order is that this sort of thing
just could not happen. Here, where things go as they ideally should,
such conflicts of permitted action choices – or even more importantly conflicts of obligation, such as my owing X five dollars
and owing Y five dollars in circumstances where I have only this
insufficient amount at my disposal – simply would not and could
not arise. In a Kantian ideal moral order it is not just the agents
who do the right thing, but here nature itself proves cooperative
as well.

Take the case of the well-intentioned lie to safeguard the potential victim of an enraged pursuer, a case which greatly interested
Kant.[17] Clearly what we have here is a conflict of situationally
discordant general obligations: to treat one's fellows honestly on
the one hand, and to safeguard them from foreseeable harm on the
other. A straightforward "conflict of obligation" ensues here with
safeguarding human life clashing with telling the truth. Here Kant
is emphatic that there is no such thing as a "right to lie." However,
the casuistical operation of an adequate excuse for lying certainly

does not conflict with this: it does not establish a right to lie, but only indicates that doing so may be excusable in certain circumstances. On such a reading, lying is not permissible (*erlaubt, gestattet*) but may nevertheless in some real-world circumstances be freed from moral culpability (*ent-schuldigt*). For in the circumstances of the case there is (*ex hypothesi*) no way to honor the overall demands of morality characteristic of an ideal order. After theoretical morality has said what it can, a "stepmotherly nature" leaves us in difficulty. The situation is one of damage control, of minimizing the contextually unavoidable wrong – of casuistry, in short. It may well be that the circumstantially acceptable (and perhaps even optimal!) thing to do – the best available resolution of a nasty situation – is to "tell a fib."[18] But being the best of a bad assortment does not make it the right thing to do, let alone establish a right to lie. Lying is not – ever – a morally good or right thing to do; but that does not mean that it is never appropriate under any circumstances.

The characteristic feature of Kantian ethics is that we must look to the ideal moral order when issues of moral theory rather than casuistry stand before us. As he sees it, the moral theoretician's prime concern is not with this rude and imperfect real-world domain of empirical existence. Because it seeks the realization of generality requisite for a "science," Kant's theory is an ideal-order morality that deals not with the reality's intractable machinations, but with a perfected order visible to the mind's eye alone.

It is concern for an aprioristic ideal-order morality that provides Kant with the requisite validation for his abstractly innocent-looking but actually portentous recourse to generalization and universalization. As he sees it, to develop an ethical theory on scientific principles we are forced to idealize. Just as physics needs its perfectly elastic bodies and chemistry its perfectly pure substances, so too does moral science require its idealizations.[19] As Kant sees is, moral theory is concerned with a priori principles, and not with their imperfect experientially a posteriori implementation amidst the empirical realities of a difficult world where we find ourselves at the mercy of a novercal nature. The damage control that must be accomplished amidst the imperfect conditions of the uncooperative world of our actual experience (the empirical order) is a matter of casuistry – something that lies outside the agenda of the moral theoretician. But such disability is a two-way street. Theorizing itself is insufficient to settle matters of the application; for this we need judgment as well, and no amount of theorizing can (or should be expected to) substitute for this.

To be sure, ethics is a practical science: it must be capable of application. But, here as elsewhere, the process of application is not part of the science itself: it becomes a matter for "good judgment" rather than "right reason." (Science delimits but does not determine its application.) For Kant, ethical theory, like physical theory, demands idealization, while casuistry, like mere engineering, deals with the inherent difficulties of a relativist empirical order. It is not that Kant is uninterested in casuistry. (His frequent forays into the field in the *Metaphysic of Morals* would clearly contradict this.) It is just that a field of deliberation very different from that of theoretical ethics is at issue here.

As Kant sees it, even as physics as a theoretical science is constrained to deal not with the real world's concrete complexities but with idealized abstractions (perfectly elastic bodies, ideal gasses, etc.), so ethics as a theoretical science is constrained to accept some degree of abstraction. It cannot grapple with the totality of real-world complexities. Moral theory abstracts and idealizes.[20] A preoccupation with the contingent concreta that define an art as contrasted with a science – technological engineering in the one case and casuistry (ethical engineering) in the other – is something else again. And so, for Kant, the requirements and ramifications of theory force the level of discussion to rise to another plane of consideration, a plane where idealization becomes a crucial factor. For him, such abstractive idealization is, in effect, an unavoidable aspect of the logic of the situation, since it alone permits the development of a systematic ethic based on scientific principles.

Some writers accuse Kant of a rigorism that is the moral equivalent of "Fiat iustitia ruat caelum." But this is gravely mistaken. What Kant does in ethics (even as in epistemology!) is to employ a two-domain approach that separates a rigoristic theory from a more flexible praxis oriented towards the real ("empirical") world.

The demands of the former are indeed rigoristic, but this rigorism cannot reasonably be extended into the practical realm of action, decision, and advice.[21]

To put it more graphically, Kant envisions a dualistic ethic. Even as man holds dual citizenship in the noumenal order projected by reason and the phenomenal order of our empirical experience, so there is a dualized ethic combining a noumenal-order morality with the casuistry attuned to the imperfect conditions of the real world of our phenomenal experience. The former, idealized domain admits of a scientific morality based on universal principles – and here alone a moral theory is possible. But in matters of application to the imperfect realm of our actual real-world experience we must make do with the compromises that are unavoidably involved in casuistry's dealings with the recalcitrant realities of the phenomenal realm.

11. BROADER IMPLICATIONS: ABSOLUTISM

Critics and opponents of Kantian ethics both rightly stress but wrongly interpret the fact that the inherent diversity of cases precludes generalizing the moral status of actions in the manner of $(\forall x)\text{perm}(x \text{ does } A)$ or $(\forall x)\text{oblig}(x \text{ does } A)$. But this sort of complaint drastically misconstrues the situation, because Kant's ethics does not deal with bare acts (as per A) but with action modalities (as per $A{:}C{:}R$), where those act-conditionalizing indications play an indispensable role. For what is pivotal from a Kantian point of view is that no matter how meritorious a type of action A may seem, the moral merit of its performance can always become unraveled if the motivation of its performance is something inherently inappropriate, such as: "wholly from selfish reasons," or "only to please a friend." Or again, no matter how heinous an action may be in the abstract, the onus of its performance can be overcome by a rationale on the order of: "inadvertently, " or "under duress," and perhaps even "to avert some otherwise unavailable horror." It is just exactly the incorporation of motives within action modalities that makes absoluteness possible with Kant, enabling him to condemn in an absolute, unqualified, and universal way such actions as

- Killing someone out of envy
- Taking advantage of people
- Inflicting pointless harm on others
- Violating a trust for personal gain
- Breaking a promise out of sheer perversity

Such ways of acting are simply wrong always, anywhere, and for anyone. But here it is the shift from acts to motive-incorporating modalities of action that is crucial.

This absoluteness enables a Kantian ethic to avert the impetus to cultural relativity inherent in the fact that different societies operate with different moral ground rules at the concretely procedural level. Agreed: some societies deem it outrageous for women to expose their faces, their breasts, their knees; others view this as altogether acceptable and perhaps even mandatory. But behind this variation stands a universal principle: "Do not wantonly violate the established rules of proper modesty, but respect people's sensibilities about proper appearance." This overarching rule is universal and absolute, although its implementation with respect to, say, elbows or belly buttons is of course something that varies with the customs and practices of the community. To be sure, the rule itself is abstract and schematic – in need of implementing criteria as to what "proper modesty and due decorum" demand in different sorts of conditions and circumstances. The matter is one of a universal principle with variable implementations subject to "locally established standards and criteria" that are grounded in the customs of the community. But as Kant sees it, whenever the issue of actual moral propriety enters in, there will – and must – stand in the background a rule (or maxim) of universal applicability and unrestricted validity with respect to the modality of action. For Kant, morality as such must address the a priori universalities of proper action and has no dependency on mere matters of person-variable ends: What he seeks is "a pure moral philosophy which is completely freed from everything which may be only empirical and thus belong to anthropology" (*Grundlegung*, p. 389, Akad.).

It is this sort of consideration that underwrites the plausibility of Kantian absolutism. For while the concrete strictures of morality – its specific ordinances and procedural rules of thumb –

will of course differ from age to age and culture to culture, nevertheless the deeper principles that ultimately define the project of "morality" as such are universal. The uniform governing conception of "what morality *is*" underpins the more concrete determination of "what morality *asks*" and suffices both to establish and to standardize those ultimate principles that govern the moral enterprise as such. Such actions as those represented by the examples of "killing someone out of envy" or "violating a trust for personal gain" are morally wrong not just for contemporary Americans, but for anyone anywhere. The variability of moral codes in point of concrete rulings thus stands in contrast to the uniform universality of moral principles and values.

There is, in consequence, a fundamental difference between morality and morals, a difference which relativism simply ignores in its tendency to identify the two. Relativism proclaims: "They have *their* moral convictions (rules, standards, values), and we have *ours*. One is every bit as good as the other. To each his own. Nobody is in a position to criticize or condemn the moral views of others." But from the vantage point of Kantian principles to take this line in moral matters would in fact be to abandon the very idea of morality. To be sure, mere custom is something else again. Variability does indeed obtain with respect to mere mores – we eat with cutlery, they with chopsticks; we sleep on beds, they in hammocks; we speak one language, they another – each with equal propriety. But this indifference does not hold for morals, for matters of moral principle, where universality does and must obtain. It is nonsense to say: "We treat the handicapped humanely; they drown them at sea to spare themselves the inconvenience of special accommodation. It's all just a matter of local custom." This sort of thing is just not viable from the moral standpoint! If crass selfishness, pointless maltreatment, wanton deceit, or the infliction of needless pain is wrong for us – as indeed it is – then it is wrong for them too; and conversely. And just this is the fundamental insight that plausibilizes a Kantian ethic with its emphasis on an absolutistic universality which has it that, at the level of fundamentals, matters of moral principle are the same universally and for everyone.

So here stands the characteristic – and ultimately right-minded insight of Kantian ethics: that when it is indeed *morals* rather than *mores* that is in view, then the issue has to be seen as one that is universal and absolute – that in this domain of morality proper what is appropriate for one must be so for all. At the level of deeper principles there is indeed a strict equality before the moral law in exactly the manner envisioned at the start of our discussion.

12. CONCLUDING OBSERVATIONS

The upshot of these deliberations is that Kant's commitment to certain characteristic principles of deontic logic, as it were, under-lies and explains many of the characteristic and controversial features that are definitive of the Kantian ethic, in particular:

- The commitment to rigid universality reflected in the Categori-cal Imperative
- The shift from concrete acts to action modalities as the units of ethical evaluation, with its consequent prioritizing of the ra-tionale ("subjective ground") of action
- The ethical focus on maxims of action
- The dismissal from moral theory of moral conflicts and dilem-mas and their consignment to the applied domain of casuistry
- The insistence on the ethical centrality not of the concrete cir-cumstances of action in the actual world, but rather in a circum-stance-abstractive ideal-order, with its correlative concern for developing an ideal state morality, relegating ethical damage control to the backwater of casuistry.

Above all, it is his insistence upon certain deontic principles that constrains Kant to shift the focus of ethical concern from real-world concreta to a transcendental (reality-detached) ideal domain where the contingent complexities that make for default excuses and for conflicts of duty simply do not arise. Kant's con-cern for the systematic, scientific level of general principles here comes to the fore once again.

And beyond this there looms a larger issue. People nowadays are reluctant to speak of the existence of significant truths in moral theory. And for this reason they are unwilling, indeed unable, to credit Kant with being a prime exponent, if not discoverer, of some of them. But if matters stood otherwise, then the following, at least, would count as plausible candidates:

- That morality roots in rationality
- That motivating rationales are paramount in moral evaluation
- That, since rationality is universal, the justifactory validation of moral appraisals must ultimately make an appeal to universal principles, so that morals are something very different from mores
- That teleology is pivotal for morality, since morality is itself a fundamentally purposive enterprise
- That a proper understanding of moral issues calls for a two-tier approach that embraces both a sector of abstract general theory developed at the level of ideals and a sector of casuistry at the level of concrete-particular rulings.

APPENDIX. ON THE COMPLEXITY OF KANT'S MORAL THEORY

Kant is seen as the father and mainstay of deontological ethics. And no wonder, when he produces passages as uncharacteristically lyrical for him as the oft-cited paeon to duty in the *Critique of Practical Reason*:

> Duty! Thou sublime and mighty name that dost embrace nothing charming or insinuating but requirest submission . . . : what origin is there worthy of thee, and where is to be found the root of thy noble descent which proudly rejects all kinship with the inclinations and from which to be descended is the indispensable condition of the only worth which men can give themselves? It cannot be less than something which elevates man above himself as part of the world of sense, something which connects him with an order of things which only the understanding can think and which has under it the entire world of sense, including the empirically determinable existence of man in time, and the whole system of all ends which is alone suitable to such unconditional practical laws as the moral. It is nothing else than personhood, i.e., the freedom and independence from the mechanism of nature regarded as a capacity of a being which is subject to special laws (pure practical laws given by its own reason), so that the person as belonging to the world of sense is subject to his own personhood as also belonging to the intelligible world. For it is then not to be wondered at that man, as belonging to two worlds, must regard his own being in

relation to his second and higher vocation with reverence and the laws of this vocation with the deepest respect. (*CPrR*, pp. 56–57, Akad.)

Accordingly, Kant is often seen as the prime exponent of an ethic based on duty, and duty alone. And this is well enough, as far as it goes. But it does not go deep enough. For behind Kant's dedication to deontology and duty there are deeper strata of thought that move in a rather different direction – namely, that of an ethic which is not merely deontological, but both axiological and quasi-utilitarian.

The dialectic of thought that is at issue here can be portrayed in the following question–answer sequence.

Q: How should I act?
A: You should – and indeed from the moral standpoint must – do your duty.
Q: But what is my duty?
A: It is your duty to maximize a certain ultimately self-regarding value – namely, your desert for happiness, through obedience to the moral law. [Note that this gives Kant's ethic an axiological cast. Moreover, it means that for Kant one's duty to others is ultimately grounded in a duty to oneself – namely one's obligation to realize one's full potential as a rational free agent.]
Q: But what must I do to deserve happiness?
A: You must act according to the "Categorical Imperative" – that is, according to an injunction to act as any rational person would in your circumstances, so that your action would be universal in an ideal moral order. [Note that at this point Kant's ethic in effect becomes an ideal-order consequentialism.]

As this dialectic indicates, Kant's moral theory encompasses overall three sequential and successively deeper stages: deontology, moral axiology, moral egoism (of a particularly enlightened sort), and hypothetical-generality consequentialism.

To fail to stress this extensive complexity of Kant's ethical thought and to class him as a deontologist pure and simple is to fail to appreciate both the subtlety and the internal richness of his position in ethical theory as an ideal-order consequentialist.

Kant himself put the matter as follows:

In an intelligible world, that is, in the moral world, in the concept of which we leave out of account all the hindrances to morality (the desires), such a system, in which happiness is bound up with and proportioned to morality, can be conceived as necessary, inasmuch as freedom, partly inspired and partly restricted by moral laws, would itself be the cause of general happiness, since rational beings, under the guidance of such principles, would themselves be the authors both of their own enduring well-being and of that of others. But such a system of self-rewarding morality is only an idea, the carrying out of which rests on the condition that *everyone* does what he ought, that is, that all the actions of rational beings take place just as if they had proceeded from a supreme will that comprehends in itself, or under itself, all private wills. [This condition is feasible] only through the necessary connection of the hope of happiness with the necessary endeavor to render the self worthy of happiness. (*CPuR*, A809–10 = B837–38)

Let us consider each of these stages in sequence:

1. *Deontology.* This is the most straightforward and least debatable aspect of Kantian morality. It emerges with striking clarity from the innumerable passages along the lines of the particularly striking specimen that I have just cited.
2. *Self-regard.* As Kant sees it, it is not the pursuit of happiness that matters for ethics, but the cultivation of one's desert for happiness. De facto happiness in this world is a matter of contingency over which we have no control and which is consequently irrelevant to moral merit. What does lie in our control is the prospect of acting so as to make ourselves deserving of happiness.
3. *Axiology.* An axiological ethic is (by definition) one that pivots on the injunction: "Act so as to maximize value." And Kant's ethic is of exactly this form, where the pivotal value at issue is desert for happiness through a conformity to the moral law.
4. *Hypothetical-generality consequentialism.* What we have in Kant is not utilitarianism: "Evaluate the consequence of your action for people in general and maximize this." Rather, what we have is a hypothetical-generality consequentialism: "Evaluate (in terms of its approximation to an ideal order of things) the state of affairs that would ensue if the maxim (the action principle) of your action were to become a general rule of conduct." Would it form part of an ideal order of things for "everyone to do like-

228

wise"? Only if the motive force of an action (its moving principle) admitted of generalization on this basis would the act possess the sort of moral worth that would qualify the agent who performed it for that reason – that is, with the maxim in view – as meritorious in point of desert for happiness.

The overall lesson of these considerations is the need to recognize the inherent complexity of Kant's position. By the time one has finished spelling out what it is that his deontology – his "Do your duty" morality – requires of moral agents, one has to traverse a wide range of ethical positions and doctrines, with both enlightened hedonism and ideal-state consequentialism playing a prominent part. To see Kant as a deontologist pure and simple is to fail badly to do justice to his position in moral theory. To characterize Kant as a deontologist is not false, but misleadingly oversimple.

Chapter 9

On the Unity of Kant's
Categorical Imperative

1. PREFACE

Commentators have repeatedly been troubled by the fact that in the *Foundations of the Metaphysics of Morals (Grundlegung)* Kant appears to offer several quite different formulations of his Categorical Imperative. Although these Kantian formulas are clearly interconnected, they seem to assert rather different sorts of things. However, as I shall suggest, there is reason to believe (1) that a single fundamental principle is basically at issue; (2) that this single imperative is a principle of rationality in general, a principle that is by no means confined to the moral or practical sphere, but holds good for theoretical reasoning and evaluative judgment as well; and (3) that the variously formulated moral categorical imperatives are not really redundant reformulations or restatements of the same principle, but, rather, are different and distinct applications or implementations of one overarching principle of rationality. The present deliberations will accordingly bear witness from yet another point of view to the systematic unity and coherence of Kant's thought.

2. STAGE SETTING

In his classic study of Kant's Categorical Imperative, the Oxford philosopher H. J. Paton begins his chapter on the formulation of the principle with the following observation: "We might have ex-

This essay is a substantially revised version of a paper "On the Unity of Kant's Categorical Imperative" published in the *Acts of the Seventh International Kant Congress, Mainz, 1990* (Bonn: Bouvier, 1991), pp. 375–95. Reprinted by permission of Bouvier Verlag.

Display 1. *Formulas for the Categorical Imperative* (CI)

CI-1   Law-Willing Formula:
       "Act only on the maxim through which you can concurrently will
       that it should become a universal law." (*Grundlegung*, p. 421, Akad.;
       cf. pp. 402 and 426)
CI-2   Law-Transmuting Formula:
       "Act on the maxim which could thereby become a universal law."
       (Ibid., pp. 436–37)
CI-3   Universal Legislation Formula:
       "So act that your will can regard itself as concurrently legislating
       universally." (Ibid., p. 434)
CI-4   Universal Law of Nature Formula:
       "Act as if the maxim of your action were to become through your
       will a universal law of nature." (Ibid., p. 421; cf. p. 437)
CI-5   Kingdom of Ends Formula:
       "So act as if you were always through your maxim a legislator [i.e.,
       law-maker] in a universal kingdom of ends." (Ibid., p. 438)
CI-6   End-in-Itself Formula:
       "So act as to use humanity, both in your own person and in the per-
       son of every other, always and at the same time as an end, and never
       simply as a means." (Ibid., p. 429)

pected Kant to be content with one formulation of the categorical
imperative. Instead, he embarrasses us with no less than five different formulae."[1] Paton regards the Categorical Imperative as
having various different formulations (which Display 1 lists in a
manner somewhat different from his). Though Paton sees these
formulas as related in various ways, he firmly refuses to take any
one of them as basic. By contrast, however, the present discussion
argues that throughout all Kant's different formulas one single
fundamental and far-reaching principle is at issue. And it will endeavor to show that this fundamental principle extends beyond
the sphere of ethics into other, very different areas of deliberation,
specifically including the theory of scientific knowledge.

3. THE FOUNDATION OF THE CATEGORICAL IMPERATIVE

As a starting point it is useful to consider Kant's initial formulation of the Categorical Imperative (CI) in the *Foundations*:

(CI-1) Act only on that maxim through which you can concurrently will that it should become a universal law.

Plainly, this is not a specifically *moral* principle at all. It is clear on even casual inspection that something much more general is at issue than anything that we would nowadays so categorize: an unrestrictedly applicable principle of action, and not a somehow narrower principle that bears particularly and specifically on issues of actions in which the well-being or interests of persons is somehow engaged. CI-1 involves nothing that would be unsuitable if the actions at issue had to do with solving a mathematics problem or investigating the behavior of magnets. After all, the maxim that governs the action at issue need not be something like "Do not lie" or "Do not steal," but could be something like "Do not perform your calculations carelessly" or "Do not clutter your statements with needless verbiage." The more one reflects on this particular formula, the clearer the realization that a very general principle of rational comportment is at issue.

What CI-1 in effect affirms is actually a conjunction of two imperatives:

(i) Act on principles – that is, on the basis of maxims that represent general rules of acting.
(ii) Make sure that these principles on which you act are of universal applicability: that they are appropriate to guide the conduct of anyone else who has to proceed in relevantly similar circumstances, in short, that they have the endorsement of reason.

The fact is that the Kantian injunction "Act always and only on law-universalizable principles" simply comes down to "Act rationally" – that is, "Act as any truly rational person would act in the circumstances." This principle is one of practice, all right – an injunction to action of a certain sort. But its scope is totally and unrestrictedly general, applying to any sort of action whatsoever, be its character specifically moral or not. And its basis is one of rationality at large. (For Kant, the consideration that indicates an action to be morally appropriate also renders it, ipso facto, the rational thing to do: morality is simply a mode or component of practical rationality.)

Such a basic imperative of "Proceed rationally" is clearly designed to govern every phase of the agency of a rational being: the particular sphere of action – whether it be in moral or in cognitive or in evaluative contexts – clearly does not matter at all. Accordingly, Kant stressed that what is at issue with such an unrestricted Categorical Imperative is a fundamental law of reason:

> The consciousness of this fundamental law may be called a given of reason, since one cannot ferret it out from antecedent data of reason, such as the consciousness of freedom (for this is not given *a priori*), and since it forces itself upon us as a synthetic proposition *a priori* based on no pure or empirical intuition. It would be analytic if the freedom of the will were presupposed, but for this, as a positive concept, an intellectual intuition would be needed, and here we cannot assume it. (*CPrR*, p. 31, Akad.)

The situation is thus as follows. The imperative at issue is effectively analytic, since rational free agents must ipso facto so act that the maxims of their actions can be willed by them (i.e., by their fully rational agents) to become universal laws (of agency for all beings) – that is, that they would deem it for the best if everybody acted on the maxim in question. However, what stops the Categorical Imperative from being altogether abstract, a merely conceptual stricture with regards to rational beings, is that it is addressed not to rational agents as such, but to us ("*You* are to act in such a manner that . . . "). It is certainly not something given from the outset – an a priori fact – that we are free rational agents; this is something we ourselves merely presume (or assume or postulate). That the Categorical Imperative appertains to rational agents is an analytic truth; that it appertains to us is not.

At the basis of Kant's theory of morality there thus lies a principle of rational procedure – a fundamental imperative that is applicable in every sphere of rational agency: a Categorical Imperative of reason in general. The autonomy of a rational agent lies in maintaining consonance with one's nature as (*ex hypothesi*) a being of this kind. Specifically this means that if, or rather since, we do (and should) see ourselves as rational beings – as intelligent, rational, free agents – we ought to act conformably with this circumstance.

The imperative at issue does not however, read: "Act as is fitting for the sort of being that you are" without tacitly adding "that you are by nature." For what "are" you? Well – you might be a lawyer or a thief. Neither is categorically incumbent on you. "Act as is fitting for a lawyer " is an imperative of merely restricted validity, conditional on your having become a lawyer. "Act as a thief would act" is not an appropriate imperative at all. The idea is not, as with Polonius, "To your own self be true," but more impersonally "To your own real nature be true." The imperative, then, is: "Live up to what you are by nature." Fine! But what sort of being are you by nature?

Well, on the one hand there is what natural science says you are – a member of the animal species *Homo sapiens,* with all the assets and liabilities appertaining thereto as a creature subject to the legislation of the order of nature. But at this level, the imperative is empty. For you have no choice but to conform to the laws of physical nature. There is no point in enjoining someone: "You ought to conform to the laws of gravitation" – for example, by falling when you slip on a banana peel. Nature sees to it that you conform to its laws; you yourself have no say in the matter. This sort of thing you do automatically, not as a matter of duty nor as a choice. Thus far the imperative is valid – but empty.

However, as Kant sees it, what you are "by nature" goes beyond the legislation of the order of physical nature. For by your nature as a human being you are not only a member of the biological species *Homo sapiens,* you are also a full-fledged member of the wider community of rational beings. Accordingly, so the fundamental principle Categorical Imperative also encompasses the categorical imperative "Act conformably to (i.e., as is fitting for) a member of a certain idealized community, viz. the community of rational free agents." In consequence of this formulation, we arrive not at the implementationally trivial "Conform to the legislation of the order of nature," but rather at "Conform to the legislation of the ideal, supranatural order – namely, the legislation of rationality." That is: "Act as a member not only of the order of causes, but of the order of reasons – the universal kingdom of ends." With W. K. Clifford, Kant sees us as subject to an obligation to rationality – an obligation whose roots are even deeper than those of the commitment to the benevolent morality that it in fact grounds.

4. THE DERIVATION OF THE TOPICAL IMPERATIVES

For Kant, then, a very general and very fundamental Categorical Imperative of rationality in general lies at the basis of the Categorical Imperative of morality. The crux of his position is that the moral Categorical Imperative, "Conform to the legislation of morality" – when viewed in the appropriate light – is simply a consequence of a more fundamental Categorical Imperative, "Conform to the legislation of rationality."

> [It] is evident that it is not only of the greatest necessity in a theoretical point of view when it is a question of speculation, but also of the utmost practical importance, to derive the concepts and laws of morals from pure reason and to present them pure and unmixed, and to determine the scope of this entire practical but pure rational knowledge (the entire faculty of pure practical reason) . . . without making their principles depend upon the particular nature of human reason as speculative philosophy may permit and even sometimes find necessary. But since moral laws should hold for every rational being as such, their principles must be derived from the universal concept of a rational being generally. In this manner all morals, which need anthropology for their application to men, must be completely developed first as pure philosophy, i.e., metaphysics, independently of anthropology (a thing which is easily done in such distinct fields of knowledge). For we know well that if we are not in possession of such a metaphysics, it is not merely futile . . . but even impossible to base morals on legitimate principles for merely ordinary and practical use. (*Foundations*, pp. 411–12, Akad.)

The starting point for morality, then, is a universal imperative of reason, a Categorical Imperative of rationality at large. The fundamental principle is, as we have seen, that of the major premise: "Conform your proceedings to the appropriate principles of reason." This general principle has a threefold application or explanation, as set out in Display 2. These three minor-premise

Display 2. *Domains of Rationality*

Case	In matters of	The rational appropriate principles of reason are the principles of
1. Cognitive	Belief	Logic/methodology
2. Practical	Action	Morality
3. Evaluative	Evaluation	Sound judgment

implementations yield (respectively) the three more specific categorical imperatives of theoretical, practical, and judgmental reason:

1. Cognitive case: Conform your cognitions to the principles of logic and rational inquiry!
2. Moral case: Conform your actions to the principles of morality!
3. Evaluative case: Conform your evaluations to the principles of sound judgment!

The three corresponding imperatives, namely, the injunctions to

> Proceed in matters of ⟨believing/acting/judging⟩ consistently with the demands of ⟨theoretical/practical/evaluative⟩ reason!

are thus simply so many distinct applicative unfoldings of one single overarching imperative of reason.

As these considerations indicate, the basis of the moral categorical imperative is not something specific to human actions or interactions, but something generic to rationality at large. The foundation of the Categorical Imperative is accordingly an imperative of rationality of the very highest generality – one that cuts across the boundaries of theoretical, practical, and evaluative reason to encompass reason of any description and thereby transcends the specifically human community to embrace every rational agent in general.

5. THE UNITY OF THE CATEGORICAL IMPERATIVE

The pervasiveness of a Categorical Imperative of rationality in general makes for a deep-rooted unification of the three Kantian domains of inquiry, action, and evaluation. For at the levels of highest generality there lies a universal categorical imperative of reason:

CI: Act always so as to foster the rational order of things.

This universal Categorical Imperative applies in every domain, be it that of theoretical reason, of practical reason, or of judgmental evaluation. To be sure, in different domains, the overarching principle takes on somewhat different forms. In the theoretical domain, it yields a categorical imperative of cognition (CI/C) that governs the entire realm of theoretical reason:

CI/C: Develop your knowledge of nature as a rational (logical) system – a logical order.

In the domain of the understanding we have a categorical imperative of teleologically evaluative judgment (CI/J):

CI/J: Develop your appreciation of the world in terms of its being a purposive order.

And in the moral domain of our practical endeavors (our actions and interactions) we have a categorical imperative of morality (CI/M):

CI/M: So arrange your agency – be it in self-regarding matters or in interaction with others – as to create and foster a moral order.

However, the same fundamental principle is operative throughout: the fostering of rational order – of system. In each case we have a topic-specific command subsumed under an overarching imperative of rationality at large that enjoins the cultivation of systematicity. And so, behind Kant's limited categorical imperative of moral agency there lies a grand unified Categorical Imperative of rationality in general: "Pursue the ideal of systematicity in every area of endeavor – alike in matters of belief, of action, and of evaluation." It is this supreme Categorical Imperative of Kantian philosophy that fuses his treatment of knowledge, of praxis, and of judgment into one seamless whole.

In particular, these considerations mean that an exactly parallel situation obtains in the theoretical order and in the practical order. As we see in the *Critique of Pure Reason,* there are also substantial maxims of theoretical reason that admit of subsumptive unification under one highest maxim of theoretical reason (the CI/C). Kant himself shows this in the following terms:

> It is the business of reason to render the unity of all possible empirical acts of the understanding systematic . . . Although we are unable to find in *intuition* a schema for understanding, an *analogon* of such a schema must necessarily allow of being given. This analogon is the idea of the *maximum* in the division and unification of the knowledge of the understanding under one single principle . . . Thus the idea of reason [as a system] is an analogon of a schema of sensibility . . . This [systematicity of reason] is achieved by bringing its employment, so far as may be possible, into connection with the principle of thoroughgoing unity, and by determining its procedure in the light of this principle. (*CPuR*, A664–66 = B692–94)

Systematic, inquiring reason is subject to regulative principles of procedure geared to comprehensiveness, systematicity, and the like, every bit as much as practical, productive reason is geared to imperatives enjoining honesty to others and the development of one's own talents.

Let us look more closely at the cognitive case. In the appendix to the "Transcendental Dialectic" entitled "The Regulative Employment of the Ideas of Pure Reason," we are instructed that in the theoretical/cognitive domain of developing our scientific knowledge of the world the principle CI/C takes effect through a host of subordinate implementing maxims that enjoin the pursuit of the parameters of

- Causal regularity
- Simplicity
- Economy
- Homogeneity
- Continuity

And Kant goes on to tell us that these "legitimate and excellent regulative principles of reason" (*CPuR*, A668 = B696) implement cognitive systematicity/universalizability in a way that exactly

238

parallels the situation on the moral side, where we find a strictly comparable impetus to

- Probity
- Reliability
- Honesty
- Trustworthiness
- etc.

These epistemic features represent regulative desiderata of cognition ("Seek simplicity, continuity, etc.") that constitute maxims of (theoretical) reason in a way which is entirely parallel to the injunctions to moral agency ("Do not lie," "Do not cheat," etc.) that constitute maxims of morality.

As Kant sees it, there is a strict isomorphism between theoretical/ cognitive and practical/procedural reason. The regulative epistemic "maxim-ology" – that is, rulishness – of human knowledge (i.e., of science) runs parallel to that of rational agency (i.e., of morals). On both sides – and on that of evaluative judgment as well – we have a strictly rule-governed praxis where rules are categorical (i.e., universalizable and impersonal) and normatively imperative (obligatory). Throughout, it is a matter of implementing the regulative function of reason:

> I entitle all subjective principles which are derived, not from the constitution of an object but from the interest of reason in respect of a certain possible perfection of the knowledge of the object, *maxims* of reason. There are therefore maxims of speculative reason, which rest entirely on its speculative interest, although they may seem to be objective principles. (*CPuR*, A666 = B694)

This approach results in a parallelism that runs across the whole range of deliberations developed by Kant in the three *Critiques* (see Display 3). The salient point is that the same fundamental drive to rational systematization is operative throughout these domains. The cognitive domain (i.e., that of science) is governed by our duty to create a system of cognitions where people's intellect can flourish in point of knowledge. The practical sphere (i.e., that of morality) is governed by our duty to create a system of

Display 3. *The Structural Isomorphism of Kantian Deliberations*

	Cognition (*Theoretical reason*)	Action (*Practical reason*)	Evaluation (*Evaluative rationality* = *judgment*)
Product	Belief	Action	Evaluation
Controlling interest	Correct belief	Fitting action	Appropriate evaluation
Governing principle	Regulative principle (of cognition)	Maxim (of action)	Standard (of evaluation)
Ruling Ideal	A logical system (of knowledge): a systematic codification of the rules of natural law	A "universal kingdom of ends": a systematic codification of the rules of moral law	A teleological system of values: a systematic codification of the rules of evaluative law
Ruling maxim	Conform your cognitions to the principles of logic (i.e., to a coherent system of natural laws).	Conform your actions to the principles of morality (i.e., to a coherent system of principles of action).	Conform your judgments to the principles of evaluation (i.e., to a coherent system of values).
Implementing desiderata	Continuity, uniformity, regularity, etc.	Reliability, honesty, etc.	Beauties (for artifacts) Sublimities (of nature) Sound purposes (for rational agents)

comportment where people's condition can flourish in point of happiness. The judgmental order (i.e., that of evaluative judgment) is governed by our duty to create a system of evaluations where people's appreciative faculties can flourish through a proper appreciation of values in the works of nature and of people.

Just as practical rationality – that is, morality – stands coordinate with our noumenal status as rational free agents, so our cognitive rationality stands coordinate with our noumenal status as members of an ideal rational order: creatures committed by their very nature to the pursuit of cognitive ideals. What is at issue either way is a matter of being true to ourselves – that is, to our noumenal potential.

Accordingly, to abandon the autonomy of the self-generated demands of reason for the lures of heteronomy (the call of instinct, habit, or authority, on the cognitive side; that of inclination, need, or desire, on the practical) would be to betray our inherent rationality and to cease to be the sorts of creatures we ought to be (and rightly see ourselves as being). Throughout, the demands of reason are paramount – to enroll ourselves in the universal (humanity-transcending) ideal confraternity of rational beings. The theoretical justification of our cognitive or our practical or our evaluative maxims is not contingently purposive (i.e., that they serve certain aims or wishes of ours), but rather mandating, because they enable us to operate on the level to which we properly and by nature belong as rational creatures. Heteronomy involves giving way to the de facto impetus of the imperfect creatures we are, autonomy lies on the ideal level to which, being capable of reason, we should and do aspire. The normative impetus is paramount: throughout the realm of rationality, the point is not what we want nor even what we are, but what we ought to be.

6. A KANTIAN RATIONALE FOR CULTIVATING COGNITIVE SYSTEMATICITY

Whereas the precritical philosophers had regarded the several parameters of scientific systematicity (unity, simplicity, and the like) as validated ontologically ("constitutively") with reference to the rational authority of a creator God, Kant sees them as validated methodologically ("regulatively") with reference to a rational inquirer's ex officio commitment to the systematicity of knowledge. On Kant's principles, we are (inter alia) inherently scientists by nature – people committed by their very nature to the project of developing their knowledge as a system. And this is so on exactly the same basis that we are inherently moralists by nature – that is, people committed to being part of a mutually supportive confraternity of interagents. For in each case it is in this way alone that we can bring to expression our most deep-rooted vision of ourselves as rational creatures committed to making systematic sense of every department of our activities.

For Kant, the human mind has an inherent tropism to rationality and thereby to rational systematization. To realize ourselves fully as what we are called upon by our nature to pursue in point of cognitive aspirations, we must heed this call to system. And so we should try in our actions to institute a system of moral laws, in our inquiries to establish a system of logical laws, and in our evaluations to institute a system of evaluative laws (of aesthetic and teleological principles). What is basic throughout is the cultivation of rational law and order that is part of the self-realization of a rational creature.

In this regard there is an aspect of the Kantian position that deserves special emphasis. Hans Reichenbach has written: "Actually in cases of inductive simplicity it is not economy which determines our choice. . . . We make the assumption that the simplest theory furnishes the best predictions. This assumption cannot be justified by convenience: it has a truth character and demands a justification within the theory of probability and induction."[2] This perspective is gravely misleading. What sort of consideration would possibly justify the supposition that "the simplest theory furnishes the best predictions"? Any such belief is surely inappropriate. Induction with respect to the history of science itself – a constant series of errors of oversimplification – would soon undermine our confidence that nature operates in the way we would deem the simpler. On the contrary, the history of science is a highly repetitive story of simple theories giving way to more complicated and sophisticated ones. The Greeks had four elements; in the nineteenth century, Mendeleyev had some eighty; we nowadays have a vast series of stability states. Aristotle's cosmos had only spheres; Ptolemy's added epicycles; ours has a virtually endless proliferation of complex orbits that only supercomputers can approximate. Greek science could be transmitted on a shelf of books; that of the Newtonian age required a roomful; ours requires vast storage structures filled not only with books and journals, but with photographs, tapes, floppy diskettes, and so on. Of the quantities nowadays recognized as the fundamental constants of physics, only one was contemplated in Newton's physics, the universal gravitational constant. A second was added in the nineteenth century, Avogadro's constant. The remaining six are all creatures of twentieth-century physics: the speed of light (the velocity of electromagnetic radiation in free space), the elementary charge, the rest mass of the electron, the rest mass of the proton,

Planck's constant, and Boltzmann's constant.[3] It would be naive –
and quite wrong – to think that the course of scientific progress is
one of increasing simplicity.[4]

Here, then the direction of Kant's thought seems profoundly
correct. We have not learned that nature works in simple ways.
We have not learned that simple hypotheses are true. We have not
learned that probability is on the side of simplicity. What favors
simplicity is not some aspect of learning about this world at all. It
is simply a matter of rational comportment, of rational economy's
insistence on the simplest means to given ends. The rational basis
for our inductive-simplicity preference lies in considerations of
the economic dimension of practice and procedure, rather than in
any factual supposition about the world's nature.

The penchant for inductive systematicity reflected in the structural dimension of information is simply a matter of striving for
economy in the conduct of inquiry. It is governed by an analogue
of Occam's razor – a principle of parsimony to the effect that needless complexity is to be avoided. Given that the inductive method,
viewed in its practical and methodological aspect, aims at the
most efficient and effective means of question resolution, it is only
natural that our inductive precepts should direct us toward the
most systematic, and thereby economical, device that can actually
do the job at hand. Our systematizing procedures pivot on this
injunction always to adopt the most economical (simple, general, straightforward, etc.) solution that meets the demands of
the situation. The root principle of inductive systematization is
the axiom of cognitive economy: "Avoid needless complications"
(Complicationes non multiplicandae sunt praeter necessitatem).
The other-things-equal preferability of simpler solutions over more
complex ones is thus obvious enough: they are less cumbersome
to store, easier to take hold of, and less difficult to work with.

Galileo wrote: "When therefore I observe a stone initially at rest
falling from a considerable height and gradually acquiring new
increases of speed, why should I not believe that such increments
come about in the simplest, the most plausible way?"[5] Why not
indeed? Subsequent findings may, of course, render this simplest
position untenable. But this recognition only reinforces the stance
that simplicity is not an inevitable hallmark of truth (*simplex*

sigillum veri), but merely a methodological tool of inquiry – a guidepost of procedure. When something simple accomplishes the cognitive tasks in hand as well as some more complex alternative, it is foolish to adopt the latter. After all, we need not presuppose that the world somehow is systematic (simple, uniform, and the like) to validate our penchant for the systematicity of our cognitive commitments. Our striving for cognitive systematicity in its various forms persists even in the face of complex phenomena: the commitment to simplicity in our account of the world remains a methodological desideratum regardless of how complex or untidy the world may turn out to be.

The point is that we should opt for simplicity (and with it for uniformity, harmony, etc.) because this is, for every relevant point of view, the rational thing to do. The Kantian commitment to cultivating systematicity lies in the inherent rationality of this course of procedure. We pursue system (and with it simplicity, uniformity, etc.)

- Because it is cognitively desirable to have information cohere in a system
- Because it is practically convenient (i.e., efficient) to have our information organized systematically
- Because it is aesthetically pleasing to have our information display a systematic harmony

Be all this as it may, for Kant, our intellectual duty and our moral duty run strictly parallel under the aegis of a quest for systemic order. Rationality's obligation to forge a cognitive order of understanding subject to epistemic desiderata such as regularity, simplicity, continuity, and the like is a sibling of rationality's obligation to forge a moral order of action subject to moral desiderata such as honesty, probity, trustworthiness, and the like. Both issue from the same duty to make the world a place that is congenial to reason.

As Kant sees it, an intelligent creature's supreme challenge and duty is to domesticate the world for reason. On the side of knowledge, this means fostering the prospect of a scientific systematization that represents the world's processes as a law-ordered complex. On the side of morality it means fostering the creation of a moral order that manifests the well-designed rules of personal interaction. Both science and morality are two sides of the same sort of process, a rationalization (of belief and action, respectively) that minimizes friction – in dealing (cognitively) with our world on the one hand and (interactionally) with our fellows on the other.

When Kant tells us in the conclusion of the *Critique of Practical Reason* that "two things" fill the mind with "wonderment and awe" – "the starry heavens above and the moral law within" – he does not stop there, but quite characteristically goes on to observe that in each case it is specifically the apprehension of lawful order that most deserves our admiration. What is most splendid for him is a grandeur apparent neither to the visual or the moral sense, but to reason, because what confronts us in each case is something that evokes our highest admiration less from our sensibilities than from our reason's inherent appreciation of rational order.

7. THE DIVERSE FORMULAS OF THE MORAL CATEGORICAL IMPERATIVE

But let us descend from these lofty peaks of larger Kantian perspectives to reappraise the local situation that we encounter specifically in Kant's moral philosophy. Exactly how and why is it that in his exposition of the categorical imperative of morality Kant presents us with those various different formulae?

The fact is that these various formulations are not so many distinct restatements of the categorical imperative of morality, but rather are explanations of its nature and bearing by way of indicating diverse implications or applications of the underlying principle at issue in the Categorical Imperative of rationality at large. The appropriate perspective is essentially as follows: A principle (maxim) of action is morally appropriate just exactly if it is such that a rational being would actually want it to become a universal law (CI-1) (of nature [CI-2]), and would choose to make it obtain if this were within his power (CI-3 and CI-4). We *should* act in the empirical order as rational legislation would have us act – that is, as the arrangements of an ideal or noumenal order *would* ordain by way of natural laws characterizing how its perfectly rational agents act. And so, as CI-5 says, we should act in line with the ideal legislation of a "kingdom of ends."

As regards CI-6, this is a fairly straightforward consequence of the preceding as per the derivation

1. Act rationally – that is, act so that your actions instantiate rationally universalizable principles.
2. A rationally universalizable principle is (by definition) one that holds good for everybody – that is, as much governs you in your relations to me as me as in my relations to you.
3. Therefore I should not treat you as a mere means to my personal ends, nor vice versa (CI-6).

Accordingly, the proliferation of "different formulations" of the Categorical Imperative that some commentators complain of are not confusingly diverse formulas but rather are diverse applications or implementations of one single overarching Kantian principle of rationality in its bearing upon issues of morality.

8. A PUZZLE

Let it be supposed that this chapter's analysis is correct, so that Kant envisions a single fundamental and overarching Categorical Imperative of rationality at large of which the various domain-limited categorical imperatives – that of morality included – are simply so many particularized subordinate exfoliations. The problem now arises, why it should be that Kant himself – the great systematizer – was not more explicit on this issue. Why does he himself not emphasize the point that the categorical imperative of morality that is at issue in the second, practical *Critique* is simply an application of a more fundamental and overarching categorical imperative of rationality that was already hard at work in the deliberations of the first, theoretical *Critique*?

The problem here, as I see it, is not why Kant presents the various different formulas for the Categorical Imperative. The answer to that question is simple: they simply highlight and emphasize different features of one basic principle of rationality in the context of morally relevant agency. Rather the real problem, in my view, is why, given the unity and coherence of those different formulations, Kant is not more explicit and emphatic about the one fundamental and overarching principle of rationality that is at issue throughout – a superprinciple to the effect: "Act always on principles, and make sure that they are rational."

I regret having to confess that I can offer no compelling answer to this question. Perhaps the best explanation is that in placing that overarching Categorical Imperative of rationality at large into sharper and more explicit focus, Kant would have had to become much more explicit about "the nature" of rational beings as such – an issue that would almost unavoidably have involved him in treading paths uncomfortably close to the sort of metaphysics that he condemned as being of the old precritical type.

Notes

1. On the Status of "Things-in-Themselves"

1. "Kant went wrong . . . in thinking that reality is an unknown of which man can say nothing, and in conceiving of thought as a form that man imposes on reality and that, therefore, prevents him from knowing of that reality," G. Vander Veer, *Bradley's Metaphysics and the Self* (New Haven: Yale University Press, 1970), p. 136. Vander Veer's discussion addresses Bradley's charge that Kant's theory of the *Ding an sich* places authentic "reality" in a realm from which man's reason is barred by the very constitution of his mind.

2. A. C. Ewing, *Idealism* (London: Methuen, 1934), p. 107.

3. "What the things in themselves may be I do not know, nor do I need to know, since a thing can never come before one except in appearance" (*CPuR*, A277 = B333).

4. A. C. Ewing, *A Short Commentary on Kant's Critique of Pure Reason* (Chicago: University of Chicago Press, 1938), p. 101.

5. On the subcategorial, schematic grounding at issue see *CPuR*, A243–44 = B301–2.

2. Kant on Noumenal Causality

1. Note that these considerations mean that there is important work for the concept of noumenal causality to accomplish in the setting of all three Kantian *Critiques*.

2. P. F. Strawson, *The Bounds of Sense* (London: Methuen, 1966), pp. 41–2.

3. The Principle of Causality schematizes and concretizes that of Sufficient Reason: it stands in back of it as its supporting basis on the realism of reason. However, Kant is not always careful to distinguish the generic (preschematic) Principle of Sufficient Reason from the specific (schematized) Principle of Causality. For example, at A201 = B246 of *CPuR*, he uses the term "Principle of Sufficient Reason" where "Principle of Causality" is obviously wanted. Note also the explicit (and favorable) mention of the Principle of Sufficient Reason as an a priori synthetic principle in the *Prolegomena* (sect. 3).

4. The entire context of this passage is important. See also the key passage at *CPuR*, A305–7 = B362–64.

5. "On the Ultimate Origin of Things" (1967), tr. in L. E. Loemker (ed.), *G. W. Leibniz: Philosophical Papers and Letters* (Dordrecht: Reidel, 1969), pp. 486–91. See pp. 486–87.

6. On the sort of "imputation" at issue cf. *The Metaphysics of Morals*, p. 222, Akad.

7. Compare the discussion of the Second Analogy at *CPuR*, A201–2 = B246–47.

3. Kant's Cognitive Anthropocentrism

1. It is generally recognized that this deduction establishes only the need for *some* categories and does not address the validation of the specific categories that Kant tabulates. (Compare A. C. Ewing's *Short Commentary in Kant's Critique of Pure Reason* [Chicago: University of Chicago Press, 1967; reissue of the original 1938 edition], p. 66.) In the so-called metaphysical deduction, Kant sought to validate the particular categories via a schematization with respect to time. But this of course subordinates them to something specifically human in the Kantian framework, namely time as a form of human sensibility.

2. *CPrR*, p. 22, Akad.

3. In a later explanation, Kant writes that "the thing *in itself* is not an existing being but = *x*, merely a principle" (*Opus Postumum*, tr. Eckhart Förster and Michael Rosen [Cambridge: Cambridge University Press, 1993], p. 175). But while it thus is a mere thought thing (*Gedankending*) we ought not to conclude that the thing in itself is a nonentity (*Unding*) (ibid., p. 181). The thing-in-itself is, after all, a creature of reason projected under the aegis of the Principle of Sufficient Reason. Cf. Chapter 2 of the present volume. While it itself does not exist in space and time, its idea provides us with a critical resource for thinking about the things that do.

4. Perhaps the occupation of East Prussia during the Seven Years' War (from early 1758 to August 1762), in whose course Kant offered mathematics courses to Russian officers, exerted some influence on his thought in this connection.

5. *CPrR*, p. 136, Akad.

4. Kant on Cognitive Systematization

1. There is an extensive discussion of Kant's theory of system in the closing chapter of H. W. Cassirer, *Kant's First Critique* (London: Allen & Unwin, 1954), entitled "The Problem of the Systematization of Knowledge." Cassirer sees Kant's theory as questionable in ways that keep Cassirer from getting an adequate grasp on it. He neither appreciates how central sys-

tematization is in the Kantian scheme of things nor how essential the cor-relativity of system and purpose is to Kant's thoroughly practical valida-tion of systematization as a theoretical resource. On the other hand, vari-ous useful observations about Kant's view on systematization are offered in J. D. McFarland's *Kant's Concept of Teleology* (Edinburgh: University of Edinburgh Press, 1970).

2. I describe Leibniz's theory of cognitive systematization in detail in my es-say "Leibniz and the Concept of a System" in *Leibniz's Philosophy of Nature* (Dordrecht: Reidel, 1981), pp. 29–41.

3. Kant develops this idea in considerable detail in the "appendix to the Transcendental Dialectic." For present purposes, however, we need not pursue these details.

4. Rational cognition through the construction of concepts is mathematical. A pure philosophy of nature in general, i.e., one that only investigates what constitutes the concept of a nature in general, may indeed be possible without mathematics, but a pure doctrine of nature concerning determi-nate natural things (doctrines of body and doctrine of should) is possible only by means of mathematics. And since in every doctrine of nature only so much science proper is to be found as there is a priori cognition in it, a doctrine of nature will contain only so much science proper as there is applied mathematics in it (*Metaphysical Foundations*, p. 472, Akad.).

5. Cassirer, op. cit., p. 353.

5. Kant's Teleological Theology

1. H. W. Cassirer, *Kant's First Critique* (London: Allen & Unwin, 1954), pp. 356–57.

2. An informative account of Kant's theory of purpose is provided in J. D. McFarland, *Kant's Concept of Teleology* (Edinburgh: University of Edin-burgh Press, 1970). See also Andrew Woodfield, *Teleology* (Cambridge: Cambridge University Press, 1976) for a modern treatment of the scien-tific issues.

3. See sect. 2 of Chapter 2 in the present volume.

4. H. W. Cassirer, op. cit., p. 350.

6. Kant on the Limits and Prospects of Philosophy

1. "Reason, when employed apart from all experience, can know proposi-tions entirely *a priori,* and as necessary, or it can know nothing at all" (*CPuR*, A775 = B803).

2. On these issues see also Chapter 3 of the present volume.

3. See the explanations cited in Rudolf Eisler's *Kant Lexikon,* (Hildesheim: Olms, 1989; reprint of the 10th [1930] edition), s.v. "Geltung."

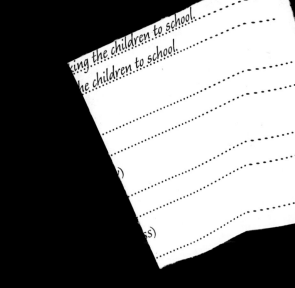

4. This analogy follows the tracks of one projected by Kant himself:

   > Ignorance . . . cannot be established empirically, from *observation*, but only through an *examination*, critically conducted, of the primary sources of our knowledge. [Such] knowledge of our ignorance, which is possible only through criticism of reason itself, is *science* . . . For I represent the earth as it appears to my senses, as a flat surface, with a circular horizon, I cannot know how far it extends. But experience teaches me that wherever I may go, I always see a space around me in which I could proceed further; and thus I know the limits of my actual knowledge of the earth at any given time, but not the limits of all possible geography. But if I have got so far as to know that the earth is a sphere and that its surface is spherical, I am able even from a small part of it, for instance, from the magnitude of a degree, to know determinately, in accordance with principles *a priori*, the diameter, and through it the total superficial area of the earth; and although I am ignorant of the objects which this surface may contain, I yet have knowledge in respect of its circumference, magnitude, and limits. (*CPuR*, A758–59 = B786–87)

5. On transcendental illusion in Kant see Michelle Grier, "Kant on the Illusion of a Systematic Unity of Knowledge," *History of Philosophy Quarterly* 14 (1997), 1–28.

6. A whole host of commentators align themselves with Kemp Smith on this issue. See F. E England, *Kant's Conception of God* (New York: Humanities Press, 1968), pp. 194–96; W. H. Walsh, *Kant's Criterion of Metaphysics* (Edinburgh: University of Edinburgh Press, 1925), pp. 244–49; R. P. Horstmann, "Why Must There Be a Deduction in Kant's *Critique of Judgment?*" in Eckhart Förster (ed.), *Kant's Transcendental Deductions* (Stanford: Stanford University Press, 1989), pp. 157–76; Paul Guyer, "Reason and Reflective Judgment: Kant on the Significance of Systematicity," *Noûs* 24 (1990), 17–43.

7. Recall the passage from the *Opus Postumum* where Kant insists that while the thing-in-itself is a mere thought object (*Gedankending*) it is not thereby a nonentity (*Unding*). Immanuel Kant, *Gesammelte Schriften*, Vol. 22 (Berlin: Preussische Akademie der Wissenschaften, 1938), p. 181.

8. P. F. Strawson, *The Bounds of Sense* (London: Methuen, 1966), p. 221.

9. See the discussion of the role of the Principle of Sufficient Reason in Chapter 2 of the present volume.

10. H. W. Cassirer, *Kant's First Critique* (London: Allen & Unwin, 1954), p. 346.

11. *Wesen* though not *Objekt*. Kant is perfectly willing to accept *Verstandeswesen*. As he sees it, *objects* require categorical conceptualization, but *beings* can be projected at the level of ideas.

12. Accordingly, Kant's contention that "the moral laws, and these alone . . . belong to the practical employment of reason" (*CPuR*, A800 = B828) is

not as restrictive as it at first view seems, since he does not hold the narrow (interests-of-others oriented) construction of the moral realm that has become common among present-day ethicists.

13. On this issue see Chapter 9 of the present volume.

14. Philosophy differs from mathematics in that "whereas . . . mathematical definitions *make* their concepts, in philosophical definitions concepts are only *explained*" (A730 = B758; cf. *CPuR*, A718 = B746). This is because philosophy does and must operate with preexisting concepts.

15. "Suppose a philosopher be given the concept of a triangle and be left to find out, in his own way, what relation the sum of its angles bears to a right angle. He has nothing but the concept of a figure enclosed by three straight lines, and possessing three angles. However long he meditates on this concept, he will never produce anything new" (*CPuR*, A716 = B794).

7. On the Reach of Pure Reason in Kant's Practical Philosophy

1. It is, of course, the case (with Kant as with Leibniz) that there will be analytic propositions in any field in which there are any definitions at all. And this will specifically include arithmetic. Thus consider the proposition $3 = (1+1) + 1$. Since 3 is (by definition) $2 + 1$, and 2 is (by definition) $1 + 1$, this result follows by definitional substitution alone and is thus analytic in Kant's sense as in Leibniz's. It must be acknowledged that this is a situation that Kant himself does not adequately take into account. He carelessly says that "[a]ll mathematical judgments, without exception, are synthetic" (*CPur*, B14). But this is to deny that definitions occur in mathematics – and that is nonsense. "A straight line is the shortest distance between two points" is indeed analytic in Kant's sense, but "A straight line makes no turns" is not. The fact is that Kant would not (any more than Leibniz) deny that definitions play a role in arithmetic. And it will be the inevitable result of this concession that there will here or elsewhere be some definitional truths that have to be seen as analytic.

2. Note, however, that we are not entitled to suppose that the organized products of nature are comparably subject to a causality of purpose. Accordingly, we cannot comparably project purposiveness from ourselves onto other things:

> If, on the contrary, we supply to nature causes acting *designedly* and consequently place at its basis teleology, not merely as a *regulative* principle for the mere judging of phenomena, to which nature can be thought as subject in its particular laws, but as a *constitutive* principle of the *derivation* of its products from their causes, then the concept of a natural purpose would no longer belong to the reflective but to the determinant judgment. Then . . . it would introduce into a natural science a new causality, which we only borrow

from ourselves and ascribe to other beings, without meaning to assume them to be of the same kind with ourselves. (*CJ*, sect. 61, at end; p. 361, Akad.)

8. On the Rationale of Kant's Categorical Imperative

1. Some prime instances of the vast literature are Bruce Aune, *Kant's Theory of Morals* (Princeton: Princeton University Press, 1979); Barbara Herman, *Morality as Rationality* (New York: Garland, 1990); Stephan Körner, *Kant* (Harmondsworth, UK: Penguin, 1959); Christine M. Korsgaard, "Kant's Formula of Universal Law," *Pacific Philosophical Quarterly* 66 (1985), 26–470, reprinted in her *Creating the Kingdom of Ends* (Cambridge: Cambridge University Press, 1996), and "The Right to Lie: Kant on Dealing with Evil," *Philosophy and Public Affairs* 15 (1986), 325–49; Onora O'Neill, *Complications of Reason* (Cambridge: Cambridge University Press, 1989); John Rawls, "Themes in Kant's Moral Philosophy," in Eckhart Förster (ed.), *Kant's Transcendental Deduction* (Stanford: Stanford University Press, 1989).

2. The textual basis of Kant's position on equality before the law is compactly summarized in Rudolf Eisler's *Kant Lexikon* (Hildesheim: Olms, 1989; reprint of the 10th [1930] edition), s.v. *Gleichheit*.

3. Instead of deriving C* via (PA) one could simply see it as itself representing a fundamental Kantian principle. However, this would leave its connection with deeper Kantian commitment less perspicuous.

4. As Körner puts it, "'conformity to law in general ranks with Kant as the necessary and sufficient condition of the morality of . . . action," *Kant*, p. 159. For an instructive discussion of this principle see Aune, *Kant's Theory of Morals*, pp. 83–90. (Regarding the point at issue see p. 122.)

5. In her stimulating essay "Kant's Formula of Universal Law," Korsgaard characterizes these three possibilities as the "logical contradiction interpretation," the "practical contradiction interpretation," and the "teleological contradiction interpretation," respectively. Korsgaard represents these as three alternative possibilities. The present interpretation, however, regards them as complementary, representing different but equally relevant ways of realizing a "contradiction." Korsgaard comes down on the side of the practical contradiction interpretation, which certainly does fit some of Kant's examples. But many other examples (the revenge killer and the talent neglecter among them) indicate that the teleological contradiction interpretation must sometimes be invoked.

6. Such a contradiction is not exactly a self-contradiction but rather a clash of wills, that is, a contradiction between the empirical and the transcendental/rational will. (See *Grundlegung*, p. 424, Akad.) Since both are constituent parts of one overarching volition, the result can, in a way, be viewed as a will at odds with itself.

7. Körner, *Kant*, p. 138.

8. Walking in David Hume's footsteps, many philosophers nowadays construe rationality narrowly, interpreting it as a matter merely of effective means to essentially arbitrary ends. But the appropriateness of the ends themselves and, above all, respect for persons as rational free agents matter crucially for the sort of rationality that is at issue in Kant's thought. (On these issues see the author's *The Validity of Values* [Princeton: Princeton University Press, 1993], especially Chapter 3, "The Rationality of Values and Evaluations.") For rational decision and action it is necessary that the propriety of ends be ensured, and so evaluation (*Urteil*) is a crucial aspect of Kantian rationality.

9. As long as there is no absolutely worst of all evils, we can always envision a situation of a circumstantially forced choice between doing *A* and doing *B* which is something yet worse. And real-world conditions can always put us into this unhappy condition. But of course this will not happen in a morally ideal order, which helps to explain why Kant is drawn in this direction.

10. On this tripartite characterization of action in terms of the formula "to do *A* in circumstances *C* in order to realize objective *R*" compare also Rawls, "Themes in Kant's Moral Philosophy," pp. 82–84. See also Herman, *Morality as Rationality*, p. 33.

11. For example, if the act is that of consoling my neighbor, Ms. Smith, for her recent loss, then the generalization-relevant action is not "consoling *my* neighbor (Ms. Smith)" but rather "consoling one's neighbor."

12. Theory, as Kant sees it, is concerned with generalities, and "exceptions would nullify the universality on account of which alone they are called *principles*." See his "On a Supposed Right to Lie from Philanthropy" (p. 430, Akad.). See also section 10 of the present chapter.

13. Universalizability, as here construed, effectively means consonance with an ideal moral order where, as Kant sees it, desert and happiness are in balance. Supererogation, if generalized, would envision an order where people are happier than they deserve to be, so that this proper balance is disturbed. Accordingly, supererogatory acts are not morally permissible on Kantian principles, seeing that supererogation engenders a teleological contradiction in the sense of note 4 to this chapter.

14. Note that this position would impel Kant into operating a nonstandard deontic logic. In standard deontic logic we have: "perm(*A*) or perm (not-*A*)": every act is such that either it or its omission is permitted. But since Kantian permission requires universalization, actions that are variably acceptable from a moral point of view (i.e., are acceptable under some condition but not under others) are never permitted outright. (For example, neither "killing another person" nor "letting another person live" is permitted outright – it all depends on conditions, circumstances, motives, and the like. Since Kant's theory is concerned not for incompletely characterized actions, but for action modalities that are fully con-

textualized in morally relevant regards, his "deontic logic" is bound to have some nonstandard features. Violation of some of the principles of standard deontic logic cannot be invoked against it.

15. Onora O'Neill, *Constructions of Reason* (Cambridge: Cambridge University Press, 1989), p. 87.

16. But of course keeping your promise to X only because you realize that this will cause distress to Y is something else again. Exactly this fact that motives matter explains why one must conditionalize. For us moderns, promise keeping is appropriate not absolutely, but "when other things are equal." And with Kant other things are always equal in an ideal moral order.

17. See in particular his late (1797) essay "On a Supposed Right to Lie from Philanthropy" (Akad., vol. 8, p. 430).

18. After all, "preserving life" can plausibly be seen as a more urgent moral desideratum than "telling the truth." And as Kant puts it in the *Metaphysics of Morals*, in situations of moral conflict "practical philosophy says, not that the stronger obligation takes precedence [fortior obligatio vincit], but that the stronger ground of obligation prevails [fortior obligandi ratio vincit]" (p. 224, Akad.).

19. This aspect of Kant comes to be emphasized in Hans Vaihinger's *Philosophy of As If*, initially published as *Philosophie des Als ob* (Leipzig: F. Meiner, 1911), English tr. by C. K. Ogden (London: Kegan Paul, 1924).

20. Moral theory does indeed conditionalize, even as does a science that maintains not that all elements conduct electricity, but that all metals do. But with moral theory this conditionalization can never be complete and will always have to omit (and thus abstract from) certain potentially relevant real-world complexities.

21. Korsgaard occupies a questionable position when she imputes "a double level theory" to Kant in "The Right to Lie: Kant on Dealing with Evil," especially pp. 341–48. It is not two levels of theory that are at issue, but rather the duality of theory and application.

9. On the Unity of Kant's Categorical Imperative

1. H. J. Paton, *The Categorical Imperative: A Study in Kant's Moral Philosophy* (London: Hutchinson, 1947), p. 129.

2. Hans Reichenbach, *Experience and Prediction* (Chicago: University of Chicago Press, 1938), p. 376.

3. See B. W. Petley, *The Fundamental Physical Constants and the Frontiers of Measurement* (Boston: Hilger, 1985).

4. This point is forcefully argued by Michael Polanyi in *Personal Knowledge* (Chicago: University of Chicago Press, 1960), pp. 16–17.

5. Galileo Galilei, *Dialogues Concerning Two New Sciences*, tr. H. Crew and A. de Salvo (Evanston: University of Illinois Press, 1914), p. 154.

Name Index

Note: Bracketed numbers following note citations indicate chapter numbers where, in the Notes section, the same note number for different chapters occurs several times on one page.

257